MERION FRIENDS' MEETING HOUSE, *CIRCA* 1830.

WELSH TRACT of PENNSYLVANIA

The Early Settlers

Extracted from the
Welsh Settlement of Pennsylvania
by
Charles H. Browning

HERITAGE BOOKS
2020

HERITAGE BOOKS
AN IMPRINT OF HERITAGE BOOKS, INC.

Books, CDs, and more—Worldwide

For our listing of thousands of titles see our website
at
www.HeritageBooks.com

A Facsimile Reprint
Published 2020 by
HERITAGE BOOKS, INC.
Publishing Division
5810 Ruatan Street
Berwyn Heights, Md. 20740

Represents the first 276 pages of
Welsh Settlement of Pennsylvania,
written by Charles H. Browning, and originally published by
William J. Campbell, 1912, Philadelphia

First Printed with Index, 1990

— Publisher's Notice —
In reprints such as this, it is often not possible to remove blemishes from the original. We feel the contents of this book warrant its reissue despite these blemishes and hope you will agree and read it with pleasure.

International Standard Book Number
Paperbound: 978-1-58549-171-1

To the memory of
SAMUEL JONES LEVICK,

a minister among Friends for forty-five years; "a man of strong and earnest convictions; deeply interested in public affairs, both national and local; active in the work of organizing charities, and an enthusiastic laborer for the abolition of slavery,"

are dedicated

these annals of the pioneer Welsh Friends of Pensylvania, from many of whom he was descended.

CONTENTS.

Arranging Welsh settlement	11- 29
Welsh land companies	33- 42
Thomas and Jones' land patent	45- 59
Merion adventurers	63- 78
Families and lands of first arrivals	79- 92
Families and lands of second arrivals	95-138
Lloyd and Davies' land patent	141-161
John Bevan's land patent	163-173
John and Wynne's land patent	175-193
Lewis David's land patent	195-203
Richard Thomas' land patent	207-212
Richard David's land patent	213-248
Welsh planters and servants	249-276
Appendix	277-281
Index	283

PICTURES AND MAPS.

Merion Meeting House	Frontispiece
Map of the Thomas and Jones tract, in 1683-4.......	31
Merion Meeting House	43
Location of Merion Meeting's land, 1695-1804	60
A section of Holme's Map of Pa., (*circa* 1688)	124
A section of Scull & Heap's Map of Pa., 1750	162
A section of Read's Map of Pa.	174
Locations of first Meeting Houses	194
Haverford tp., (1690), east part	204
Haverford tp., (1690), west part	232

WELSH QUAKER
EMIGRATION
TO PENSYLVANIA

WELSH SETTLEMENT OF PENNSYLVANIA

FRIENDS IN WALES

In Pensylvania, there is no more ancient public building preserved, that is so intimately associated with the settlement of the State, in its provincial period, than the Merion Meeting House, a stone-built house of God. It is one of the very few remaining links suggesting the days of William Penn, and it is the oldest.

The march of public improvement and progress is passing, leaving it the same House, growing older, but not decaying, of hallowed memories, which was the first permanent place for public religious meetings of the first settlers of the region in which it stands, ever an interesting relict of days long passed, of early colonial, or provincial times and customs of the greatest of the American commonwealths.

Its oldest part, completed in the year 1695, as its datestone tells, the possible successor of a more modest and unpretentious Meeting House, stands as a firm, rock-built, permanent land-mark, in Lower Merion township, Montgomery county, at the intersection of Montgomery avenue, and Meeting House Road, a short distance from the city line.

'Twas on one of those

"Fair First-day mornings,
Steeped in summer calm,"

that I made my first visit to this Friends' Meeting. Any day it is worth more than the time you will spend on a visit

WELSH SETTLEMENT OF PENSYLVANIA

there, "for conscience sake," if not out of interest, or curiosity.

You will find a large, double iron gate, just west of the picturesque and quaint "General Wayne Inn, Established in 1704," that yields to pressure, for it's never locked, and admits you to a clean, rolled gravel driveway leading upwards through a well kept lawn to the old building, past the usual shelter for horses, for the merciful are merciful to their beasts, shaded by tall sycamore, or buttonwood trees, native to the soil, ancient you may see, for their girths are near twenty feet, which have witnessed the passing to worship, or to mourn, of many generations of Friends.

You will find that the Meeting House seems to stand on a natural elevation, but the ground is really only a part of the level fields about it, and that it is the bounding roadbeds that here have been cut down to a plane which gives it the apparent elevation. The lawn about the old building has a luxuriant growth of clover, and is sufficiently shaded by trees not so old as those you have passed under, and, on the whole, is a restful spot, "far from the madding crowd," that has been enjoyed by thousands in days gone by, and is likely to be for longer, for there is never any lack of funds to keep the place in perfect condition and beauty.

This lawn on which the old house stands, to one side, is of the shape of a triangle, being bounded on two sides by the intersecting public roads, while the third, or base, may be said, rests on an end of the rectangularly spaced grave yard. All about the property is a strong, stone retaining wall, which it was necessary to build when the public roads were cut down and leveled, topped with an iron fence, which gives the grounds a park-like appearance, and, with the Meeting House, makes it notable in this locality, to the thousands motoring and driving on the adjacent avenues.

Outwardly you will find the Meeting House attractive in appearance for it has some architecturally distinctive marks and features, absent in the usually plain, unpretentious Friends' Meeting Houses, which suggests that its builders were men of refined taste, who could design and erect a meeting house at once plain and unassuming, but at the same time attractive to the senses. Yet, withal, it is a little modest stone building that has withstood the elements for over two centuries. and so will probably remain to the end, an accommodation for all of its congregations, a quaint and charming bit of colonial architecture, with its three gables, and as a whole, a remarkable one, for it is the only Friends' Meeting House erected into the shape of a T, or of a "tau cross," the "crux commissa," which latter design is so incongruous with Friends' taste, it must be considered an accident that this Friends' Meeting House was built cruciform.

In a general description, the Meeting House faces the South, and the transept, east and west, a gable pointing towards three of the chief points of the compass. In the western gable end of the transept may be seen a small stone, set into the wall, above a window, with the legend:

BUILT
1695
REPAIRED
1829

And on the lintel of the window in the Eastern gable may be seen the engraved date, "1829." Of these dates, and what they indicate, will be told further on.

A generous "front-door" on the South side of what may be presumed to be the stem of the cross, opens on a covered wooden stoop, and two side doors are sheltered by the stiff hoods common to the Meeting House of early construction.

Anciently, this may have been an ideal spot for a Friends' Meeting House, but now it seems better adapted for a mission, since its nearest neighbors are a tavern, "where they sell liquor," but a quiet, orderly place, and not unlike the

WELSH SETTLEMENT OF PENSYLVANIA

road-houses of England, and a popular race track. But to maintain the religious atmosphere, its third neighbor is the great convent house and estate of the Sisters of Mercy, a teaching order. Between the walls of the convent grave yard, where Sisters are buried, and the Meeting House, lays the "Friends' Ground," the grave yard of the Merion Meeting, protected from trespass by a stone wall, surmounted by an iron fence.

Passing through its ever open iron gates, unheeding the weather beaten warning, "All Trespassing Forbidden," and going up the long, straight gravel walk, bisecting the grounds, where

> "Round about, the old Friends sleep,
> Grave women, earnest men,"

you may notice that innovation has reached this long-time secluded spot, as it has other Meetings' grave yards, for there are inscribed stones marking graves, something the Founders and early members of this Meeting would not have tolerated. However, these cannot be classed as tombstones, or monuments, for they are little, modest affairs, never taller than two feet which superceded equally low head and foot boards to the graves, and for this reason many have sank as if ashamed, so that the grass hides them, and the simple legends they bear are difficult to read. There are only about 200 graves thus marked, which is but a small percentage of the thousands of people here interred, one above the other, in two centuries, and, singular to relate, one-third of the stones tell they are in loving remembrance of people who died over eighty years of age, thus evidencing, as claimed, that "Quaker habits promote longevity." These modest grave-stones tell the barest details of the departed; only their names and span of life, engraved on the upper edge, in the strata, and for this reason are soon rendered unreadable by the elements of the weather.

As the majority of the stones tell of Friends who died after 1830, it may be presumed it was about that decade of

ARRANGING WELSH SETTLEMENT

the last century, shortly after the Society became divided into two branches, generally known as "orthodox" and "Hicksites," and the latter Friends, who, however, do not recognize this appellation, calling themselves simply "Friends," got control of this Meeting, they being more liberal in their views of such matters, when non-Friends, but descendents of members of the Society, began to be buried here, and the taste and desire for marble marking stones prevailed, for the stones recording earlier decease may have been erected long subsequent to the event, since they do not have the appearance of more age than their neighbors of later dates, and there are several that tell of deaths in the last decade of the 18th century.

And it is also notable that such members of the Friends' families who served as soldiers in the Civil War, are buried here, and bear the little marker-flags placed by the loving hands of their living companions, the members of the Society of the Grand Army of the Republic on Memorial Day.

This spot, hallowed by dear and sad memories, may in a few years be in the midst of a dense population, the overflow from the city, but now, of a summer's day, only the far-off ring of a blacksmith's hammer, or the occasional tap of the convent bell, or the quick rush of an "auto," is the only commotion that disturbs its continual calm.

In some respects, this may be like a hundred other Friends' Meeting Houses, which called for the lines from the Quaker poet, John Russell Hayes:

> "I love the old Meeting Houses,—how my heart
> Goes out to these dear, silent homes of prayer,
> With all their quietude and rustic charm;
> Their loved associations and pathetic solitude;
> Their tranquil and pathetic solitude;
> Their hallowed Memories!"

But the old Merion Meeting, and its house has enough personality to make it distinguishable.

No picture of the neighborhood, in which this ancient House stands, can be painted better by the pen, to compare its site with what it was in the extreme past, than the commercial statement, the land in its vicinity, which was bought from Penn for only five pence an acre, is now being sold for more than five thousand dollars an acre, and a mile beyond, at Wynnewood and at Ardmore, for fifteen thousand dollars an acre! Which means, the inhabitants of Penn's "City of Brotherly Love," once miles away, and whose buildings could be counted on the fingers of one hand when the Welsh Quakers pitched their tents here, have brought it into sight of the door of the old Meeting House, and have thus enhanced the value of the land about it. The suburban population surrounds it; villages have grown-up about it; it has become accessible by steam and electric cars, and by well-kept avenues, this ancient, vine-grown old stone Meeting House, to which Friends for years came afoot and horse-back, along the bridle-paths and lanes through the wild woods, but whose descendants now roll up to meetings in luxurious limousines.

This Merion Meeting House, as it stands, was not only the first place of public worship erected for the original settlers of the territory west of the Schuylkill river, distant from the limit of the proposed city of Philadelphia, and just without its present bounds, by the Welsh Friends, who began to remove here in the summer of 1682, but the first public house of worship or church building put up in the Commonwealth, and, as may be seen hereafter, it was also the first "town hall' erected in it. And I understand it was the first permanent Meeting House for Friends erected in America.

The story of the experiences of the earliest Welsh settlers in "Merioneth Town," or "Merion Town," as the district in which this Meeting House stands, was at first called, in honor of the shire in Wales from which its first settlers came, or Merion township, as it came officially to be designated, and of the "towns" of "Harfod," or Haverford, and Radnor, continguous to it, from the year of first settlement,

ARRANGING WELSH SETTLEMENT

1682, will be told by their extant letters written to friends at "home," has none of the thrilling tales of hardship and adventure, of "battle, murder and sudden death," that embellishes, and saddens those of the first comers into Virginia and New England, a half-century earlier, nor those of the pioneers of the Cumberland Valley, the Valley of Virginia, or of Kentucky, when beginning the "winning of the West," a half-century later. Nor did these Friends—"those devil-driven heretics," as the Rev. Cotton Mather, of New England, called the Quakers in his "Magnalia,"—have to suffer from the "sharp laws" of Massachusetts, and New England Puritan intolerance, and any there who did, soon found their way to Pennsylvania.

Writing of these early days, with his facile pen in his "Quaker School Boy," Friend Isaac Sharpless says, "It was a venture, as all emigration is, but the results were happy. There was none of the suffering of Massachusetts and Virginia. The wise arrangement of Penn had made the redmen more than friends. The Quaker home, and children, were left in perfect security, while the adult attended Quarterly Meeting."

And the Welsh Friends were hardly forerunners even in the land, for the way had long been made clear for their peaceful entrance into their purchased lands, and many were able to be seated at the very first on old "Indian fields," and on clearings made by their predecessors, the Swedes, Dutch and early English, who came up here from the old settlements on the lower Delaware. But as these choice spots were, as we may see, soon claimed by Penn as his private property, their tenure of them was brief. That Penn appreciated them highly may be seen from his letter of 16, 8mo. 1683, to the Free Society of Traders in Pensylvania, in which he says, "There are also very good peaches, and in great quantities, not an Indian plantation without them, they make a pleasant drink," hence the "insidious punch" of peach brandy and honey.

WELSH SETTLEMENT OF PENSYLVANIA

The Delaware river country had been opened for fifty-odd years to settlers, on both of its lower banks, and considerable land was being cultivated and farmed, in peace, without fear, though not comfort possibly, as we understand it, when the Welsh Friends removed to Penn's new province, where he "would found a free colony for all mankind that shall go thither," as his land-sale advertisements stated. Therefore, the story of their first years in America is almost devoid of especial interest in respect to what makes that of older colonies here so prominent.

Yet, although it may be only that of domesticity—simply the transfer of "home" across the sea, from one peaceful site to another, with only discomforts incidental to removal and travel, and re-establishment, to enliven it, theirs is the story of active participation in the founding of the Commonwealth of Pensylvania.

They had longed
> "For a lodge in some vast wilderness,
> Some boundless contiguity of shade,"

and they certainly were accommodated, these Welsh of English nationality, but their settling in Pensylvania was not a complete severance from "home," to which kin and ancestors still bound them for several generations.

Although, like the Swedes of the "South River country," and the Dutch of New Netherlands, the Welsh of the Schuylkill, who, however, ceased coming over in any great number after the "sufferings" were stopped in their native land, or when they learned that Penn had not kept to his promises to the early colonists, as will be explained hereafter; were engulfed, disappearing as a separate race in a few years, in the great flood of English to our shores, and lost their identity, and Welsh characteristics, swallowed up by the cosmopolitan development of our country, and even the use of their distinctive tongue. * The moral influence and teachings

---

*The Welsh language may have been understood, spoken and written and read and preferred by the Welsh Quakers generally in Pen-

ARRANGING WELSH SETTLEMENT

the Welsh members of the religious Society of Friends, "the people vulgarly called Quakers," with their Cymric blood, an industrious, hardy race, were instilled into the community of strangers which grew up about them, and in which they were finally absorbed, grown into the fibre and woof of our great nation, for, there is hardly a present-day family of any prominence, or social pretentions, in Pensylvania, or in the "West," having colonial ancestry, that cannot claim, with truth, an ancestor among the early Welsh Friends of this Commonwealth, and they are proud in being able to do so for reasons that may appear hereafter. ‡ In this connection the late Dr. Levick said in a public address, "The early Welsh settlers of Philadelphia, and its vicinity, belonged to a race which has left its impress, in a very marked manner, on the character of its descendants to the present day."

---

sylvania, for, as will appear, they desired, and expected that the civil affairs of the whole Welsh Tract would be determined by officers and juries "of our language." But English was the prevailing language with the Welsh Quakers in the "Haverford and Merion towns," as the earliest settlers therein were of the upper, educated class of Wales, and were often at London, and among the English. But in Radnor Township there were many Welsh who did not understand English, for, as late as in 1707, the Welsh Episcopalians then petitioned the Bishop of London to send them a rector who could read and speak both Welsh and English. They were the founders of the P. E. Church of St. Davids. In other parts, and in the Gwynedd settlement, however, the Welsh language and customs obtained distinctively for many years, and many of the wills, and documents issued by the people of the latter section were in the Welsh tongue, as, for instance, as late as 1712, the subscription paper passed around, for collecting funds to rebuild the Gwynedd Meeting House, in which House ministers had to speak alternately in Welsh and English, in the same address.

---

‡The Welsh origin for the Pensylvania families of Adams, Apthorp, Arnold, Bevan, Cadwalader, David, Davies, Evans, Ellis, Edwards, Foulke, Floyd, Griffith, Guinn, Gwynne, Hughs, Humphreys, Howell, Hewes, Henry, Harry, Jones, John, Lloyd, Lewis, Morris, Morgan, Owen, Price, Powell, Paul, Penn, Pugh, Richards, Rice, Reese, Roberts, Thomas, Williams, Wynne, etc., can easily be imagined.

WELSH SETTLEMENT OF PENSYLVANIA

And Mr. Benjamin H. Smith, in an interesting article in a recent number of the magazine of the Historical Society of Pensylvania, concerning the lands in Merion of the first coming Welshmen, whose sturdy honesty and integrity he recognized, says, "they were prominent and respected citizens in their own country," and "those who came to Pensylvania took a leading part in the development of the new colony, and many of their descendants have borne distinguished names in literature, science, and public affairs."

Before entering into sketches of the Founders of the Friends' Merion Meeting, and of their Meeting House, and of the people prominently connected with it in its earliest years, and of its present-day members, and the same, incidentally, of the other meetings composing the Haverford or Radnor Monthly Meeting, it should not be uninteresting to review some of the events leading up to its establishing as introductory to them.

Immediately after William Penn was in full possession of the Royal Grant for the territory in America, then named, and so written for fifty years subsequently in public documents, and frequently in preserved private letters of the Quakers, "Pensylvania," he began to advertise, and canvass for purchasers and settlers for it. He first began his efforts within the Society of Friends, of which he was a prominent minister, and well known to thousands, advertising his province as an ideal asylum, or home, for them, with life there everything they might desire, appealing especially to those who were unhappy and dissatisfied, for various reasons, more or less serious, with their conditions in life.

Though it is unnecessary to bring to mind the many, many "sufferings" experienced by the Friends when the "church people" must have studied Collier's "Art of Ingeniously Tormenting," because of dislike to military duties; objections to paying tithes to support the "Established Church," their piety, and especially their public worship, a matter that was positively forbidden by acts of parlia-

ARRANGING WELSH SETTLEMENT

ment, one of these edicts to suppress "seditious conventicles," however, it is proper to mention here, as in it are the names of Welshmen who removed to Pensylvania, or the fathers of others.

This particular "edict" is dated 20 of May, 1675, and is signed by Humphey Hughes and John Wynne, constables. But it is not the notice that these Welshmen "met unlawfully under pretence of religion," and that the constables were ordered to "levy on them by way of distress," but it is the list of names given in the schedule, accompanying it, of those on whom they were to levy the fines, that is of interest.

"The names of those that unlawfully met together att Llwyn y Braner, within ye parish of Llanvaur, upon ye 16th day of May, being Sunday, 1675. Oathes being made they were present formerly in unlawful meetings within three months.

"First conviction on the oathes of Owen D'd, and Thomas Jones.

"Second conviction, and warrant of arrest for the Double fine, on oath of Robert Evans."

(Each of these following was fined ten shillings.)
"John David John, and his wife, of Cilltalgarth.
Hugh Roberts, and his wife, of the same place.
Cadwalader Thomas, of the same place.
Robert David, of the same place.
Robert Owen, of Vron Gôch.
Elin Owen, of the same.
John Thomas ap Hugh, of Llaythgywm.
John ap Edward, of Nanlleidiog.
Evan Edwards, of Cynlas.
Peter Owen, of Bettws y Coed.
Robert John, of Pen maen.
Margaret John, of same place.
Hugh John Thomas, of Nanlleidiog.
His sonne and daughter.

WELSH SETTLEMENT OF PENSYLVANIA

Litter Thomas, of Llandervel.
Jane Morris, of Pen maen.
Edward Griffith, of Llaetgwm.
Edward Reese, of Llantgervel.
John James, of the same.
William Morgan, of Llanecill.
Owen David, of Cilttalgarth.
John William, of the same place.
Anne, verch David, widow, of Pen maen."

This schedule, with the order, is preserved among the mass of MSS. which the wife and widow of John Thomas brought over here in 1683, now in possession of Lewis Jones Levick, Esqr., of Bala, (Philadelphia), who inherited them. It came into John's possession while serving as constable, and he endorsed on it:

"Evan Owen ye son of a widow called Gainor, whose late husband was Owen ap Evan, of Vron Gôch, was convicted by oath to be present at a meeting, though but 9 or 10 years old."

Penn's advertisements of his American possessions (he was his own sales-agent), readily appealed to Friends of every race, but the very first to take advantage of his generous and alluring offers, which he well knew how to make attractive, for he had had only recently some valuable experience in getting settlers for West Jersey when attending to Friend Billing's embarrassed estate there, and which suggested to him the scheme of having a great American territory for himself, and selling it out, giving him a permanent income in quit-rents, were the Friends in Wales.

But, to go back a little of this story of Welsh interests in Pensylvania.

The principal missionary of introduction of the teachings and belief of Friends into Wales was one John ap John, of "Plas Ifa" (Plas Eva, or Plas Evan), at Trevor, a hamlet near Ruabon and Wrexham, in Langollen parish, Denbighshire, then a pastoral country, but now given over to

ARRANGING WELSH SETTLEMENT

brickyards. He was born at Trevor Issa, about 1625-30, and baptised at the parish church, and became a member of a non-conforming congregation in the parish of Wrexham, in Denbighshire. In some way, the tenets and teachings of the learned apostle of Quakerism, George Fox, had reached this assembly in fragments. The meager reports of the lectures of this eminently successful minister seemed plausible and pleasing, but to be better instructed, the minister of the congregation, the Rev. Morgan Lloyd, sent this John, of "Plas Ifa," with a companion, to attend some of the meetings and make himself familiar with the precepts taught by Mr. Fox, and report them to it. Telling of this John ap John, Mr. Fox says he had been a "minister." He was probably of the Parliamentary party, and may have been a chaplain at "Bewmarres," or Beaumaris, where he lived, in the army in the latter years of the Protectorate.

The result of this mission is thus noticed by Mr. Fox in his "Journal," (p. 123, of London, 1694, edition): "When these triers came down among us the power of the Lord overcame them, and they were both of them convinced of the Truth, they returned into Wales, where John ap John abode in the Truth, and received a gift in the ministry, to which he continued faithful."

Thus it came about that John ap John was the founder of the Society of Friends in Wales. Small Meetings were organized everywhere by him and co-laborers, at first secretly, but it was not till after the "toleration" act of Parliament was passed, that the Society became regularly organized into "Quarterly Meetings," and irregular "Yearly Meetings" were held at Swansea, in 1681, and at Redstone, near Narberth, in Pembrokeshire, on 5 2mo, 1682. But the first Yearly (or Half-Yearly) Meeting regularly organized according to Friends' rules was held at the house of Ellis Morris, at Dolgyn, near Dolgelly, in Merionethshire, on 7, 3mo, 1683. In 1684, the Yearly Meeting was at Haverfordwest, at which William Humphrey, of Llanegryn,

WELSH SETTLEMENT OF PENSYLVANIA

Merioneth, promised and undertook to write up the "sufferings" of the Welsh Friends, in the years past. A subject so enlarged, subsequently, by Friend Besse, that it is only contained in two large printed volumes, since he records the sufferings of Friends in all lands. At the Yearly Meeting at Garthgynvor, near Dolgelly, in 1685, there were in attendance these "gentlemen," who had a part in the founding of the Merion Meeting. Charles Lloyd and Richard Davies, from Montgomeryshire; Roger ap John, and John ap John, and Richard Davies, from Denbighshire. The delegates to the great Yearly Meeting, at London, in 1688, when the Welsh Friends were first represented were Richard Davies, representing North Wales, and James Lewis, South Wales.

And of this John the son of John, the late Dr. Levick, of Philadelphia, said in an address delivered before the Historical Society of Pensylvania, 13 month, 1893*: "He was the Apostle of Quakerism in Wales," and he "was the direct agent, under Providence, in bringing about changes which resulted in the settlement so largely by Welsh emigrants of the Township of Merion."

And this is the good authority for John ap John, the first minister among Welsh Friends, having been the Father of the "Welsh Tract" in Pensylvania, and of the variously called Merion, Haverford, or Radnor Monthly Meeting, in it, and it was natural that he should head the committee of Welsh Friends who first interviewed Penn about buying some of his land in America, and removing thither, and as this was but shortly after he had entered into possession, it is possible that John was in Penn's confidence, and had the earliest information of the consummation of his bargain with the King, and suggested to the Welsh to secure the best lands.

---

*Pensylvania Mag., XVII, 385, etc.

†See further as to John ap John in *The Journal of the Friends' Historical Society*, London, Supplement, No. 6, 1907.

ARRANGING WELSH SETTLEMENT

The material inducements to purchase his land, and remove to it, that Penn offered, no doubt was made to the Welsh Friends through John ap John, and they can be imagined. Surely they were sufficiently attractive, for a committee, probably gotten together by John, and representing Monthly Meetings of a half dozen Welsh shires, decided upon going to London to interview him personally before investing, for the Welsh were ever a cautious race.

The gentlemen,—who may, or may not have gone in a body,—who sought this conference with Penn on the part of themselves, and the Meetings of which they were members, is the first Roll of Honor connected with "New Wales," "Cambria," or "The Welsh Tract," as the lands, in Penn's Province, in which they became interested, were variously known at first.

These delegates, on the part of the Welsh Friends, who went on this mission, gentlemen all according to land deeds, were:

John ap John, of Ruabon, Denbigshire.
Dr. Thomas Wynne, of Caerwys, Flintshire.
Richard ap Thomas, of Whitford Garne, Flintshire.
Dr. Griffith Owen, of Dolserre, Merionethshire.
Dr. Edward Jones, of Bala, Merionethshire.
John ap Thomas, of Llaithgwm, Merionethshire.
Hugh Roberts, of Llanvawr, Merionethshire.
Thomas Ellis, of Dolserre, Merionethshire.
Charles Lloyd, of Dolobran, Montgomeryshire.
Richard Davies, of Welshpool, Montgomeryshire.
John Bevan, of Treverigg, Glamorganshire.
Lewis ap David, of Llandewy Velfry, Pembrokeshire.

There were others, among them Edward Prichard, William Jenkins, and John Burge, who went to talk with Penn about the same time, but the list aforesaid includes the leaders in the movement for Pensylvania land (although there is evidence that John Roberts and Robert Owen, who

WELSH SETTLEMENT OF PENSYLVANIA

came over to Pensylvania, were also present), and who had the interview with Penn, in London, in May, 1681, of which, unfortunately for the Welsh, no written report was kept, and was, as will be explained, the cause of a serious misunderstanding subsequently.

Of these gentlemen, the three "practitioners in physics," and Messrs. Bevan, Roberts, Ellis and Owen, removed to Pensylvania and aided in settling the Welsh people on the lands purchased from them.

What Penn particularly promised these gentlemen, if they would induce the members of their Monthly Meetings to buy his land, and settle upon it, other than its fine quality, and his liberal guarantee of freedom from certain annoyances they had to put up with in Wales, was shortly, and is yet, partly a matter of conjecture and surmise as to its details and particulars, for Penn's promises to them were only verbally made. But these certain great expectations, with which these Welsh gentlemen claimed Penn had lured them to America, had vouching only by slender circumstantial evidence, and hearsay, his English lieutenants and alleged friends in Philadelphia held. Nevertheless, the Welshmen averred, and stuck to it, though little good it did them, as we shall see, that Penn's encouragement was, in part, they should have their whole purchase, the "Welsh Tract," as a "Barony," or State, as it were, within his Province, "within which all causes, quarrels, crimes and disputs might be tried and wholly determined by officers, magistrates, and juries of our language."

However, this committee having engaged to take and try to dispose of by sale to the other Welsh Friends, 40,000, or more acres, of Penn's land, returned to their several Monthly Meetings, and reported, and published Penn's "Articles of Conditions and Concessions" concerning his Province, to which they had subscribed before leaving London,—ideas of settlement he had re-written from the "Articles of Freedom and Exemption" compiled by the Dutch West India Company for a like purpose. So alluring were their statements, based on Penn's promises, fresh in their recollections, they had no trouble in getting Friends to subscribe immediately, till their sales, and the lands they themselves would take, amounted to 30,000 acres, and thus it was that these well known, reliable gentlemen, in six Welsh counties, became the first Pensylvania real estate agents.

The men who interviewed Penn, and those concerned with them, were nearly all of the highest social caste of the landed gentry of Wales, as has been frequently proved in recent years on investigation, for it is well known that in Wales the upper class readily embraced Quakerism, through the teachings of John ap John, one of themselves, while in England the gentry did not, as there converts were confined entirely to the "plain people"—the small lease-holding, the yeomandry, farmers, tradesmen, and shopkeepers,—and this fact has occasioned the astonishment that William Penn, an aristocrat by birth and association, against the wishes of his family, became a Quaker. So it may be understood that the committee of Welsh Friends were equals and peers of Penn, and for this reason he may have readily agreed to any propositions they made, though afterwards he certainly was most jealous of concessions.

Surely, he must have been pleased to have the Welsh gentry head his list of grantees, and promise to remove their families to their purchases, for it would have a good effect on his sales, especially when it became known that the best class of the Welsh were going, carrying refinement and education into his Province, for his was a tremendous proposition to undertake single-handed, and the countenance of his scheme by gentry was a great help to him.

It was a great disappointment to all, but John ap John, of "Plas Ifa," who was indirectly the progenitor of the Haverford Monthly Meeting, did not remove to Pensylvania. Concerning him, the late Dr. Levick said in an address, that after a long search he learned that John died on 16, 9mo,

WELSH SETTLEMENT OF PENSYLVANIA

1697, at the residence of his son-in-law, John Miller, of Whitehough Manor, and was buried in Friends' ground at Bashford, near-by, in Staffordshire, where no stone, or memorial marks the grave of this first apostle of Friends' teachings in Wales. He also learned that in 1712, the Friends' Yearly Meeting, of North Wales, desired to collect and acquire his MSS. to preserve them, but they could never be found. Since Dr. Levick's investigations and death, the interest in John ap John, which he started, has continued, and the following further data has been discovered of him.

He married about 1664, Catharine, either daughter of John Trevor, of Trevor Hall, and Valle Crucis Abbey, or daughter of Roger ap John, of Ruabon. About 1653, Roger ap John and John ap John were signers of a positive denial that certain Quakers came into Wrexham to gain proselytes at their meetings, and that "after a long silence, sometimes one, sometimes more, fell into great and dreadful shakings, with swellings in their bodies, sending out skreekings and howlings!"

An extant paper, at the Devonshire House, London, (Gibson Bequest MSS. II, 33), has been discovered, signed by John ap John, saying that, in the year 1653, his "understanding was opened." And, "In my Jvgment I have byn perswaeded vnto the Establishment & setelment thereof & as occasion served, both in Words & praodies J denied ye paement of tithys & becos of ye same Denial i cam to siffer ye loss of corn, hay, lams, peegs, yieves, kids & mvch thretnings with pikyls and other waes."

In another paper he mentions his conversion to Quakerism as follows: "The 2 day of ye 5 month, 1673. This time 20 years Agoee was ye time that I John Ap John was at Swart Moore with George ffoox in Lankashire. Yt was ye ffvrst time yt I soe Go ffox."

From sundry mention of him, it is learned that sometimes with Mr. Fox, but more often alone, he traveled all over Wales, preaching to any that would listen to him. But he

ARRANGING WELSH SETTLEMENT

did not accompany Mr. Fox in England. At Brecknock, in 1657, he "was moved of the Lord to speak in the Streets," which occasioned a tumult. At Tenby, he "went to the Steeple House" to speak, which was not unusual at that time, as, when the "priest" had finished his services, the church could be used by Presbyterians, or Independents, but John was arrested and jailed till Mr. Fox got him released. At several other places he was arrested for "speaking through the Town," and at his sometime home, Beaumaris, he was imprisoned "for public speaking." John also traveled through Wales preaching with John Burnyeat, in 1674, after Burnyeat's second return from America. Together, they attended a Quarterly Meeting at the home of Charles Lloyd, at Dolobran. Besse's "Sufferings" of the Quakers, of course, tells more of John ap John's experiences as a minister among Friends, and his are the earliest instances of persecution and annoyance in Wales.

John ap John had only one child, Phoebe, who married, 8, 3mo. 1689, John Mellor, or Miller, of the manor of Whitehough in Staffordshire, at the home of Richard Davies, in Rhuddalt. John ap John, as above, died at Whitehough, where he lived after the decease of his wife, Catharine, who died at Rhuddalt, 9, 11mo., 1694, and was buried at Trevor. Mr. Mellor died 3, 1m, 1718, aged 66 years and his wife Phoebe died 22, 8mo, 1734, at Leek, aged 69 years. Both buried at Basford. They had six children.

Charles

96
64
64
224

20° of y 3 p.m. $\bar{r}$.

According to A Warr^t from Capt Thomas Holmes Surv^r Gen^{rall} Bearing date the 24th of 4: th m^o 84 directed unto me for the Surveying of 2500 Acres of Land for Edward Jones & Company upon the west side of Skool-kill river. ffalls Contigous unto the City Liberty I have Survey^d and Laid out and subdivided the said quantity of Land, unto the persons mentioned above and unto every man by proportion, as by these severall figures doth appeare with their bounds and courses exprest in y^e figur by a skale of 80 perch in an inch.

Ja. Jowell

Sur^d p. War^t pr me date$d$ 24: 6mo 82 directed to C. Hson
Chr p. Warr^t from y^e Gov$r$ until 22 c: 1 mo 83. y^e p$r$ticlrs in Chr. abst Lipag 1

The City Liberty

N
S
E
W

[30]

		Nor: Not W	
	32	32	32
W:S:W 796 perch			
Evan Rees 153¼			256 ps
Hugh John Thomas 76½	396 ps	John Watkin 76½	377 ps
William Jones 76½	388 ps	Thomas Lloyd 76½	376 ps
Cadwallader Morgan	236 ps	Gauron Robert 76½	
	32	32	32
N.W.W.	N.W.		N.N.

Map of the Thomas and Jones tract, 1683-4.

Note with the orientation of the map the southern part of the tract nearest the Schuylkill River appears at the bottom.

WELSH LAND COMPANIES

The patentees for 30,000 acres of the "Welsh Tract" lands granted by William Penn, to whom deeds were made out, may be considered self-constituted heads of seven "companies" for the division and sale of this land to the Welsh whom Penn and they hoped would be actual settlers on it, were, with the number of acres each "company" had for sale, as follows:

Co. 1. John ap Thomas, of Llaithgwm, Merionethshire,
     Dr. Edward Jones, of Bala, Merionethshire. 5,000
Co. 2. Charles Lloyd, of Dolobran, Montgomeryshire,
     Margaret Davies, widow, of Dolobran...... 5,000
Co. 3. John Bevan, of Treverigg, Glamorganshire. 2,000
Co. 4. John ap John, of Ruabon, Denbighshire,
     Dr. Thomas Wynne, of Caerwys, Flintshire. 5,000
Co. 5. Lewis ap David, of Llandewy Velfry, Pembrokeshire, ... 3,000
Co. 6. Richard ap Thomas, of Whitford Garne, Flintshire, ... 5,000
Co. 7. Richard Davies, of Welshpool, Montgomeryshire 5,000

It was one of Penn's earliest intentions to sell his land in blocks of 5,000 acres, he having adopted the Dutch plan of "patroon concessions." He certainly made his offer attractive to the Welsh by this "concession." It may not have been stated in so many words, but the purchaser of such block was a "patroon" after the Dutch idea, since those with whom he divided the land settled with him, in his grant, and looked on him as their leader, and it was not necesary he should remove to, and reside with them on his purchase.

It may be seen that nine of the party of Welsh gentlemen who interviewed Penn, in May, 1681, and engaged to take 30,000 acres of land in his province, became concerned in these "companies," and real estate agents. The balance of 10,000 acres conditionally engaged by them and others present, was disposed of subsequently by Penn himself, or his agents, in small lots to actual settlers, and to parties who bought for speculation only, and 10,000 acres reserved in addition, also in the "Welsh Tract," were taken up in a few years by Welshmen, making their total purchase of 50,000 acres, the extent of this "Welsh Tract."

Excepting for names and amount of land, the patents to the first purchasers from "William Penn, of Worminghurst, in the county of Sussex, Esq.," were nearly all of even date, namely, "the Fifteenth Day of September, in the year of our Lord One thousand six hundred Eighty and one in the CCCIII yeare of the Reigne of King Charles the Second over England".

But there was an important difference in the deeds to these "first purchasers," which turned out to be the cause of considerable trouble in after years, as we may see, and was particularly disappointing to the heads of "Companies" No. 1 and 4, and their grantees. From the deeds of "Thomas & Jones," and "John & Wynne" to their grantees, it appears that they and others made up by subscription the purchase money for the two blocks they took, and that they were only "trustees" in the matter of the purchase, and, like the other subscribers' purchase money, only interested to the amount contributed, whereas the heads of the other five "companies" bought on their own accounts, hoping to sell off what land they did not wish to retain. But Penn, and his representative in Pensylvania, considered all the heads of these companies to be "trustees," and treated them alike, and if they had not been Quakers there would

ADVENTURERS FOR LAND

have been much litigation over land claims. As it was, Penn's commissioners, and the Board of Property, had much difficulty adjusting them.

Penn's deeds to the "trustees" cite the date and consideration, the location of the territory, etc., granted to him, by Royal Letters Patent, 4 March 1681, from which he conveyed to them the various amounts of their purchases, of course, without giving their locations, and the conditions and restrictions under which he made the conveyances. The consideration being £100 sterling for each tract of 5,000 acres located in one lot, "if possible, in his province, and subject to quit-rent of one shilling for every hundred acres of the said five thousand acres att or upon the first day of March for ever."

The deeds to the "companies," as well as those from them to those who bought of them, were long afterwards recorded in Philadelphia County, and were confirmed by Penn's land commissioners. At first, much to their astonishment and disappointment, half of the land called for in "Welsh Deeds" was laid out to the "first purchasers" in the townships of Merion, Radnor, and Haverford, and subsequently the balance was laid out in the townships of Goshen, New Town, or Uwchland in the Tract.

For two years and a half this method obtained, and Penn had given no order to survey the 30,000 acre tract bought, so the Welsh could know exactly its bounds, and if they lay within their rights. Urged by them to do this, Penn gave finally the following warrant for survey, to Thomas Holmes, his surveyor general:—

"Whereas divers considerable persons among ye Welsh Friends have requested me yt all ye Lands Purchased of me by theos of North Wales and South Wales, together with ye adjacent counties to ym as Herefordshire, Shorpshire, and Cheshire, about fourty thousand acres, may be lay'd out contiguously as one Barony, alledging yt ye number allready come and suddenly to come, are such as will be capable of planting ye same much with in ye proportion allowed by ye custom of ye country, & so not lye in large useless vacancies.

"And because I am inclined and determined to agree and favour ym wth any reasonable Conveniency and priviledge:—I do hereby charge thee and strictly require thee to lay out ye sd tract of Land in as uniform a manner as conveniently may be, upon ye west side of Skoolkill river, running three miles upon ye same, and two miles backward, & then extend ye parallel with ye river six miles, and to run westwardly so far as this ye sd quantity of land be Compleately surveyed unto ym.

"Given at Pennsbury, ye 13th 1 mo. 1684."

Under instructions from the surveyor-general, dated 4. 2mo. 1684, his deputy, David Powel, laid out the tract, "in method of townships lately appointed by the Governor, att five thousand acres for a township." But it was not until 25. 5mo. 1687, that the bounds of the Welsh Tract were defined, and publicly known.

The next item found concerning the "Welsh Tract," three years later, is a minute of the Commissioners' meeting, held "in ye Council Room at Philad'a ye 25th of ye 5 Mo. 1687". It mentions the "Tract of Land, about 40,000 acres, w'ch was laid out by vertue of a warrant from the proprietary and Governor, bearing Date ye 13th day of the first month, 1684, for the Purchasers of North and South Wales and adjacent Counties of Herefordshire, Shorpshire, and Cheshire, * * * it is bounded:—

Beginning at the Skoolkill [at the Falls], thence running West [by] South West, on the City Liberties, 2256 Perches [a little over seven miles, along Township, or City Line Road] to Darby Creek.

Thence following up the several courses thereof [i.e. Darby Creek] to New Town, 988 Perches [a little over three miles], to a Corner post by Crumb Creek.

ADVENTURERS FOR LAND

Thence down the several Courses thereof [Crum Creek], 460 Perches, [not quite a mile and a half].

Thence West and by South, by a line of Trees, 2080 Perches [six miles and a half].

Thence North [by] North West, by a line of Trees, 1920 Perches [six miles].

Thence East, and by North, by a line of Trees, 3040 Perches [nine and a half miles].

Thence East and by South 1120 Perches [three and a half miles].

Thence South [and by] South East 256 Perches [about a mile and a quarter].

Thence East [and by] North East 640 Perches [not quite a mile and a half].

Thence South [and by] South East 1204 Perches [a fraction over three and a half miles].

Thence East [and by] North East 668 Perches [a little over two miles] to the Skoolkill.

Thence down the several courses thereof [Schuylkill River] to the Place of beginning."

This tract covered 62½ square miles.

So it was not till six years after the Welsh gentlemen engaged to take 40,000 acres, that the tract was surveyed for them. There is a plot of the tract in the Surveyor General's office, at Harrisburg, but it does not agree with the bounds given above. The survey included the townships of Lower Merion, a portion of Upper Merion, Haverford, Radnor, Tredyffrin, Whiteland, Willistown, East Town, Goshen, and part of West Town.

But in all these years, the Welsh were not idle, nor was Penn. All interested were "booming" the land. The Welsh trustees had disposed of their trusts, and Penn had sold a million acres.

This was not the only "Welsh Tract" in Pensylvania. Subsequently lands were sold to other Welshmen, and we

WELSH SETTLEMENT OF PENSYLVANIA

had "Welsh Tracts" in Chester Co., and at Gwynedd, or 'North Wales," and then in New Castle Co. (Delaware). The Carolinas also had "Welsh Tracts," but with these Penn was not concerned.

The material side of immigration was made as attractive as possible by nicely gotten up pamphlets issued by Penn, or his agents, setting forth, in addition to his advertising, in glowing terms, the general recommendations of his Province and land, the social advantages gained by removal there, and the approximate outside cost of it; in detail, just how to conduct a farm in the new country and make it pay. One of his advertising papers, addressed "to such persons as are inclined * * * to the Province of Pensylvania,"* tells attractively what expense a man with £100 cash would be under if he bought from him 500 acres, and transported himself, wife, a child, and two men servants to his purchase. It being understood that "500 acres of uncleared land is equivolent to 50 acres of cleared English, or Welsh land."

By taking along to Pensylvania certain small articles, cloth, clothes, harness, implements, etc., and selling them there the land would be paid for by the 50% profit derived. The transportation of the party would cost not more than £38.2.6, with new clothes, "Shurtes, Hatts, Shooes, Stokins, and Drawyers," a ton of things to sell, and "four gallons of Brandy, and 24 pounds of Suger for the Voyage." Arriving at the purchase in early summer, encamping and clearing fifteen acres for plowing, cutting out best timber for house, according to directions, planting, erecting the log-cabin, and getting in the crops, brings the experience of this party up to winter, when the prospect is not pleasant, as they have only green wood to burn. The barn is built, and in the spring stock is bought, and first crop sold.

---
*Pa. Mag., IV., p. 331.

ADVENTURERS FOR LAND

Now, the settler takes "account of stock." He finds he has paid out from his £100, in one year:—

"To Passage and Cloaths	£38.02.06
"To House and Barn	15.10.00
"To living expenses one year	17.17.06
"To Stock	24.10.00
	£96.00.00

His receipts and assets, "per Contr. Creditor," he finds as follows:—

Crop valued at	£59.10.00
House and barn, value,	30.00.00
Stock, cost,	24.10.00
Land, with 15 ac. improved,	26.05.00
Remaining cash	4.00.00
Total assets	£144.05.00

It may thus be seen the immigrant has had a good first year, "on paper." The receipts from crops paid for the fifteen-acre field (the profit of goods brought over having paid for the tract), and for the house and barn. Is it any wonder that the humble Welsh willingly removed.

The directions for building the log house are particular as to trees, how to get them ready, etc. It should be "thirty foot long and eighteen foot broad," "with a partition neer the middle, and an other to divide one end of the House into two small Rooms," and a loft over all, the floor of which to be of "clapbord," but "the lower flour is the Ground." "This may seem a mean way of Building, but 'tis sufficient and safest for ordinary beginners." "An ordinary House, and a good Stock, is the Planters Wisdom."

Only three years after immigrants began coming into Pensylvania, there were "evil reports" given out in England "by many Enemies to this new Country," because it promised to be a growing colony of non-conformists, and because others had other colony schemes they were trying to float. Then there were those who could not believe Penn's astonishing statements in his advertisements of his land, and these were as much to be dreaded as the "Enemies."

In order to head-off these aspersions against Pensylvania, Governor Penn asked some of the leading men in the Province to give him their opinions of the country from personal observation and experience. One, Dr. Nicholas More, wrote him, "Green Spring, 13 Sep. 1686," for publication it may be imagined, a long, cheerful account* reciting the "evil reports," "as if we were ready to Famish, and that the Land is so barren, the Climet so hot, that English Grain, Roots, and Herbs do not once come to Maturity, and what grows, to be little worth." This he pronounced bosh. And he gave prices current here for a hundred products and articles, and all possible profits on them.

But what would most appeal to farmers, Welsh or English, was what he wrote of grain crops. He said, "I have had seventy Ears of Rye upon one single Root, proceeding from one single Corn; 45 of Wheat; 80 of Oats; 10, 12, and 14 of Barley out of one Corn; I took the Curiosity to tell one of the twelve Ears from one Grain, and there was in it 45 Grains on that Ear; above 3,000 of Oats from one single Corn." ["Quaker Oats"?], etc. "But it would seem a Romance rather than a Truth, if I should speak what I have seen in these things."

This must have convinced the Welsh farmers.

In referring thus to Penn's advertising his lands, I do not lose sight of the fact that his Pensylvania scheme was "in the course of his pious life,"—"continually and various ways were employed in promoting the happiness of mankind, both in their religious and civil capacity," and attribute any sordid aspects to it. The advertisements

---
*Pa. Mag., IV., p. 447.

ADVENTURERS FOR LAND

are only mentioned to show the method pursued in trying to sell, and to also show that he knew how to "sell without samples," and that he was a pioneer in the real estate business, if not in the "mail-order business," and that as an all-round business man he was "far and away ahead of his time," and would have been the first great "captain of industries" if he had had faithful lieutenants, or, if, in a word, his whole endeavor had not been a chimera.

However, his real estate venture throughout was "clean." There is no evidence of any scandals connected with it. He may have had paid agents to sell his land for him, and he may have paid commissions on sales, and the "trustees" may have sold some lands at advance prices, and some may have bought to speculate, but what of it? Such methods then were as proper as they are to-day.

The "company," some of whose members were the first to come over, and have land laid out in the Welsh Tracts, was that of John ap Thomas and Dr. Edward Jones. This was in August, 1682, a year after Penn's first ship-load of colonists had arrived here, and two months before he himself came on his first visit to America. There has been much told of these very first arrivals in three ships, so it is only necessary here to repeat that the first boat-load arrived in the Delaware in August, 1681, and the third in the following December, and that the immigrants landed at Upland (now Chester), and remained there, supposing it to be the site of the city Penn had said he was going to lay out, till after the first surveyor came over, in June, 1682, up to which time twenty-three other immigrant ships had arrived.

The surveyor, Thomas Holme, after looking around, probably told some one that he was going to recommend that the city be located further up the river, at the Swede's farm, called Wicaco, for in July there was a great scramble of immigrants to that locality. Here Dr. Jones found them when he arrived in August, 1682.

WELSH SETTLEMENT OF PENSYLVANIA

When Penn came in the following October, 1682, he found his first English colonists, like squatters, living in huts and "caves," on the Delaware, where they supposed the city would be laid out, and, as first arrivals, they would have the choice lots. This may, or may not have influenced him to order his city laid out here, but it was months before it was plotted. The site of the new city seems to have been known or well guessed at two months before Penn came, as Dr. Jones mentions "the town of Philadelphia" in his letter, hereafter given, written 13, 6mo. 1682. For this reason it has been believed that the Doctor selected or suggested the site of the city, and possibly named it, as Penn tells it was named "before it was born."

Now, that we have reviewed the inception, founding, and establishing of the "Welsh Tract," on and beyond the Schuylkill, we proceed to consider its first and pioneer settlers, "the company of Thomas and Jones"—the builders of the Merion Meeting House.

MERION FRIENDS' MEETING HOUSE, *CIRCA* 1830.

THOMAS & JONES' LAND PATENT

Beginning with the Thomas & Jones "Company," and land, which was "ye first within ye tract of land in the Province" to be laid out, we will consider the companies in succession.

There are extant documents like confirmatory deeds, each having the title, "An Indenture where severall are concerned," and bearing date of March 18th, others "The first day of Aprill, in the four and thirtieth year of our sovereign Charles, Second," [1682]. They recite the conveyance of the 5,000 acres of land by William Penn to John ap Thomas and Edward Jones, and that "there have been two severall Indentures, ye one of bargain and sale for one year, bearing date ye 16th day of September in the three and thirtieth year of his majesty's reign [1681]*, the other bearing date ye 17th day of the same month and year," both made between William Penn and John ap Thomas and Edward Jones. And, "that for and in consideration of the sum of One Hundred pounds of good and lawfull money of England to him in hand paid by Jno. T. & Edw. Jones, he did grant [to them] the full portion of 5,000 acres of land, * * * ye first within ye tract of land in the Province," "bearing date ye 11th day of July then last past, paying one shilling for every one hundred acres of ye said 5,000 upon the first day of March forever."

This deed then recites that "others than John ap Thomas and Edward Jones have contributed towards this £100

---

*Charles the Second began his first regnal year in 1660, but as it was his restoration, his first regnal year was called in documents the 12th year of his reign, making his reign date from 30 Jan. 1648-9, the beginning of the Commonwealth. Therefore, in the above deed, the 33 Charles II. was 1681.

of purchase money," and that "the said John and Edward are as Trustees," they being personally responsible for the amounts to which the others and themselves have individually subscribed. That "for £25 which John ap Thomas has subscribed, he shall have 1250 acres [one-fourth interest], and Edward Jones in like proportion, and that the residue of the land be of equal goodness."

These documents are confirmation that 16 September 1681 was the date of the original grant to John ap Thomas and Dr. Edward Jones, or the "Thomas & Jones Co.," which for convenience, and because its land was the first laid out, and its subscribers the first to arrive here, and founded the Merion Meeting, we will call "Company No. 1."

Company No. 1. There were seventeen Welsh Friends, one a woman, who subscribed to the £100 purchase money for the 5,000 acres in the Welsh Tract, which John ap John and Dr. Edward Jones engaged for them. The names of these subscribers and purchasers are preserved in a memorandum written by John ap Thomas, found among his papers, entitled:—

COMPANY NUMBER ONE

"An account of wt sum of money every ffriend in Penllyn hath Layd out to buy land in Pensylvania & wt quantity of Acres of Land each is to have and wt sum of Quit Rents falls upon every one."

	Pounds.			Acres.	Quit Rent.	
John Tho	25	0s	0d	1250	12s	6d
Hugh Robt	12	10	0	625	6	3
Edd Jones	6	5	0	312 1/2	3	1 1/2
Robt Davis	6	5	0	312 1/2	3	1 1/2
Evan Rees	6	5	0	312 1/2	3	1 1/2
John Edd	6	5	0	312 1/2	3	1 1/2
Edd Owen	6	5	0	312 1/2	3	1 1/2
Will Edd	3	2	6	156 1/4	1	6 1/3
Edd Rees	3	2	6	156 1/4	1	6 1/3
Will Jones	3	2	6	156 1/4	1	6 1/3
Tho Rich	3	2	6	156 1/4	1	6 1/3
Rees John W	3	2	6	156 1/4	1	6 1/3
Tho lloyd	3	2	6	156 1/4	1	6 1/3
Cadd Morgan	3	2	6	156 1/4	1	6 1/3
John Watkin	3	2	6	156 1/4	1	6 1/3
Hugh John	3	2	6	156 1/4	1	6 1/3
Gainor Robt	3	2	6	156 1/4	1	6 1/3
	£100	0	0	5000	£2	10

From this MSS. and from the deeds for this land to the subscribers, we have the names, locations of their residences, their stations in life, and number of acres bought by each of the subscribers to the fund of £100.

"John Tho". "John ap Thomas, of Llaithgwm, gentleman," took 1250 acres, paying £25.

"Edd Jones". "Edward Jones, chyrurgion, of Bala," the partner in the trusteeship, took for himself only 312½ acres, paying £6.5.0.

"Hugh Robt". Hugh Roberts, of Kiltalgarth, gentleman," purchased 625 acres, paying £12.10s.

WELSH SETTLEMENT OF PENSYLVANIA

The following each bought 312½ acres, each paying £6. 5s.:

"Robt David". "Robert ap David, of Gwern Evel Ismynydd, yeoman."

"Evan Rees". "Evan ap Rees, of Penmaen, grocer."

"John Edd." "John ap Edwards, of Nant Lleidiog, yeoman."

"Edd Owen". "Edward ap Owen, 'late of Doleyserre,' gentleman."

The following each bought 156¼ acres, each paying £3. 2s. 6d.:

"Will Edd." "William ap Edward, of Ucheldre, or Ueneldri, yeoman."

"Edd Rees". "Edward ap Rees, of Kiltalgarth, gentleman."

"Gainor Robt". "Gainor Roberts, of Kiltalgarth, spinster."

"Will Jones". "William ap John alias Jones, of Bettws, yeoman."

"Tho Rich". "Thomas ap Richard alias Prichard, of Nant Lleidiog, yeoman."

"Hugh John". "Hugh ap John alias Jones, of Nant Lleidiog, yeoman."

"Rees John W". "Rees ap John ap William, alias Rees Jones, of Llanglynin, yeoman."

"Tho lloyd." "Thomas Lloyd, of Llangower, yeoman."

"Cadd Morgan". "Cadwalader Morgan, of Gwernevel, yeoman."

"John Watkin". "John Watkins, of Gwernevel, 'bathilor'."

As the homes of all of these subscribers were in the hundred of Penllyn, in Merionethshire, it was natural that the township in Pensylvania, where their land lay, should be given the name Merion by the surveyor-general, and sub-

COMPANY NUMBER ONE

sequently so many settlements in it should be called after Merionethshire places.*

Although the deeds of lease and release from Penn to Thomas & Jones for over 5,000 acres, were executed 16 and 17 September 1681, about four months after they had the interview with Penn in London, the transfers, by deeds, from them, of their proportions, to the several subscribers were not made till the following Spring, as these latter deeds of conveyance (copied into Books C.I and C.II in office of the Recorder of Deeds, Philadelphia), all bear dates between 28 February and 1 April, 1682, and they were not recorded till 22 3mo. 1684, but the confirmative patents were not granted till in 1702-1703. These deeds from Thomas & Jones have the same witnesses who were some of the others of these grantees, excepting, of course, the parties to the deed, and are all drawn very particularly as to facts, containing the "tripping clause," to wit: "Whereas besides the said John Thomas and Edward Jones, chirurgeon, others have contributed some part and proportion of the said sum of £100 for and towards the purchase of the premises, and whereas, though the said John Thomas and Edward Jones

---

*Some of these Welsh Friends of Merionethshire, who were signers of a marriage certificate, in 1mo. 1678-9, at the Penllyn Monthly Meeting, it will be seen came over and settled in the Welsh Tract.

Owen Humphrey.	Cadwalader Thomas.
John Humphrey.	John Thomas.
Richard Humphrey.	Elizabeth Thomas.
Humphrey Owen.	Rowland Ellis.
Rowland Owen.	Hugh Roberts.
John Owen.	Edward Vaughan.
Anne Owen.	Ellis Rees.
Elizabeth Owen (*bis*).	Ellin Rees.
Evan John.	Gwen Rees.
Rees John.	John Howell.
Gainor John.	Daniel Samuel.
Humphrey Reynolds.	Joseph Samuel.
Rees Evan.	Lydia Samuel.
John William.	Rebecca Samuel.

WELSH SETTLEMENT OF PENSYLVANIA

were intrusted to take the conveyances of all the said premises, yet they only intended to have their separate shares and proportions of the said 5,000 acres, according to the said sum they have laid out as part of the said £100 as only Trustees as to the rest of the said 5,000 acres, and for that it was also agreed that no benefit or survivorship should be taken between them." Mr. Thomas had paid in only £25, as mentioned, and Dr. Jones £6.5.0. This identifying Messrs. Thomas and Jones as only "trustees," was a serious matter to them, as will appear.

This distribution cleaned up these 5,000 acres, and reimbursed the trustees, Messrs. Thomas and Jones, for the £100 they had advanced to pay Mr. Penn.

Several of these purchasers did not remove to Pensylvania, but their land was laid out and surveyed along with the rest, and subsequently they sold out to others, who did remove and settle on it, or to their fellow contributors, as will appear later.

The earliest mention found, outside of the "trustee's deeds," which did not, however, give the locations of the lands, which was to be determined "as soon as the 5,000 acres is laid out," as the deeds state, is in a letter of Dr. Edward Jones, dated "Skoolkill River, ye 26th of ye 6mo. 1682," wherein he mentions the 2,500 acres on the Schuylkill as "ye Country lots." From the wording of the Doctor's statements, in this letter, given elsewhere, it would seem he thought his company's land, or at least the half of it, 2,500 acres, should have been laid out in "ye town lot," (in Philadelphia) "called now Wicoco." The earliest location of the land on a map was on that of Pensylvania, made by the surveyor-general of the Province, Thomas Holme, which he began to compile after Penn's first departure from America. But it is here only in outline, and indicates the land of "Edward Jones and Company 17 Families." Next, there is the unsatisfactory original draft of the lands included in this Welsh Tract, preserved at Harrisburg, which desig-

COMPANY NUMBER ONE

nates the land of "Edward Jones and Company, containing 2,500 acres, being 17 devisions." and then Powell's rough draft of the 2,500 acres, on the "city liberties's" line, and the Schuylkill river. Although a block of 5,000 was bought, it was told at the time to Dr. Jones, that because of the great demand for land in the Schuylkill neighborhood, by Penn's order only half of this amount could be laid out there. This, as will appear, was a cause of much dissatisfaction, as only part of purchase would be near the city, and the balance, away off in the wilds of Goshen, where the city of West Chester has grown up.

It is written on this extant draft or plot, preserved at Harrisburg, made by a deputy surveyor, David Powell, of the half of the total purchase made by Thomas & Jones, which lay on the west side of the Schuylkill, from above the Falls and up the river, that the first, or rough survey, was made by Charles Ashcom, on warrant from Mr. Powell, dated 24, 6mo. 1682, and that another rough survey was made on warrant "from ye Gov'r, date 22d 1 mo. 83."

From the Thomas & Jones deeds to each other, and from them jointly to the other parties to this purchase, comes the knowledge that the lots, of whatsoever size, when conveyed, were numbered, and only the number of a deed and the amount of acres going with it were given to the first surveyor, who laid them out accordingly, so the various grantees in this transaction had no part in selecting their land, and it was a lottery in what position, as to the others in this "company," the land would be laid out. The only stipulation on this point in the deeds was, it shall be "land of equal goodness with the residue, or as shall fall out by lot." This was very likely not a satisfactory arrangement, and may account for the many exchanges and sales between these lot holders soon after coming into possession, and getting acquainted with the quality and lay of the land.

Mr. Powell's mem. on the final and extant plot, dated "20th of ye 3d mo, 84," says, "According to A War't from

[51]

WELSH SETTLEMENT OF PENSYLVANIA

Capt Thomas Holmes, Survey'r Genrall, Bearing dat the 24th of ye 1st mo. 84, directed unto me for the Subdividing of 2,500 Acres of Land for Edward Joans & Company upon the west sid of Skoolkool above fals Contageous unto the City Liberty. I therefor Laid out and Subdivided the said quantity of Land, 25th of 1st mo. at the befor mentioned place, and unto every man by proportion as by these sevrall figure doth now at large Apeer with their bounds and courses enterd in ye sd figur by a skale of 80 perch in an inch. Da Powell."

In a general way, these 2,500 acres were bounded at first as follows: North, "Vakant Land," East "Skoolkool" river, South, "The Citty Libarty," and West, two tracts of Charles Lloyd and Thomas Lloyd, or Company No. 2.

This first draft of the sub-divisions of the "Thomas & Jones" land is here reproduced. The dimensions of the 17 lots may be given correctly, but the map certainly is not drawn to "skale of 80 perch in an inch." It has been worked out that "the areas of the several lots aggregate 2,444¾ acres," which was a fairly good survey of 2,500 acres at that time, though the area by modern survey would amount to about 3,200 acres. The charges for making the first survey for Dr. Jones was over £25, but he hoped "better orders will be taken shortly about" the bill, and he would not have to pay so much. But from his own account, he was lucky in getting the work done so soon after he arrived, as there were hundreds demanding surveys. To correct this first hurried survey of Mr. Ashcom, in 1682, the draft of Mr. Powell was made in 1684, naming the owner in 1682.

In all of Penn's deeds to the first Welsh companies and to other settlers, and in their deeds to their grantees, there is a safe-guarding clause that protection is guaranteed against Indian claims to the lands conveyed. This was because Penn had not yet purchased the land from the Indians as he proposed doing.

COMPANY NUMBER ONE

After his arrival here, in October, 1682, he began at once to enter upon treaties with the Indian chiefs for the purchase of their domains, taking for granted they were the proper ones to pass the titles, so as to extinguish their rights, and make good the deeds he had issued. The boundaries of the tracts the Indians resigned were, of course, vague, as were the original surveys made of the lands for Penn's grantees, since the stations were natural objects. As to the land bought by Thomas & Jones, and then occupied by it, and some of the other tracts beyond the Schuylkill:

1683, June 25, William Penn bought from Chief Wingbone, whose "autograph" is extant, all his rights and claims to the land lying on the west side of the Schuylkill, beginning at the Lower Falls, and "up the river," and "backward."

1683, July 16, William Penn brought from the chiefs named Secane and Idquoquehan, all the land lying between the Schuylkill (at Manayunk) and Chester Creek, and as far up the Schuylkill as Conshohocken Hill.

On 22 December, 1701, the minutes of the Commissioners of Property record that grantees of John ap Thomas and Dr. Jones tract were the first of the Welsh to have their deeds confirmed to them, when there was a possibility of losing their lands, of which elsewhere.

Those who appeared, and to whom warrants of resurvey were issued at this time, 1701-2-3, their lands being made up partly of the original purchases, and what was acquired subsequently:—

"To Hugh Roberts for 549¾ acres in Goshen, 482 thereof [bought] of Jno. ap Jno's.

"To Robert Roberts and Owen Roberts 200 acres each, in Meirion.

"To Edward Reese 205¼ acres, in Meirion.

"To Edward Jones' Survey on 200 acres in Goshen, and a Resurvey on 151¼ in Meirion, and 153 in Goshen.

WELSH SETTLEMENT OF PENSYLVANIA

"To Edward Jones, Jun'r, 306¼ acres, half in Meirion, ½ in Goshen.

"Robert David, 274¼ acres in Meirion, and 234½ in Goshen.

"Richard Walter 100 acres in Meirion.

"Richard Rees als Jones, 137½ in Meirion, and 75 in Goshen.

"To Cadwallader Morgan 202 acres and ½ in Meirion.

"To John Roberts, malter, 306 acres and ½, ¾ thereof in Goshen, ¼ in Meirion.

"To Hugh Jones 768 and ¼ acres in Meirion.

"To Griffith John 194 acres.

"To Rob't William 76¼ acres in Goshen.

"To Ellis David 151 acres and ½.

"To Thomas Jones, Robert Jones and Cadwallader Jones, 1225 acres, ½ thereof in Meirion, and ½ in Goshen, left them by their father, John Thomas, the original Purchaser.

"To John Roberts, Cordwainer, of Goshen, 78¼ acres in Goshen."

Only seven of these were original grantees in the tract.

From the Commissioners' "Minutes of ye Welsh Purchasers," we find further as to the distribution of the land of the original contributors, and who got some of this tract:—

Hugh Roberts had by deed, dated 28 February, 1681-2, from Thomas & Jones, 625 acres, laid out, on warrant of 1683, half in Merion and half in Goshen township. He also by deed, 17.6.1694, bought of William Edward 76½ acres, and by deed, 1 April, 1682, from John Watkin, 156 acres. He had in all 842½ acres net. He gave 200 acres out of the 625 acres to his son Robert Roberts on his second marriage, in 1689, and 200 acres out of the balance of the 625 acres and what he bought of Edwards, to his son Owen Roberts on his marriage in 1696. He also sold 100 to Edward Griffith, and 100 to Robert William, and 100 to Thomas Griffith. He further bought 156 acres "of J. Walk"

COMPANY NUMBER ONE

[John Walker?], and sold 74 acres to Abel Thomas. Reported, that he had sold 776½ acres, and had only 67¾ acres remaining. The land he sold to Messrs. Edward and Thomas Griffith, and Robert William, lay in Merion township, and also all but 67¾ in same place.

William Edward, who bought 153½ acres, through Thomas & Jones, with a questionable right to certain "liberty land," sold 76 acres, as above, and 76 acres in Goshen township, to Robert William.

Edward Rees had deed, 1.2mo. 1682, from Thomas & Jones, for 156½ acres, plus, as supposed, some "liberty land." He sold 76 acres in Goshen township to Ellis David. Of the balance, 78¼ acres and 125 acres he bought from Thomas Lloyd, being out of the purchase of Charles Lloyd and Margaret Davies, and two acres from Dr. Jones, all 205¼ acres located in Merion township.

Edward Jones, the doctor, as above, took for himself only 312½ acres, which came out only 306¼ acres on survey. He sold two acres as above and had 151¼ acres left in Merion, and 153 acres in Goshen township. Later, he bought 200 acres in Goshen from Richard Thomas.

Edward Owen, by deed 1 April, 1682, bought through Thomas & Jones, 312½ acres. By deed, 1.1.1694-5, he sold 150 acres in Merion to Robert David, all he had there. The balance of his land lay in Goshen township.

John ap Edward, by deed 18.1.1681-2, from Thomas & Jones had 312½ acres; half was located in Merion, and rest in Goshen township. His son, Edward Jones, inherited all in 1686-7.

Robert David, by deed 18.1.1681, from Thomas & Jones, received 312½ acres, located half in Merion, half in Goshen. He sold, by deed 1.10mo. 1694, 25 acres of his Merion place to Richard Walter, and had remaining 281 acres, to which he added 156¼ acres, bought, by deed 18.5.1683, of Evan Rees. He also had 150 acres from Griffith Owen. After deductions and allowances and additions and sales, he had

WELSH SETTLEMENT OF PENSYLVANIA

274½ acres in Merion, and 234½ acres in Goshen. Richard Walter bought as above from Robert David, 25 acres and 75 acres. These parcels lay in Merion township.

Rees Jones, by deed 18.2.1682, bought through Thomas & Jones, 156¼ acres in Merion. He sold 50 acres to Cadwalader Morgan, and by his will bequeathed his land in Goshen to his sons John and Evan, and 100 acres to his son, Richard Rees Jones, who bought from "John Roberts, cordwainer," 37½ acres (part of the Thomas & Charles Lloyd land), which land "the said Thomas [Lloyd] bequeathed by will to the said Jno Roberts, his nephew." So Richard Rees Jones held 137½ acres in Merion township. He also held 75 acres in Goshen township, granted to him by his Uncle, Evan John William, by deed, which lot was a portion of the Richard David purchase.

Thomas Prichard bought through Thomas & Jones, 156¼ acres. By his deed of 16 July, 1684, he conveyed the same to Rees Jones, who then had 306½ acres.

Cadwalader Morgan bought, by deed, 1.2mo. 1682, from Thomas & Jones, 156½ acres. He sold 76½ acres in Goshen to "John Roberts, malter," and retained balance in Merion township. He increased his Merion holdings with 50 acres bought of Rees Jones, and 76½ acres in Merion, which he had by deed 18.4.1684, from John William, so had 202½ acres in Merion township.

Gainor Roberts, spinster, bought by deed, 1.2.1682, from Thomas & Jones, 156 acres. One-half lay in Merion, and "John Roberts, the malter, held balance, in Goshen township. John Roberts, malter, had 75 acres from Gainor Roberts, 75 acres from Cadw. Morgan, by deed of 7.7.1687, and on this date he bought 75 acres from Hugh Jones. So he held 306½ acres, one-fourth in Merion, balance in Goshen.

"Thomas Lloyd (not the Presid't)," was a grantee, by deed of 1 April, 1682, from Thomas & Jones, for 156 acres. He bequeathed his land to his nephew, "John Roberts, cordwainer," who sold of his inheritance 37½ acres to Richard Jones, and 37½ acres to Griffith John, of Merion. So he held 78½ acres in Goshen township.

William Jones' son, John William, inherited of the Thomas and Jones tract, 156¼ acres, three acres was his estimated share of the "liberty land," as in each case of this amount, "liberty land," when allowed always reduced township holding. He sold all his land; to Cadwalader Morgan 76½, and balance to Edward Rees, who sold to Ellis David.

John Watkins received by deed, 1 April, 1682, from Thomas & Jones, 156¼ acres "less 3 acres of liberty land." He sold all to Hugh Roberts, by deed dated 23.4.1684.

Hugh Jones received by deed, 18 March, 1681, from Thomas & Jones, 156¼ acres. He sold John Roberts, malter, 76¼ acres. He and his son held the rest, in Merion township.

Evan Rees received by deed, 18 March, 1681-2, from Thomas & Jones, 312½ acres, "less 6¼ ac. of liberty land." By deeds dated 18.3.1683, he sold out to Robert David and Griffith John. The latter bought 156¼ acres from Evan Rees, and 38 from "John Roberts, shoemaker," of Goshen township.

But these conveyances are given more fully in the sketches that follow of these original grantees. These transfers of land are of much genealogical interest, for they give the names of newcomers, and approximate the time of arrival here.

There is plenty of evidence in the Philadelphia county land records, as may be seen, that the early Welsh Friends made many changes in their holdings in the twenty years following their removal here. Some increased their acreage, some decreased to strengthen the balance, some sold out entirely and settled elsewhere outside of Merion. The land transactions were freqently before the Board of Land Commissioners for adjustment and settlement. It found it

WELSH SETTLEMENT OF PENSYLVANIA

necessary finally, for its own better understanding of the situation in the Welsh "Towns" to learn as near as possible in whose names was the land Penn had granted them. In this matter, the Board, in its Minutes, under date of 22nd 10br 1701, recorded:

"Order issued the 1st inst. for taking some Measures to regulate the Welsh Tract; some of the Chiefs of that Nation in this Province having met and concerted the Methods to be taken in order to the Regulations, it was agreed: That, in as much as the Welsh Purchasers of the Propr'ry were by large Quantities of acres in one Pair, by Deeds granted to one or two Persons only, under which several other Purchasers had a Share, the Gen'l Deeds of one Purchase should be first brought in with an acc't of all other Persons who had a Share in such Purchase, also an account in whose possession the Respective Lands of every under Purchase now are."

"As for the Merion land holders in 1701, "the Propr'ry Deeds to John ap Thomas and Edward Jones for 5,000 acres was brought in with all such necessary acc'ts".

From their statement we learn that about 1,884 acres of their patent was not located in Merion township, but in Goshen township, and that the following number of the original Welsh Friends and descendants only held land in Merion township, the total of their holdings being about 3,000 acres. Newcomers holding about 445 acres.

The Merion holders and acreage being, about January, 1700, n. s.:—

"Robert Roberts, 200.
"Owen Roberts, 200.
"Edward Rees, 205¼.
"Edward Jones, 151¼ and 353 in Goshen township.
"Edward Jones, Jr., 158⅛ and 158⅛ in Goshen township.
"Robert David, 274¼ and 234½ in Goshen township.

"Richard Rees Jones, 137½ and 75 in Goshen township.

"Cadwalader Morgan, 202½.

"John Roberts (Pencoid), 76½ and 230 in Goshen township.

"Hugh Jones, 768¼.

"Thomas Jones, Robert Jones, Cadwallader Jones, 612½ (left to them by their father, John ap Thomas); and the same amount in Goshen."

Other land owners in Merion township, at this time, were Richard Walter, 100 acres; Griffith John, 194 acres, and Ellis David, 151½ acres, and in Goshen township, Hugh Roberts, 67 acres; Robert William, 76¼ acres, and John Roberts, the shoemaker, 78¼ acres, who sold inherited land in Merion to "John Roberts, Gent."

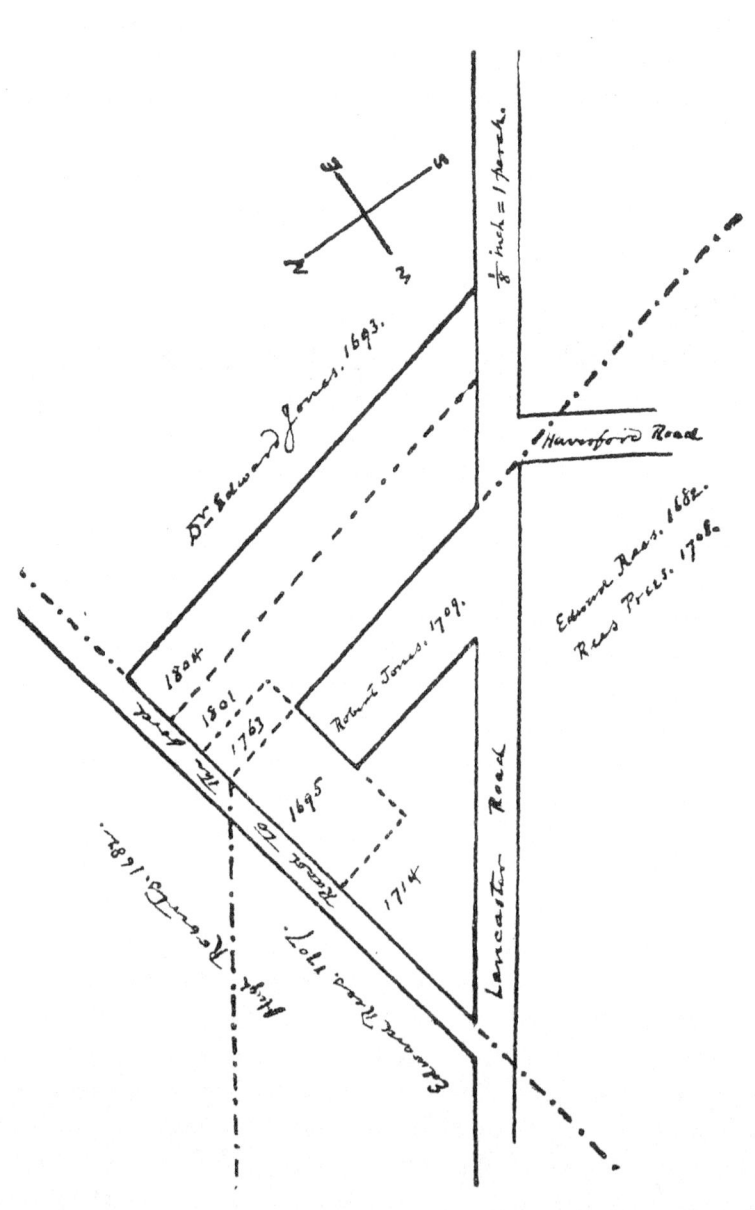

FAMILIES AND LAND
OF FIRST ARRIVALS

MERION ADVENTURERS

The following information concerning the aforesaid Welsh Friends, the "first purchasers," "ye first within ye tract of land in the Province" to have their land beyond the Schuylkill laid out, the first settlers in the Welsh Tract, and in Merion township, the founders of the Merion Meeting, has fortunately been preserved, and gathered together from many sources, more or less reliable.

The sketches of these founders are not only of biographical and genealogical interest, for they show the gradual and sure development of Merion, and of the Welsh Tract, now the "garden spot" of Pensylvania, if not of America, and incidentally the part taken by them in laying the foundation of the Commonwealth.

These first four sketches are of the four Welshmen and Friends, and their families, who were the first to remove here from Wales, and arrived at Upland (Chester), on the Delaware, 13 August, 1682, namely, Dr. Edward Jones, William ap Edward, Edward ap Rees, and Robert ap David.

DR. EDWARD JONES. He was described as "chyrurgion," and removed from Bala, in Merionethshire, and was the founder of "Merion in the Welsh Tract." Nothing is preserved of his ancestry, or antecedents. He filed with the Merion Preparative Meeting, or the Haverford Monthly Meeting, on 8. 10mo. 1704, according to its minutes, an account of himself and wife, and of their life before coming over, as all other members did, but such accounts have disappeared from the Friends' archives. His fame was as the one who selected the land to be settled upon by himself and his confrères, and as the founder of the most important settlement in "New Merion."

WELSH SETTLEMENT OF PENSYLVANIA

As told already, he was one of the Welsh gentlemen who visited William Penn in London, in May, 1681, about buying some of his land, and how he was one of the adventurers and trustees, with John ap Thomas, for 5,000 acres, taken up by "Edward Jones & Co.," located part in Merion, on the Schuylkill, and part in Goshen township, because Penn's agent here, according to instructions from Penn, of course, would not survey or lay out so large a tract in one place.

Where Edward ap John, or Edward Jones, studied medicine has not been discovered, but it may be supposed he had medical skill as a barber-surgeon, and practiced his profession among Friends in and about Bala, from whence he came, and later in Merion and Philadelphia.

He and his party, "40 souls," were the first of the Welsh Friends to remove to Penn's Province. The names of all who composed Dr. Jones's party cannot now be determined, and it is only positively known that on this trip of the ship Lyon there were as passengers Dr. Jones and his wife, and two small children; William ap Edward, and his second wife, and two children by his first wife; Edward ap Rees, and his wife, and three children, and Robert ap David, and his wife, and one child, and that they were the "first class passengers."

These four men were the only ones of the seventeen "shareholders," purchasers of the land Thomas & Jones engaged, who made the first settlement in Merion. This accounts for sixteen souls, and the others of the forty were farm-hands and servants.

Dr. Jones, and his party of first Merion settlers, sailed from Liverpool, in the latter part of May, 1682, in the ship Lyon, Captain John Compton, master, and arrived at Upland, now Chester, in the Delaware, 13. 6mo. (August), 1682, two months before William Penn's first arrival.

Among the papers of his "partner," John ap Thomas, brought to America by his widow, is preserved a letter written by Dr. Jones to him, whom he had left very ill at

COMPANY NUMBER ONE

home, thirteen days after reaching his destination. Some extracts from this interesting letter have been give above, but as it was an account of the experience of this first party, as well as the Doctor's earliest opinion of his new home, his letter is given in full. It was written apparently after the men of the party had gone out to inspect the tract assigned to them on the west side of the Schuylkill, at and above the Falls, where subsequently they took their seats close together, and camped with their families, till their comfortable log houses were built, for it was mid-summer, and therefore no great hardship at first.

An account of another family tells that these first comers "dug caves, walled them, and dwelt therein a considerable time, where they suffered many hardships, in the beginning, —the next season being wet and raining about their barley harvest [time]."

It is unfortunate that the Doctor's first letter he refers to has not been preserved, or did not reach John Thomas.

This second letter is addressed in this quaint manner:—

"These ffor his much esteemed friend John ap Thomas of Llaithgwm neer Bala in Merionethshire, North Wales, to be left with Job Boulton att the Boult and tun in Lumber Street London, and from thence to William Sky Butcher in Oswestrie, to be sent as above directed and via London— with Speed."

"My endeared fr'd & brother, my heart dearly salutes thee, in a measure of ye everlasting truth, dear fr'd, hoping that these few lines may find thee in health, or no worster yn I left thee.

"This shall let thee know that we have been aboard eleaven weeks before we made the land, (it was not for want of art, but contrary winds,) and one we were in coming to Upland.

"Ye town [the future Philadelphia] is to buylded 15 or 16 miles up ye River.

"And, in all this time, we wanted neither meate, drink, or water, though several hogsheds of water run out. Our ordinary allowance of beer was 3 pints a day, for each whole head, and a quart of water; 3 biskedd a day, & some times more. We laid in about a half hundred [weight] of biskedd, one barrell of beere, one hogshede of water,— the quantity for each whole head, & 3 barrells of beefe for the whole number—40—and we had one [barrel of beef] to come ashoare.

—"A great many could eat little or no beefe, though it was good. Butter and cheese eats well upon ye sea. Ye remainder of our cheese is little, or no worster; butter & cheese is at 6d per lb here, if not more. We have oatmeale to spare, but it is well yt we have it, for here is little or no corn till they begin to sow their corn, they have plenty of it.

"The passengers are all living, save one child yt died of a surfeit.

"Let no frds tell that they are either too old, or too young, [to come over]. for the Lord is sufficient to preserve both to the uttermost.

"Here is an old man about 80 years of age; he is rather better yn when he sett out. Likewise here are young babes doing very well, considering the sea diet.

"We had one tun of water, and one of drinke, to pay for at Upland; but ye master [of the ship] would faine be pd for 13 or 14 hogsheds yt run out by ye way, but we did not. And about 3 quarters of Tunn of Coales we pd for. We laid in 3 Tun of Coales, and yields no profit here.

"We are short of our expectation, by reason that ye town [future Philadelphia] is not to be builded at Upland; neither would ye Master bring us any further [than Upland], though it is navigable for ships of greater burthen than ours.

COMPANY NUMBER ONE

"Ye name of ye town lots [where they imagined, for some reason, the city would be laid out, as the site was not positively decided till after Penn's arrival] is called now Wicoco. Here [at the supposed town-site] is a Crowd of people striving for ye Country land, for ye town lot is not divided [that is the future Philadelphia was not yet laid out in lots, and was not until the following winter], & therefore we are forced to take up ye Country lots [first].

"We had much adoe to get a grant of it [that is, a warrant to locate and survey the land, from Penn's deputy, young Markham, directed to the official surveyor, Thomas Holme, or Holmes, who had been here only about six weeks, and was filled with engagements]. But it Cost us 4 or 5 days attendance [on the officials] besides some score of miles we travelled [forth and back to the Falls of Schuylkill and to the surveyor], before we brought it to pass [before the site was selected].

"I hope it [the Thomas & Jones lands, and its location] will please thee, and the rest yt are concerned, for it hath most rare timber. I have not seen the like in all these parts. There is water enough besides.

"The end of each lot will be on a river, as large, or larger than the Dye, at Bala. It is called Skool Kill River.

"I hope the Country land [the land the Doctor selected] will within this four days [be] surveyed out. [It seems that Ashcom, a Deputy Surveyor, made a rough survey of this land on 24 August, but probably had not returned when the Doctor wrote this on 26 August.] The rate for surveying 100 Acres, twenty shillings. But I hope betters orders [terms] will be taken [made] shortly about it" [the charge].

At this point there is a long paragraph in Welsh (the major part of the letter being English), and so written to make his remark secret and private, as the Doctor's letter was to be carried to England by the man he referred to, the captain of the ship in which he came over:—

WELSH SETTLEMENT OF PENSYLVANIA

"We liked him, the Captain, well enough when eating our own victuals; but beware of his provisions [a warning to Mr. Thomas, or any who might sail with him], because it was only bread and salt meat, with little beer, and foul water usually. But he made a great fuss over me and my wife, and over most of those who could talk with him [in English]. There is another Captain living in the same town [Liverpool], and passengers [some of Penn's first colonists] from Carmarthenshire came over with him on his provision, and they spoke well of him, but they paid him £4. 10. 00; early [for young] children, under 12 years of age, 52 shillings, and got plenty to eat, and good drink. The name of this good man is Captain Crossman. It is cheaper to furnish our own provisions than to pay £4. 10.

"I think most of the things [dry goods, utensils, implements, etc., brought over to sell to colonists] will not be sold until you come over, because so many things had previously been brought here."

All these suggestions may have been useful to others coming over. He suggested to bring for sale some white fustian, serges to make clothes, men's hats, saddles, bridles, shoes, etc. "Blue flannel is most called for here, but all colors are used," he wrote. "Don't bring much white flannel with you. Stuff dyed blue we like best."

"Compel the master of the ship to come to the town of Philadelphia with your goods [it appears from this, and Penn said, the town received its name before its site was selected]. I had to pay to the other [another] party 30 shillings for hauling the things up. and be sure to pay for carrying your luggage, and everything else that you start with, to the Captain."

Then continuing in English:—

"The people [about where the tract lay] generally are Swede, which are not very well acquainted [with our language].

COMPANY NUMBER ONE

"We are amongst the English which sent [send] us both venison, and new milk, & the Indians brought [bring] venison to our door for six pence ye quarter.*

"And as for ye land, we look upon it a good & fat soil, generally producing twenty, thirty, & fourty fold. [This may mean that in the tract were old Indian fields of this quality, or reputation.]

"There are stones [for houses] to be had enough at the falls of the Skool Kill, that is, where we are to settle, & water enough for mills. But thou must bring Mill-stones, and ye Irons that belong to it, for Smiths are dear [in charges here]. (This was a useless suggestion, as may be seen elsewhere.)

"Iron is about two and thirty, or fourty shillings per hundred. Steel about 1s. 6d. p. l.

"Ye best way is to make yr picken axes when you come

---

*That is, they were then stopping "in town," and had not yet moved out to "ye country lots," with the squattors on the site where they supposed "ye town" would be laid out, who were living in dug-out caves, on the bank of the Delaware, or in lean-to shacks. Near the Thomas and Jones grant, was Peter Cock, a Swede, who had about 200 acres, west of Mill Creek, *i.e.*, Cobbs Creek, in Blockley tp., Phila. Co. Later the Swansons became neighbors across the Schuylkill, having been forced to exchange their land on the Delaware, for the city's site, and take land on both sides of the Schuylkill, from Fairmount to the Falls. The one Englishman in this neighborhood was William Warner, who, with his son, held three large tracts of land, extending from the Schuylkill half-way to Cobbs Creek, along the future Haverford Road. It is presumed that Warner came here by the way of New England, and bought land from the Indians, or the poorer Swedes. On 3 April, 1678, the Upland Court confirmed 100 acres to him, and on I June, 1681, he was an applicant to this Court for further confirmations of purchases. After Pen'n entered into possession, Mr. Warner became a member of young Gov. Markham's Council, 3 Aug., 1681, and on 13 Sep. following, he became a justice, and was a member of the first assembly held in Philadelphia, 10 March, 1683. He called his land, which lay in the "City Liberties," in Penn's time, "Blockley," from the place of his nativity, in Worcestershire, and it gave name to the township in which it lay, extending to the present 52d Street.

WELSH SETTLEMENT OF PENSYLVANIA

over, for they cannot be made in England; for one man will work with ym as much as two men with ours.

"Grindle Stones yield good profit here.

"Ordinary workmen hath 1s. 6d. a day [wages]. Carpenters 3 or four shillings a day.

"Here are sheep [belonging to the settlers on the lower Delaware river], but dear—about twenty shillings a piece. I cannot understand how they can be carried from England.

"Taylors hath 5s. & 6s. a day [wages].

"I would have you bring salt for ye present use;—here is coarse salt; sometimes two measures of salt for one of wheat [in exchange], and sometimes very dear.

"Six penny, & eight penny nails are most in use.

"Horse shoes are in no use.

"Good large shoes [for people] are dear.

"Lead in small bars is vendible; but guns are cheap enough.

"They plow, but very bungerly [here], & yet they have some good stone.

"They use both hookes and sickles to reap with.

"Time will not permit me to write much more, for we are not settled.

"I [send] my dear love, and my wife's unto thy selfe and thy dear wife, and the rest of my dear friends, H. Ro., Rich: P., Evan Rees; J. ap E., Elizabeth Williams; E. & J. Edd., Gainor R., Ro.: On., J.: Humphrey; Hugh J. Tho., and the rest of fr'ds as if named.

"I remaine thy Lo' friend & Bro while I am,

"Edd Jones."

"My wife desires thee to buy her one Iron Kettle, 3s or 3s. 6d., 2 paire of shoes for Martha [a little child], and one paire for Jonathan, let them by strong and large [which confirms they had only two children at that time]; be sure and put all yt goods in cases, if they be dry, they keep well, otherwise they will get damp and mouldy [on the voyage].

This is ye 2nd letter, Skool Kill River.

Ye 26th of ye 6mo. 1682."

COMPANY NUMBER ONE

Dr. Jones, and his companions, Edward Rees and William Edwards, (or the surveyor, Ashcom, assigned the lots to the partners in this purchase, as Dr. Jones gave him the number of acres each bought) selected adjoining lots in their tract, he having laid out to himself here 156½ acres (and the same amount was divided between the other two), which upon Powell's resurvey, he made 153¼ acres, supposing three acres were to be in the Liberties. It was a narrow strip, extending from the river into the back country, 788 perches, or about two and one-half miles, and beyond the present Montgomery avenue, the successor of the Lancaster road. The remainder of Dr. Jones's purchase was laid out in Goshen township (about West Chester) subsequently.

Dr. Jones had two tracts in Goshen of 125 acres and 400 acres, made up of his original purchase, and of land he bought of "Edward Jones, Jr." and Richard Thomas.

"Edward Jones, Jr.," (son of John ap Edward), having procured a resurvey on 306½ acres in two tracts of 153¼ acres, one in Goshen township, the other in Merion township, one parcel was 20 acres over, and the other 28 short, it was ordered 20. 2. 1703, that patent for the whole be issued to "Edward Jones, the elder," to whom "Edward Jones, Jr.," had sold.

On same date, Edward Jones, Sr., it appears had 150 acres in Merion township, and 153 acres in Goshen township, and 200 acres more in same township, which he had purchased of Richard Thomas.

Of these properties, he sold, in 1707, to Robert Williams, 300 acres, and the balance, in 1720, to Ellis Williams. Dr. Jones also owned 160 acres in Blockley township on the old Lancaster road and the Merion line.

From his confirmation patent for this Merion land, where he resided over fifty-five years, dated 22. 4mo. 1703, after the third, and final, survey, it would seem that he had bought from his adjoining lotholder on the South, Ed-

WELSH SETTLEMENT OF PENSYLVANIA

ward Owen, the back half of his purchase of 156¼ acres, and had sold the front half of his own first selection, and on this date, had added 188 acres, purchased from Edward Jones, Jr. (adjoining his purchase from Owen), which land lay on the Haverford and Merion road, going East from near the Merion Meeting House, and extends over the Pensylvania Railroad at Narberth. His deed for his original purchase, dated 1 April, 1682, was from John Thomas, and was witnessed by John and Robert Lloyd, Griffith and Reece Evan, and William John.

Dr. Jones was honored with the appointment of a Justice of the Peace in the Welsh Tract, and was chosen as one of its representatives in the Pensylvania Assembly.

According to Penn, in his long letter addressed to the London members of the Society of Free Traders of Pensylvania, dated at Philadelphia, 16. 6mo. 1683, "Edward Jones, son-in-law to Thomas Wynne, living on the Sculkil," was a good farmer. As Penn says: "He had with ordinary cultivation, for one grain of English barley, 70 stalks and ears of barley."

The Doctor died at his Merion home, in February, 1737. His burial is recorded on books of the Merion Meeting: "Edward Jones, Doctor, aged 80 years," 12mo. 26. 1737.

Friend Thomas Chalkley, of "Chalkley Hall," in Frankford (Philadelphia), in his "Journal" records: "The 26th of the 12mo., 1737, being the first day of the week, there was buried at Merion, Edward Jones, aged about 92 (*sic*) years. He was one of the first settlers of Pensilvania, a man much given to hospitality, a lover of good and virtuous people, and was beloved by them. I had a concern to be at that meeting before I left my home at Frankford, and before I heard of this Friend's death. There were many hundreds at his funeral."

His will, signed 27. 3mo. 1732, was proved at Philadelphia, 2 August, 1738, witnessed by John Roberts and Esther Thomas (marked). He was described as surgeon,

COMPANY NUMBER ONE

and aged and infirm. He named his sons Jonathan, Edward, Evan, Thomas and John Jones, the youngest son, and desired that John should continue to feed, clothe, and support his brother Thomas. His wife Mary was to have his estate during her life, and then it was to go to son John. He gave son-in-law, John Cadwalader, some land in the center of Philadelphia, and negroes to each of the Cadwalader girls, Mary, Rebecca, and Hannah, and one to each grandson, Thomas Cadwalader, and Martha Roberts. He named daughters Martha, Elizabeth, and Mary, and appointed his wife, sons Jonathan, Edward and Evan, and John Cadwalader, executors.

Dr. Jones married, possibly in Denbighshire, Mary, a daughter of Dr. Thomas Wynne, also one of the Welsh adventurers for Penn's land ("Company No. 4"). It is not known when she died. She probably survived her husband, and it is supposed she was buried in the ground of the Merion Meeting. Of her it is said (see "The Philadelphia Friend," XXIX, 396, which dates her decease 29. 7mo. 1726, which is, of course, an error) : "She was an approved minister among Friends, and zealous for the promotion of the truth." Of their eight children* named in the Doctor's will:—

---

*Among the present day descendants of Dr. Edward Jones are:

Mrs. Robert R. Corson.	Mrs. William Cresson.
Mrs. Howard Comfort.	Mrs. James Yocum.
Dr. George Smith.	Mrs. Richard Day.
Frank Foulke.	Dr. Richard Foulke.
Abraham L. Smith.	Mrs. Charles L. Bacon.
Benj. Hayes Smith.	Mrs. Charles W. Bacon.
Rodman Wister.	William Wynne Wister.
Alex. W. Wister.	Mrs. Richard A. Tilghman.
Edward Browning.	Dr. Owen Jones Wister.
Mrs. Jawood Lukens.	Mrs. Israel J. Wister.
Mrs. Arthur V. Meigs.	Robert Toland.
Mrs. Charles Richardson.	Charles Follen Corson.
Mrs. George B. Roberts.	Dr. Joseph K. Corson.

WELSH SETTLEMENT OF PENSYLVANIA

Martha Jones, for whom her father asked, as above, two pair shoes be forwarded from Wales, just after her arrival here. She married, seventeen years after coming here, at the Merion Meeting House, on '26. 10mo. 1699, the young school teacher, John Cadwalader** who it is supposed had been living at her father's house for two years. He died 16. 2mo. 1747.

John Cadwalader, although he was never a land owner in Merion, but because of his relationship to many of the families here, and his marriage among them, Merion has ever claimed him as belonging there by rights.

The exact date of his birth has not been preserved, but he was born about the year 1677-78, probably at Kiltal-

---

**Some descendants of John Cadwalader, who are also descendants of Dr. Edward Jones:

Mrs. Henry B. Robb.	Mrs. Archibald McCall.
Mrs. Edw. Fenno Hoffman.	Mrs. William Schley.
Mrs. John Hone.	Mrs. Philemon Dickinson.
Mrs. Samuel Chew.	Mrs. Richard F. Stevens.
Mrs. William Pearsall.	Mrs. Henry J. Rowland.
Mrs. John Steinmetz.	Wm. Cadwalader Schley.
Mrs. S. Bevan Miller.	Mrs. William Woodville, Jr.
Mrs. Roland L. Taylor.	Mrs. Arthur S. Johns.
Mrs. Fred Rhinelander Jones.	Mrs. Charles W. Ross.
Mrs. John Travis.	Mrs. George N. Schrew.
Dr. Thomas Cadwalader, 1707-1779.	Harmon Pumpelly Read.
Col. Lambert Cadwalader, 1732-1813.	Mrs. Garret D. Wall Vroom.
Gen. John Cadwalader, 1742-1786.	Mrs. Samuel Meredith.
Gen. Thomas Cadwalader, 1795-1873.	Mrs. John Read.
Judge John M. Read, 1797-1874.	Samuel Reese Meredith.
Col. George A. McCall, 1802-1868.	Admiral Cadwalader Ringgold.
Judge John Cadwalader, 1805-1879.	Mrs. William Henry Rawle.
Gen. George Cadwalader, 1806-1879.	Travis Cochran.
John Cadwalader.	William Cochran.
Dr. Charles E. Cadwalader.	George Cochran.
Richard M. Cadwalader.	Arthur Potts.
John Lambert Cadwalader.	Mrs. Samuel E. D. Hankinson.
Mrs. William Greene Cochran.	Mrs. John Graham.
Mrs. Samuel L. Shober.	

COMPANY NUMBER ONE

garth, Llanvawr, Merionethshire, where his father lived. He brought his certificate of removal from the Pembroke Quarterly Meeting, dated in 1697, which states he had attended school there. He probably came over soon in this year, and lived in the family of some relative on the Schuylkill, till he received the appointment as a teacher in the Friends' Public School, in Philadelphia, which he had, on motion of Griffith Owen, in the Philadelphia Monthly Meeting, 29. 1mo. 1700, who recommended him as "a person fit for an assistant in the school."

Having received this appointment, he probably moved into town, for in July, 1705, he was admitted as a freeman of the city. In 1718-33, he was a chosen member of the City Council, and of the Pensylvania Assembly, in 1729, in which body he served till his decease, intestate, on 23 July, 1734.

He purchased 200 acres of land in "Ughland," Chester county, on warrant from the Land Commissioners, paying £12. 10s. per 100 acres on 22. 9mo. 1715.

Jonathan Jones, eldest son, who came over with his parents, and for whom his father desired that a pair of strong and large shoes be sent from Wales, although he was only two years old. He was born at Bala, Merionethshire, on 3. 11mo. 1680; died 30. 7mo. and was buried at the Merion Meeting House, 8. 8mo. 1770, aged 90 years. His will, dated 19 May, 1768, was proved at Philadelphia, 1 September, 1770.

Jonathan was given some of his father's estate, and bought from his brother-in-law, Evan Owen, the plantation of about 450 acres, which included the seats subsequently called "Wynnewood," and "St. Mary's," East of Ardmore, and North of the Pensylvania Railroad, which, it being a part of the Charles Lloyd tract, Thomas Lloyd had conveyed by deed, dated 5. 6mo. 1691, to Robert Owen, who settled it on his son, Evan Owen.

WELSH SETTLEMENT OF PENSYLVANIA

Jonathan Jones married at the Merion Meeting Gainor Owen, b. 26. 8mo. 1688, daughter of Robert Owen, of Merion.

This union of scions of two of the most important families of the Welsh Tract, naturally brought to the wedding a great concourse of English and Welsh Friends, as may be judged by the signers of their extant marriage certificate, which is of longer form than now used, beginning:— "Whereas, Jonathan Jones, son of Edward Jones, of Merion, in ye Welsh Tract, Chyrgeon, and Gainor Owen, daughter of Robert Owen, late of ye same place, yeoman, deceased, having declared their intention of marriage with each other before several Monthly Meetings of ye people of God called 'Quakers, in ye Welsh Tract aforsayd," etc., "Now these are to certifie to all whom it may concern, that for ye full accomplishment of their said intentions this 4th day of ye 8th mo in ye year 1705, they ye sayd Jonathan Jones & Gainor Owen appeared in the publick meeting of the said People, and others met together, at the public meeting place at Merion aforsayd & ye Jonathan 'Jones taking ye sayd Gainor Owen by ye hand did in solemn manner openly declare that he took her to be his wife, promising to be unto her a faithful and loving husband until death separate them & then and there in ye sayd assembly ye sayd Gainor Owen did in like manner declare that she took ye sayd Jonathan Jones to be her husband & promising," etc., The names of the signers are given elsewhere.

They had eleven children, of these:—Mary, *m.* Benjamin Hayes; Edward Jones, *d. unm.;* Rebecca, *m.* John Roberts, Jr., of "Pencoyd"; Owen Jones, (*m.* Susanna Evans,)* who

---

*Owen Jones, 1711-1793, a provincial treasurer of Pensylvania, and a "Tory," *m.* 30. 3mo. 1740, Susanna, daughter of Hugh and Lowry Evans, of Merion, had Jane, *m.* Caleb Foulke; **Lowry**, *m.* Daniel Wister; Owen, 1745-1825, *d. s. p.,* Susanna, *m.* John **Nancarro;** Hannah, *m.* Amos Foulke; Rebecca, *m.* John Jones, *d. s. p.,* **Sarah**, *m.* Samuel Rutter, and Jonathan, 1762-1821-2, father of Col. Owen **Jones,**

COMPANY NUMBER ONE

received 350 acres from his father, and added about 120 acres by purchase from brother Jonathan,—his possessions included much of Wister's "St. Mary's," and "Wister's Woods," and Wynnewood, which had been the estate of his brother-in-law, Evan Owen, and is still, in part, occupied by descendants; Ezekiel Jones, Jacob Jones; and Jonathan Jones, Jr., who received about 120 acres at Ardmore from his father, some of which was owned by the Glenn family, but is now divided among many newcomers.

Elizabeth Jones, wife of Rees Thomas, Jr., of "Rosemont" plantation, in Merion.

Mary Jones.

Edward Jones, Jr., of Blockley township. By gift from his father he had some of his father's land, along with the other sons. His will, signed in the presence of Martha Palmer, John Winne (marked), and Jonathan Hood, 14 November, 1730, was proved 30 September, 1732, by wife Mary. He names children Aquilla, Penelope, Salvenas, Beula, and Prudence; his brothers, Jonathan and John; his father-in-law, William Palmer; Brother-in-law, John Cadwalader; Trustees, Jonathan and John Jones, William Palmer, and John Cadwalader.

Thomas Jones, named in his father's will, 1732, and was probably an invalid.

Evan Jones. He *m.* first, Mary Stephenson, of New York, and *m.* secondly, a daughter of Colonel Matthews, of Fort Albany, New York.

M.C., deceased, whose son, J. Awbrey Jones, *d. s. p.*, at "Wynnewood," which property reverted, by the latter's will, eventually to the Toland family of Philadelphia, which was distantly related to him through the *m.* of Robert Toland and Rebecca, daughter of John Price Morgan, and his wife, Susan, daughter of Lowry Jones and Daniel Wister, aforesaid.

WELSH SETTLEMENT OF PENSYLVANIA

John Jones, of Philadelphia. He received from his father's estate the farm of 188 acres, bought of "Edward Jones, Jr." (son of John ap Edward), as above. This was included in the following sale:

By deed dated 15 October, 1741, "John Jones, late of Lower Merion, and of Philadelphia, yeoman, (youngest son of Edward Jones, late of Merion, Chyrurgeon, deceased), and Mary, his wife," conveyed "to Anthony Tunis, late of township of Germantown, now of Lower Merion," 402 acres of land, "late estate of Dr. Edward Jones," for £812 Pensylvania money. The abutting properties on this land were owned by John Roberts, Hugh Evans, Rees Price, Richard George, and Thomas Davids. "The Road," the old Lancaster pike, was a prominent bound, that is, this property lay "along the Road dividing this land from Edward Price's, south and west, to the Meeting House Ground, thence by the same, south and east, by the Road to Haverford, south and west, by Rees Price's land."

MERION ADVENTURERS

Of the three other gentlemen and their families who accompanied Dr. Edward Jones, and were founders of the Merion Meeting, namely:—

Edward ap Rees, or Edward Price,
Robert ap David, or Robert Davis,
William ap Edward, or William Edwards,

there is preserved the following information. They were all, of course, Friends, and members of the Penllyn Monthly Meeting, and resided in the old country in the same neighborhood, near Bala, where they were free-holders of land, and gentlemen farmers.

EDWARD AP REES, or Rhys, or "Edward Prees," and "Edward Price," as he is variously known (whose descendants assumed the surname "Price"), was a yeoman, and a minister among Friends, and a founder of Merion Meeting, came with his wife and two children, in Dr. Jones's party, from Kiltalgarth, Penllyn, in Merionethshire. He was the son of Richard Rhys (ap Grywwyth), of Tyddin Tyfod, in Merioneth, whose will, signed 26 January, 1685, was proved at the St. Asaph registry, and brother to Jane, wife of Cadwalader Morgan, and to Hannah, wife of Rees John William, all first settlers of Merion.

On request he filed with the Merion Preparative Meeting, of the Haverford Monthly Meeting, on 2. 12mo. 1704-5, according to the minutes, an account of his parentage, his home, marriage, education, &c., which unfortunately has not been preserved, or cannot be found.

His first Merion land, about 76 acres, which he had by deed, dated 1 April, 1682, recorded 11. 4mo. 1684, witnessed by John Lloyd, Robert Lloyd, Griffith Evan and Reece Evan,

WELSH SETTLEMENT OF PENSYLVANIA

was not located on the Schuylkill, but back of the purchase of William ap Edward, and between the lands of Dr. Jones and Hugh Roberts.

By deed dated 5. 5. 1691, he acquired 125 acres of the land of Governor Thomas Lloyd, part of Charles Lloyd's purchase from Penn ("Company No. 2"), which adjoined his original land on its west end, and also two acres from Dr. Jones, and received, on resurvey, a confirmatory patent, dated 1 January, 1703-4, for all his land, then amounting to 190 acres here. In 1707, he purchased 222 acres from Robert Roberts, north of his Lloyd land, and 10 acres on Mill, or Cobb's creek, in Blockley township.

The balance of his original purchase, or his Goshen land, 76 acres on Chester creek, and 78 acres which he bought, in 1697, of John William, of Merion (who in 1 mo. 1717-8, had patent for 400 acres on a branch of French creek), he sold, by deed of 9 January, 1708-9, to Ellis David, whose son, called David Ellis, held it in 1735.

Edward Rees resided on his first purchase, some of which lay on both sides of the Lancaster Road, which remained in his family for two centuries, in a stone house, erected about 1695, standing till recently northwest of the Merion Meeting House.

He was, of course, one of the organizers and first members of the Merion meeting. On the northeast corner of his land, and near a path, across his land, succeeded by the old Lancaster road (or Montgomery avenue), was the site selected as best, and most convenient for the public meeting house of the Merion Friends. He sold, for a nominal sum, one-half acre, and by deed, dated 20. 6mo. 1695, conveyed it to the trustees of the Merion Peculiar, or Preparative Meeting, Messrs, Robert Owen, Edward Jones, Cadwalader Morgan, and Thomas Jones, but it is uncertain whether the stone Meeting House, then probably nearly completed, was erected on this lot, or it was land added to the graveyard.

COMPANY NUMBER ONE

Edward Rees was a man of education, and considerable property, as the inventory of his personalty, taken after his decease, shows he owned Bibles and other books of history, in Welsh and English, and considerable cash in his house. Like some others of these early settlers, he revisited his Welsh home, when advanced in years, with Benjamin Humphrey. He was buried at the Merion Meeting House, 6. 13. 1728. His will, signed 6 January, 1727-8, was proved at Philadelphia, 23 November, 1728. Overseers, Jonathan Jones and Samuel Humphrey; witnesses, Robert and Jon. Jones.

He was twice married. He married first in Wales, Mably, or Mabby, daughter of Owen ap Hugh Ievan, and niece of "Thomas ap Hugh, gent," of Wern Fawr, Merionethshire, and married secondly, in 1713, Rebecca, daughter of Samuel Humphrey (ap Hugh), of Haverford. She survived him, and died without issue; her will signed 18. 3. 1732, proved 19 January, 1733; she named as executors, Ellis Price, brothers Daniel and Benj. Humphreys, and sisters Ann Hogg, of New Castle, and Lydia; gave money to school at Haverford.

By his first wife, who came over with him, and was buried at the Merion Meeting House, 23. 8mo. 1699, he had one son and two daughters:—

Rees Price, mentioned as "Rees Rees," in his father's will, *b*. 11. 11mo. 1678. His father conveyed some land to him, by deed of 7 August 1708. He married three times. His children were:—(named in their grandfather's will) Edward Price; Mary, *m*. Rees Harry; and Margaret, *m*. first, ——————— Paschall; *m*. second, William Montgomery; issue by both husbands, and, it is said, Jane, John, and Ellis Price.

He *m*. first, at Radnor Meeting, 6. 10mo. 1705, Sarah, daughter of David Meredith, of Radnor.

[81]

WELSH SETTLEMENT OF PENSYLVANIA

He *m.* secondly, at Haverford Meeting, 9. 10mo. 1718, Elizabeth, daughter of Ellis Ellis, of Haverford, and his wife, Lydia, daughter of Samuel Humphreys aforementioned. She was buried at the Haverford Meeting House, 12mo. 5. 1733-4. Ellis Ellis' will, signed 13. 6. 1705, proved 6 April, 1706, names wife and son Thomas only. Overseers; Rowland Ellis, John Richard, Rees Price, and Benjamin Humphrey.

He *m.* thirdly, at Haverford Meeting, 10. 3mo. 1737, Ann Scotharn, a widow, of Darby.

Rees Price was the second landlord of the Blue Anchor tavern, on Dock Creek (now Dock street), Philadelphia, where Penn landed on his first visit to his city, when the tavern, standing by the public landing place, was a little house, 22 feet on Dock (Street) creek, and 12 feet on Front Street, and was kept by Mr. Guest.

His descendant, Esther Price, *m.* at Merion Meeting, 16. 10mo. 1834, Benjamin Hunt, and this, it is claimed, was the last marriage at this Meeting.

Catharine Price, d. an *infant,* and was buried on her father's land, in Merion, 23. 8mo. 1682. This was the first death and burial in this little settlement, at the Falls of the Schuylkill, two months after arrival here.

Jane Price, b. 11. 9mo. 1682. This was the first birth in this settlement, three months after arrival, according to her transmitted birth date. She was buried at the Merion Meeting House, 10mo. 13. 1769, the record saying:—"Jane Mares, widow of George Mares. Born on the banks of Schuylkill in a Stone Hut in 1683. She was the Daughter of Edward Rees, after called Edward Preist, and then Price." She *m.* first, Jonathan Hayes, *d.* before 1727, and *m.* secondly, George Marris, or Mares.

ROBERT AP DAVID, or Robert David, and Davis, as his descendants were called, was living at Gwerneval (Gwerevol) Ismynydd, Penllyn, Merionethshire, when he pur-

COMPANY NUMBER ONE

chased from Thomas & Jones 312½ acres, paying £6. 05. 00, and decided to remove to this purchase in Penn's Province.

He was apparently a young married man, with one child, when he and his wife joined Dr. Jones's party at Liverpool, about the middle of May, 1682, and took passage in the "Lyon," for America. Arriving, in health, like the others of the party, in August he went up the Schuylkill with them, and settled on his land here, which on resurvey amounted to 148½ acres here, the balance of his purchase being subsequently laid out in Goshen township.

He may have been the Robert David, "of Tuyn y nant, Merioneth, who filed Certificate from the Men's Meeting, Penllyn, dated 18. 5mo. 1683, with the Haverford Monthly Meeting, and had sent for it, which was signed by Robert and Evan Owen, Richard Price, Morris Humphrey, Thomas Prichard, Evan Rees, Reece Evan, Roger Roberts, Hugh and Edward Griffith, Griffith and David John, and William Morgan.

His land on the Schuylkill, which had been assigned to him by the surveyor, extended back from the river only 386 perches, to the land allotted to and taken up by John ap Edward, and succeeded to by "Edward Jones the younger." Here he resided as a gentleman farmer for fifty years, the balance of his life. He died in October, 1732, and was buried at the Merion Meeting House.

By deed, dated 1. 1. 1694, he added to his farm, by purchase from Dr. Griffith Owen, the 153¼ acres, extending inland from the river 690 perches to Lloyd's land, and adjoining his original purchase on the North, which was the original purchase of Edward Owen through Thomas & Jones. Of this tract, Robert sold in the same year, 25 acres to Richard Walter.

By deed dated 20. 5. 1683, recorded 28 October following, Robert David bought 156¼ acres (76½ acres of the lot being unimproved land in the Thomas & Jones tract), from Evan Rees, the Penmaen grocer, for £3. 2. 6. Witnesses, Hugh Roberts, John Owen, Ellis Davis, and Maurice Davies. The receipt for the purchase money is in Latin. This land he exchanged for the same amount with Gainor Roberts, which latter land he also sold to Richard Walter, (with the 25 acres which adjoined it,) by deed of 1 December, 1694. Mr. Walter had his purchase resurveyed, and received patent, dated 8. 4. 1703, for 117 acres. The land is all near and on the old Lancaster road, near the City Line.

Robert David's holdings in Goshen township, on Chester creek, were at one time, 346 acres, made up of 234½ acres, his original purchase, and 88½ acres bought of Richard Thomas, Jr., and 23 acres allowed him by the Commissioners.

His final patent, dated 20. 5. 1703, for his Merion land, called for 280 acres and for his Goshen land, 346 acres, although on 12. 2. 1703, he claimed only 275½ acres in Merion, and 243 acres in Goshen, or 509½ acres.

Robert David, of Merion, bequeathed all his estate to his only son, Thomas Davis, by his will, signed 26 April, 1732, witnessed by Robert Evans, Rees Lloyd, and Robert Jones, and proved 18 October, 1732. He mentions his wife, Elizabeth, and daughters Elizabeth and Jane, and grandchildren (Jane's children), and Elizabeth, Jane and Robert, David, kinswoman Margaret Roberts, and his brother Ellis; gave some money for the graveyard at the Merion Meeting House; and named as executors his wife, and daughter Elizabeth, and as trustees, John Cadwalader, Robert Roberts, and Robert Jones. His wife, "Elizabeth Davis"'s will, signed 4 June, 1734, present Thomas and John Cadwalader, was filed 31 July, 1734, mentions son Thomas Davis, daughter Elizabeth Davis, executrix; mentions grandchildren Robert Roberts, Elizabeth Evans, and Jane Roberts.

The brothers, *William ap Edward*, and *John ap Edward*, it has long been supposed, both came over in Dr. Jones's party, arriving here in August, 1682. William, there is good evidence, certainly did come with the Doctor, but John did not, as we shall see.

They were sons of Edward ap John, a free-holder, of Cynlas township, in Llanddervel parish, Merionetshire, and who lived near Bala, and was buried, according to the register, at the parish church, on 1 March, 1667. He had two other sons, Evan Edward, who came over before 1704, and Thomas Edward, of Llanllidiog, in Llanddiervel, 1686.

WILLIAM AP EDWARD, a yeoman, was described as of Ucheldri, and of Nantlleidiog, and Cynlas, and he was sometimes known as "William Bedward," *ap* and *ab* being interchangeable. His descendants assumed the name "Williams." A more particular account of him and his brother, John, we are unable now to learn, as the account of himself and brothers, John and Evan, and their families, and old home life, filed with the Merion Preparative Meeting, by William, 2. 1mo. 1704-5, has disappeared from the Meeting archives.

William ap Edward was twice married, and in May, 1682 with his second wife, Jane, and two daughters by his first wife, Katharine, he embarked for America, with Dr. Jones's party, on the "Lyon," and with others of this company settled on his purchase on the Schuylkill, in the Fall of 1682. Here he lived about ten years only, and sold his 76½ acres in Merion, on the Schuylkill, by deed dated 17. 6. 1694, to Hugh Roberts, whose land adjoined his on the North, and removed to a tract which he purchased in the Liberty Lands, or Blockley township, surveyed 23. 2. 1692, and confirmed by deed to him, 27. 10. 1693. A part of the village of Overbrook is on his land.

His Blockley land was made up of the 100 acres of "Liberty Land," which he bought, (said to have been the same claimed, on account of the purchase of 5,000 acres, by Thomas & Jones), and 30 acres on account of the original purchase of 1,000 acres by William Jenkins, and 20 acres on

WELSH SETTLEMENT OF PENSYLVANIA

account of Jonah Hasting's purchase of 1,000 acres, and this tract of about 150 acres seems to have been all he owned in 12mo. 1701. This land, where he lived and died, subsequently was included in the great estate of the George family—the families intermarried—and "Overbrook Farms."

By deed of 21 January, 1703, he conveyed his 75 acres, on Chester Creek, Goshen Township, to Robert William.

William ap Edward's will, dated 29 December, 1714, was proved by his wife, at Philadelphia, 29 January, 1714-5.

He mentions his son Edward, daughters Mary, and Elizabeth, wife of Thomas Lloyd, Katharine, and Sarah, gives money to the Merion Meeting, and appoints as overseers, his son Edward, and William Thomas Lawrence, Henry Lawrence, and Thomas Lloyd, and friends David Jones and Thomas Jones. Witnesses:—James Hinton, Jenkin David (marked), and Abel Thomas.

He was buried at the Merion Meeting 10mo. 31. 1714, (John George was also buried here on this day). His wife, Jane, was buried here, aged 93 years, on 8mo. 3. 1745.

He *m.* first, Katharine Robert, *d.* in 1676. She was a sister to the Friends' minister, Hugh Roberts, and Gainor Roberts, both of the Thomas & Jones purchasers' colony, and had by her, two daughters, namely,

Elizabeth Williams, b. 14. 3. 1672, who came over with her father. She *m.* Thomas Lloyd, "not the President," who was one of the original purchasers from Thomas & Jones, but resided about a mile North of the village of Bryn Mawr.

Katharine Williams, who came over with her father, and *d. s. p.*

He *m.* secondly, about 1681, Jane, daughter of John ap Edward, (who, of course, was not his brother), a farmer near Bala, and had by her, who came over with him, four children:—

COMPANY NUMBER ONE

Sarah Williams, b. 20. 8mo. 1685, in Merion. She m. Thomas Lawrence, son of David Lawrence, and his wife, a daughter of Thomas Ellis.

Edward Williams, only son, b. 7. 12mo. 1689; he received from his father his Blockley land; will proved at Philadelphia, 21 February, 1749. He was very particular as to bequest to his wife, leaving her "a clothes-press in the parlour," and his "white mare and colt, and new blue-plush side-saddle." He m. Eleanor, daughter of David Lawrence, of Haverford. *Issue*: Joseph, father of Rebecca, m. Amos George; Eleanor, m. Joseph Bond, and Sarah, m. Edward George) Daniel, Sarah (wife of Joshua Humphreys) Edward and Jane (wife of Evan Thomas).

Ellen Williams, b. 19. 4mo. 1691, m. Henry Lawrence.

Mary Williams, b. 11. 11mo. 1694, m. Richard Preston, of Haverford.

JOHN AP EDWARD, the brother of William ap Edward aforesaid, was another of the parties to the "Thomas & Jones tract," but he did not come over with him in the Dr. Jones party, arriving in August, 1682, as supposed. In the testimony before Penn's Commissioners, of Dr. Jones, in June, 1702, taken in the matter of a servant of the late John ap Edward claiming his "time" was up and desiring to be relieved from further servitude, the Doctor declared that this servant man "came to this Province about the year 1683, as the servant of John ap Edward," and there is evidence that John brought over four servants, therefore, if John ap Edward and servants came over with the Doctor in 1682, I think he would have so stated, and not have put his arrival "about the year 1683." Nor did John ap Edward come over in the party of Hugh Robert, bound for the Thomas & Jones tract, because his will is dated 16 October, 1683, when he was very ill, and the Roberts party was then at sea, having sailed in September, 1683. The reference

WELSH SETTLEMENT OF PENSYLVANIA

in John's will that he had brought servants over, is proof that the will was written here after arrival. Nor should I imagine that he arrived in 1683 after Roberts arrived, for, being ill in October, he would hardly have sailed in time to arrive "about the year 1683." Therefore, I judge that John ap Edward arrived here, in some party coming out to Philadelphia, between August, 1682, and October, 1683. The two witnesses to his will were probably servants, possibly his, as the names of only two of his, a man and a maid, have been found.

When John ap Edward arrived, he found his land laid out for him. He had, as we have seen, contributed £6. 5. 0. towards the fund to buy 5,000 acres of Penn's land through Mr. Thomas and Dr. Jones, and that his share amounted to 312½ acres, for which he received the deed, dated 18 April, 1682. When Ashcom roughly laid out the Thomas & Jones purchase into lots, 24 August, 1682, he assigned, by order of the surveyor-general, only half of this purchase (as was the treatment of all the other Welshmen, much to their disgust, for they had been given to understand, and it was not absurd, that the purchaser of each lot would have all of his land in one place), 156¼ acres to John ap Edward, who found it laid out about 1 1/5 mile from the Schuylkill river, and the balance was a right to the same amount to be laid out in Goshen township, miles away, which was not a pleasant surprise for a practical farmer, one that would expect his farm should be in one tract, or at least, in contiguous parcels. However, as this was the misfortune of the other Welsh farmers, John accepted his allotment.

On Powell's map of the Thomas & Jones tract, John is credited with only 153½ acres, as Powell supposed he was entitled to three acres of Liberty Land, and that his land stands in the name of "Edward Joans, Jun'r," who was his son who succeeded to it on the decease of his elder brother. As this draft was made by Powell in 3mo. 1684, Evan, the

COMPANY NUMBER ONE

heir, and his father were then both dead, and Edward, a minor, was the heir apparent.

When John ap Edward came over, he brought with him four servants, possibly three men, farm hands, and his wife's maid. He found his land, though far from the great natural highway, the river, of quality equal to any other's, as was the bargain, and much better than most of it, for we know it lay in the beautiful, rolling country near our Merion settlement. He apparently lived only long enough to see one crop gathered. From his will it may be known that he was a shareholder in the Free Society of Traders in Pa., and was a prosperous man, and a Friend, and a founder of the Merion Meeting.

His will, dated 16. 8mo. 1683, when he was "weak of body"; witnessed by Gabriel Jones and William Morgan (probably servants), was not proved until 8. 2mo. 1686, by his brother, "William Edward, of Merion."

To his eldest son, Evan Jones, he gave the 312½ acres, which he had "purchased from William Penn."

To his youngest son, Edward Jones, he gave "the land due me for bringing over of servants, 200 acres," [that is, he brought four servants, receiving the usual allowance of fifty acres for each], and in addition his interest, or shares, "in the Society Trade of Pensylvania," [*i. e.*, Free Society of Traders], valued by him at £5.

He gave to his daughter, Elizabeth, £15 "of English money," with two feather beds, and bed clothes belonging to them, two brass pans, two pewter dishes, and one large trunk.

The balance of his personal estate, and his interest in the servants, he desired to be sold to pay his debts, and if anything remained, he desired his sons to have it.

He gave ten shillings to "my nephew John Evan."

He appointed "my beloved brethren Evan and William ap Edward, and my trusty friends Hugh Roberts, David Davies, John Roberts, and Hugh John Thomas," to be his executors, (although none but William was in this country, but he had reason to expect they would come), "to whose care I leave my children," as they were minors at that time. He desired that the monthly meeting decide what it was best to do with his estate should both of his sons die young, and without issue. As this will was written a month, or more, before the presumed time of organizing the Haverford Monthly Meeting, he may have expected it, or referred to the Burlington Monthly Meeting, which covered the meetings then in Pensylvania.

"My maid, Mary Hughs, [or Hughes] the sum of two pounds at the expiration of the time of her apprenticeship."

The executed will has not been preserved, but there is a copy of it on file, which shows he marked his will with simply a large E. In the package of testamentary papers connected with the settlement of his estate, at the office of the Register of Wills, Philadelphia, is the original rough draft of the will, unsigned, and undated. Also the original inventory of his personal estate, made as it says by Thomas Ellis, Hugh Jones, and John Roberts, on "the 3 day of the first month 1683-4," which is evidence that John died between 16 October, 1683 and 3 March, following.

It seems that all the personal property was sold in a lump per inventory, after John's death, and that the appraisers filed a copy of the inventory on 20 February, 1702-3, when the heir, Edward, became of age, to show the sum derived from the sale, and stated:—"The Inventory was cast up and found to be £63. 15. 9, according to English money, which being reduced to pensilvania money is £79. 14. 8. five pounds of English money being allowed to the buyer of the said Inventory by the trustees, [which made the sale net] £73. 9. 8."

The value of the unexpired time of the servants is given:—"The Soms of the Servants being £30. 15. 0."

COMPANY NUMBER ONE

which is in addition to the aforesaid valuation of the personalty. From the inventory, we learn that John was well supplied with agricultural and household implements, bedding, clothing, and some grain, cows, and horses, and harness, and that there were sold his pair of spectacles, children and women's clothing, pewter, a gun, powder, four powder horns, fishing tackle, "leathen dresses," and "lethern waistcoats."

There is also preserved the receipt of Elizabeth Jones, endorsed "no part of the record," that is of the original testamentary proceedings, "Received from William Edward administrator of the Estate of my Father, John Edward, the Summe of fifty pounds, seven Shillings currant silver money of Pensylvania, in full of all bequests and Legaceys bequeathed to me by my sd father in his last will & testament bearing date of sixteenth day of the eight month in the year 1683, and in full of the shars that befell me of my deceased brother Evan Jones his estate, and I do acquitt and discharge the said William Edward his heirs, of all trusts and Legaceys, dues, debts, and demands from the beginning of the world to this day, 22 of 3mo. 1699." She wrote her name "Elizabeth Jones," and was then twenty-eight year of age, and apparently unmarried. The witnesses to this receipt were the same as those to the copy of the inventory mentioned, namely, Hugh Jones (marked), Thomas Jones, and Robert Jones.

The name of the wife and mother of his children of John ap Edward has not been found. She was apparently deceased when he made his will. His descendants assumed the name "Jones." Of his issue:—

Evan Jones, eldest son, b. 2. 2mo. 1677, mentioned in his father's will, died young and unmarried before 3mo. 1684.

Edward Jones, second son, and youngest child, b. 5. 8mo. 1681. He succeeded to all of his father's land when he became of age, in 1702-3. According to a note, he had his father's will copied into the records.

By deed, dated 13. 2mo. 1702-3, he conveyed all of the lands of his inheritance to Dr. Edward Jones, of Merion, giving "Receipt of Edward Jones, of Philadelphia, only son of John ap Edward, deceased, and nephew of William ap Edward, of Blockley," dated 23 January, 1702, Recorded in Philadelphia County Deed Book, No. C. II., fo. 198. His Merion tract of land extended from about the old Lancaster Road (Montgomery Avenue), across the Pensylvania Railroad between Merion station, and the borough of Narberth.

Elizabeth Jones, first child, b. 18. 12mo. 1671. She *m.* after 22 May, 1699, John ap Robert ap Cadwalader, or "John Roberts," of the Gwynedd settlement. They were the founders of the Roberts family of "'Woodlawn" plantation, in Whitpain township, Montgomery county, Pensylvania.

Sarah Jones, b. 8. 11mo. 1673, not named in her father's will.

FAMILIES AND LANDS
OF SECOND ARRIVALS

MERION ADVENTURERS

The second party of Welsh from Merionethshire, members of the Penllyn Monthly Meeting, who were purchasers of land in the "Thomas & Jones Tract," to remove here, were:

  Hugh Robert.   Cadwalader Morgan.
  Edward Owen.   Hugh John.
  William John.   Katherin Thomas.
     Gainor Roberts.

This is the party generally known as "Hugh Roberts's party."

They came over in the ship Morning Star, of Chester, Thomas Hayes, master, sailing from Mosson, in September, 1683. After a voyage of two months, uneventful, excepting for several burials at sea, they arrived in the Delaware, and at Philadelphia, 16-20 November following.

There was a large passenger list, outside of the Roberts' party, in which there were 50 souls, or more, including servants, Welshmen and their families, coming over to settle somewhere in the great Welsh Tract, who all may have come under Proud's description:—"Divers of those early Welsh settlers were persons of excellent and worthy character, and several of good education, family, and estate."

Of the most noted of those coming in this vessel, at this time, were John Bevan ("Company No. 3"), and his family, and party; John Roberts, of "Pencoyd"; Thomas Owen, who came to open-up Rowland Ellis's land; Rees Thomas, a future man of affairs in the Welsh Tract; Ralph and William Lewis; the Humphreys, Richard, John, and Samuel, the noted men of the Friends' Haverford Meeting;

WELSH SETTLEMENT OF PENSYLVANIA

Griffith John ap Evan, Robert ffloid, William Morgan, Evan John, brother of Rees John William, of Merion, etc., all became land owners, prosperous farmers, "good men and true," in townships of Merion, Haverford, or Radnor, and elsewhere in the Welsh Tract.

HUGH ROBERTS, Hugh Robert, or "Hugh ap Robert, of Kiltalgarth, yeoman," headed the second party of settlers from Merionethshire bound for the Thomas & Jones tract. In his immediate party, were his mother, his wife, his sister, Ganior Roberts, five children, and four servants.

Hugh Roberts was a man of education, a pleasant writer, and an eminent minister among Friends, whom he joined in 1666, and many sketches of his ministerial life have appeared in Friends' publications.

But little is now known of his ancestry, excepting that he was the son of Robert ap Hugh, or "Robert Pugh, gent," of Llyndedwydd, a leased farm, near Bala, and the lake, in Penllyn, Merioneth, by his wife, Katherine Roberts, who, then being a widow, accompanied her son to Pensylvania, and was buried at the Merion Meeting, in 1699. She was the daughter of William ap Owen, of Llanvawr parish, in Penllyn, where Hugh Roberts resided when he set out for America.

Katharine Robert, of Llaethgwn, widow, and her daughter, Gaynor Robert, of Kiltalgarth, spinster, both brought Certificates, dated 18. 5mo. 1683, from the Men's and Women's Meeting, Penllyn, and signed by the same Friends, namely:—Robert, Ellin, and Janne Owen, Richard Price, Evan Rees, Reece Evan, Elizabeth William, Elizabeth John, Gainor John, Hugh and Edward Griffith, Cadwalader Ellis, Thomas Prichard, William Morgan, Roger Roberts, David John, Margaret John, Margaret David, and Margaret Cadwalader.

Hugh Roberts, being so prominent a Friends' minister, in North Wales, suffered annoyances, fines, and imprisonment. He brought a certificate of membership, for himself, wife, and family, from the Men's Meeting, Penllyn, Merioneth, dated 2. 5mo. 1683.

Some members of this Men's Meeting at this time were:

Robert Owen.	Hugh Griffith.
Evan Owen.	Edward Griffith.
Richard Price.	Morris Humphrey.
Cadwalader Ellis.	Thomas Prichard.
Evan Rees.	David Jones.
Rees Evan.	William Morgan.
Ellis David.	Griffith John.
Thomas Ellis.	Roger Robert.
Rowland Ellis.	Owen Humphrey.

Nearly all of these were signers of Mr. Roberts's certificate, in which he was described as of Llanvawr parish, Merioneth.

He soon became well known in America as a travelling public minister, and in 1688, and 1697-8, made missionary visits to North Wales. On this last trip, he kept an interesting journal of his travels, beginning on 15. 12mo. 1697, which took him to England and Wales by the way of Maryland and Virginia, which is still extant.

This interesting journal, printed in full in the periodical of the Historical Society of Pensylvania, begins:—"In the year 1697, the 15th of ye mo. I set out from home to visit Friends in England and Wales, Samuel Carpenter and John Ascue accompanying me to Maryland." He held meetings *en route,* and in Maryland visited Mordecai Moore, Samuel Galloway, David Rawlins, the Widow Blackstone, "who was no Friend." From her home, where he stopped two days, he went to the Rapahannock river, alone, through the woods, on foot, "to one Captain Taylor, who was very kind to me." Thence "to a friend, George Wilson, a place where I had been before." "Here I had a very open Meeting amongst ye people of ye world." Then to New Kent county, "Where there is a meeting of Friends," and next day to a Monthly Meeting at Curles on James river, "met dear James Dickinson," "And I went to Edward Thomas at James river, Charles Fleming coming along with me," and attended a Quarterly Meeting at Tenbigh. Then visited Alexander Llewellyn. "We travelled that same day 46 miles, besides keeping ye Meeting, and it was not hard for us to do it because ye Melting love and power of God was set over all." From this Welsh settlement, Mr. Roberts went over the James river to Walter Bartlet's, "and so on to Sevenech, where I had a good meeting at ye Meeting House." Visited to homes of Henry Wiges, William Cook, Richard Ratcliff, Daniel Sanburn, and John Coopland, and held a Meeting at Chuckatuck. Went to the homes also of William Scot, Leven Buffstin, Elizabeth Gallowell, and Elizabeth Hollowell, having Meetings at each house, "from thence on board ye ship, which was to ye mouth of James river, where ye Fleet met, we stayed on board 15 days before we sailed, and had several Meetings from ship to ship, and upon ye 7th day of ye 3d month we sailed." Next, he saw land on 17. 4mo. and arrived at Plymouth on 22. 4mo.

Resuming his travels, Mr. Roberts visited many Friends, and places in England, and at Bristol, "we met our dear friend William Penn, and were not a little glad to see one another." Entering Wales, he visited many Meetings, one at "Trefrug, where John Bevan liveth, and glad we were to meet one another." Together, they made the rounds of many Meetings, at James Lewis's, Rediston; at Owen Bowen's, near Carmarthin; at James Preece's, City Boom. In Radnorshire, he visited Roger Hughes; at Lanole, Ed-From North Wales he travelled to many places in South Wales, then back to Merionethshire, in the North, where ward Jones, David Powel, Thomas Goodin, near Llwyn-du. "Penllyn where I was born and bred," and visited there his he visited Lewis Owen, near Dollegelley, then to Bala, and old friend, Robert Vaughan, and then made another pilgrimage through Wales.

On his return here, he brought over a large party of people from Merioneth, and North Wales. But many died at sea. He arrived at Philadelphia 7. 5mo. 1698, and settled the surviving emigrants, some in Merion, and others at Gwynedd, of which settlement he is considered the founder.

Half of Hugh Roberts's original purchase from Thomas & Jones, by deed dated 28 February, 1681, recorded 16 April 1684, witnessed by Daniel Jones, Robert Owen, William Jones, Reece Evan, Thomas John, and William Apedd (ap Edward), was laid out for him before his first arrival, on the Schuylkill. This parcel of land, surveyed 306 acres, was along the side of the estate of the widow of his dear friend, John ap Thomas, and like hers, extended back to the lands of Thomas Lloyd, the Governor.

For no other reason, as no evidence has been found in either case, than because he was a minister, it is assumed that the Merion Friends held all their Meetings, before the present Meeting House was erected, in 1695, in his house, and that the early weddings took place in the home of the Widow Thomas, because her house was most convenient, and more cheerful. However this may be, there is no documentary proof for the assumptions, and the preserved records of the earliest functions in Merion are described as taking place in the "public Meeting House."

The Pensylvania land records of his day show that Hugh Roberts was a land speculator, as well as a minister, to the day of his death. But space permits only to transcribe a few of his land transactions, especially those connected with the the neighborhood of the Merion Meeting House.

In addition to his original purchase of 312½ acres in Merion, he bought the Merion share, 76½ acres (about the present Overbrook), of John Watkins, 23. 4mo. 1684. By deed of 1. 4mo. 1688, he bought from the Commissioners,

WELSH SETTLEMENT OF PENSYLVANIA

200 acres, in Merion, for which he had warrant to survey, and 100 acres "liberty land." Of this 300 acre lot, 100 acres he had bought for, or did sell to the Widow Thomas, which sale was confirmed to her sons, Thomas and Cadwalader, 22. 12. 1702. By deed of 17. 6mo. 1694, he purchased his brother-in-law's, William Edwards's, original purchase, 76½ acres, adjoining his land, on the Schuylkill.

The aforesaid 100 acres of "liberty lands," were in right of the Richard Thomas purchase from Penn, and lay on Indian creek and the Mill Creek, (now Cobb's Creek). When Penn was here he sold to Hugh 200 acres of liberty land, on the west side of the Schuylkill river, for which he was to pay £150. He gave Penn £60 cash in hand. On 26. 11mo. 1701, he asked for further time, as he could not raise the balance due. The Commissioners ordered him to furnish good bond, and they would give him an extension till 29. 7mo. next.

Hugh Roberts also bought of Peter Young 500 acres, and of Francis Cook 400 acres, that is 900 acres of the original tract of John & Wynne ("Company No. 4"). This purchase lay in Blockley and Merion townships, and in other places. Of his Merion lands, he sold 295 acres to Cadwalader Ellis, and 335 acres were confirmed to his executors, by a patent, dated 26 March, 1706.

Of his Blockley purchase above, 200 acres became the seat called "Chestnut Hill," along the old Lancaster road, which his youngest son, Edward Roberts, inherited. Part of this tract is now included in Fairmount Park. In 1721, a portion, that including what is known now as "George's Hill," in the West Park, was purchased (300 acres altogether) from said Edward by Edward George (son of Richard and Jane George, who came from Llangerig, in Montgomeryshire, about 1707-8), whose descendants, Jesse and Rebecca George, gave it to the city forever for a park. Mr. Roberts also had 300 acres in Radnor in 1717.

COMPANY NUMBER ONE

Hugh Roberts had at one time altogether 1349¾ acres in Merion, and tracts of land in the townships of Duffryn Mawr, and Goshen, on Ridley Creek, some of which he disposed of to Cadwalader Ellis.

Hugh Roberts, it has been said, died at the house of John Redman, in Long Island, New York, when on a visit, in 6mo. 1702, and his remains were brought over from Long Island and buried at the Merion Meeting House, on the 20th. August, "after a large meeting was held."

But a letter from Judge Isaac Norris, to Jonathan Dickinson, dated 11. 6mo. 1702 ("Penn-Logan Correspondence"), says:—"Dear Hugh Roberts is, we think, very near his end. I was to see him on First-day, and then took a solemn and tender farewell, his soul being resigned, earnestly desiring and expecting his change; as in his life he was a preacher of Love, so now, in his latest moment does he continue to be so."

Therefore, it is most probable that he died at home, in Merion. The entry on the Merion Meeting minutes is "Hugh Roberts departed this Life 6mo. 18. 1702."

His will, signed 20. 5mo. 1702, was proved at Philadelphia, 7 December, 1702. He names his children, and distributed about 1200 acres in Merion, and 1100 acres in Goshen township, a meadow called "Clean John," &c. He bequeathed £5 to the Merion Meeting. He mentioned his servants, namely, two men, Morris Robert, and John Robert, and boys, Griffith and Morris. He named as trustees, John Roberts (of "Pencoid"), Cadwalader Morgan, Griffith John, and Griffith Owen. Witnesses:—Samuel Bowne, Griffith Owen, and Samuel Jennings.

Hugh Roberts was twice married. He *m.* first, Jane, daughter of Owen ap Evan Robert Lewis, of Fron Gôch, in Merioneth. She was a sister of Robert Owen, of Merion. She came to Merion with him, and brought the certificate above mentioned, and died 1. 7mo. 1686, and was buried at Merion Meeting House. He *m.* secondly, 31. 5mo. 1689, at

WELSH SETTLEMENT OF PENSYLVANIA

the Llwyn-y-Braner Meeting, in Penllyn, Merionethshire,. when on a visit, Elizabeth vch. John, or Elizabeth Jones.

His six children, all by his first wife, Jane Owen, who was of Royal Descent, assumed the surname "Roberts." Of them:—

Robert Roberts, b. 7. 11mo. 1673. By his father's will, he and his brother Owen received jointly his Merion land.

On 26. 1mo. 1706, this land was patented to them, in two tracts, of 222 acres, and 31 acres each, and by deed of 16 October, 1707, "Robert Roberts, of Maryland," conveyed his 222 (220) acres, which lay along the Lancaster road (Montgomery avenue) from the Meeting House to the Gulf road, and 10 acres, called "Clean John Meadow," on the "Upper Mill Creek," to Edward Rees.

Robert Roberts was twice married, and is supposed to have removed to Maryland, and died there. He *m.* first,. Catharine Jones, and *m.* secondly, Priscilla Jones.

Ellin Roberts, b. 4. 10mo. 1675.

Owen Roberts, second son, b. 1. 10mo. 1677. He inherited some land from his father, as above, but entering on mercantile life in Philadelphia, was never a Merion planter. There was in 1716, an "ould Grave Yard" on his Merion property, from which bodies were removed to the ground of the Merion Meeting. He was the worthy son of his father, and was honored by being made the high sheriff of Philadelphia county, 1716-23; the treasurer, 1712-16; collector, 1716-23, a member of the city council, 1712, and of the Assembly, 1711, &c.

He owned 231 acres, of the east end of his father's original land, and by deed of 14 October, 1726, his relict, Ann,. then residing in Nantmell township (Chester county), conveyed the same to Jonathan Jones, of Merion.

His will, signed 31. 1mo. 1706, witnessed by Griffith John,. Evan Owen, John Roberts, and Robert Jones, was proved at

Philadelphia in 1723. He named brother Edward, and appointed trustees, brothers-in-law Evan Bevan and Robert Jones, with uncle John Roberts and Griffith John. He *m.* 23. 1mo. 1696, Ann, daughter of John Bevan, one of the early settlers of Merion, who died after 1723. Issue, six children. His infant son, Owen Roberts, was buried at Merion Meeting, 7mo. 25. 1707, but he had another Owen, *b.* 23. 8. 1711. Other children were Hugh Roberts, *b.* 30. 5. 1699. John Roberts, *b.* 12. 8. 1701, *m.* Mary Jones, and Awbrey Roberts, *b.* 24. 4. 1705.

Edward Roberts, third son, *b.* 4. 2mo. 1680. He received the "Chestnut Hill" place from his father, in 1702, but resided in Philadelphia, where he was a member of the City Council, in 1717, and Mayor, in 1739-40, having served as alderman, and a justice. He used for his seal "a rose, under a crown, between two human hearts." His will was proved 6 May, 1741.

He *m.* first, Susanna Painter, buried at the Merion Meeting House, 10mo. 3. 1707, daughter of George Painter, and *m.* secondly, Martha Hoskins, and *m.* thirdly, Martha Cox. He had four children: Hugh, Jane, wife of William Fishbourne, Mayor of Philadelphia 1719-21; Mary, and Elizabeth Bond.

William Roberts, *b.* 26. 3mo. 1682; *d.* in 1697.

Elizabeth Roberts, *b.* in Merion, 24. 12mo. 1683, named in her father's will.

EDWARD OWEN was residing in Dolserey, or Doleyserre, Merioneth, and described as "Gentleman," when he bought, by deed, dated 1 April, 1682, 312½ acres through Thomas & Jones. He was a son of Robert Owen (ap Humphrey), of Dolserey, by his wife, Jane, a daughter of Robert Vaughan, of Hengwrt.

Edward Owen came over in Hugh Robert's party in 1683, and found his land laid out on the Schuylkill, 153¼ acres, adjoining that of Dr. Jones, and the balance in Goshen tp. He probably never resided on this estate, as he sold it to his brother, Dr. Griffith Owen, by deed dated 9. 1mo. 1684-5, and according to it, was then living on Duck Creek, in New Castle Co. (Delaware). His Goshen rights he also conveyed to this brother, who had the land laid out, subsequently, on Chester Creek.

Dr. Griffith Owen, with his wife, Sarah, who survived him, son Robert, d. before 1717, and two daughters, Sarah and Elinor, and seven servants, from Prescoe, in Lancashire, came over (with his parents, and brother Louis Owen, who settled in New Castle Co.), in the ship Vine, of Liverpool, sailing from Doleyserre with a large party bound for the Welsh Tract, and arrived at Philadelphia 17. 7mo. 1684.

Besides the land he had fom his brother, which Dr. Owen, by deed dated 1. 1mo. 1694-5, conveyed to Robert David, whose land adjoined, the Doctor bought some from Richard Davies and John ap John, and the Land Commissioners (of which Board he was a member in 9ber, 1701), in Goshen, and had 775 acres, in one tract, which was confirmed to him, by patent dated 13 Dec. 1703. The Goshen Meeting House was built in the center of this tract, on land donated by the Doctor.

Dr. Owen died in Philadelphia in 1717, aged 70 years, and was one of the earliest physicians here, others being Dr. Edward Jones, Dr. John Goodson, Dr. Thomas Wynne, and Dr. Graeme. His will, signed 3 Jan. 1717, proved 6 Jan. named wife and children, Edward, Griffith (both became "practitioners in physick" in Philadelphia), John (a mariner), Sarah, wife of Jacob Jonathan Coppock, and Ann, wife of John Whitpaine. Son-in-law William Sanders, and "daughter-in-law, Mary, wife of Samuel Marriot."

WILLIAM AP JOHN, or William Jones, a yeoman, and widower, was residing in Bettws, in Merioneth, when he became a purchaser of 156¼ acres, in the Thomas & Jones tract, for £3. 2. 6. Witnesses to his deed, dated 1 April,

COMPANY NUMBER ONE

1682, being John Lloyd, Griffith Evan, Robert Lloyd and Reece Evan.

He came over in the "Morning Star" with the Hugh Roberts party, in 1683, bringing his children, and found 76½ acres laid out for him on the Schuylkill. He had about the same amount assigned to him in Goshen tp. There seems to be no proof that he ever resided on his Merion land, as he died shortly after coming over, his nuncupative will being sealed and proved at Philadelphia on 1. 1mo. 1684-5. He bequeathed his lands to his son, "John Williams," and appointed Hugh Roberts and John Roberts, (of "Pencoid"), trustees and guardians of his minor children. His wife is mentioned in his will as "Ann Reynald, deceased."

Of his children:—

John Williams, as above said, inherited all his father's lands. By deed, dated 18. 4mo. 1694, he conveyed his Merion land to Cadwalader Morgan, whose land adjoined his, and his Goshen land, 78 acres, he sold, 13. 6mo. 1697, to Edward Rees, of Merion, who conveyed it, 9 Jan. 1707-8, to Ellis David.

The other children, "who took the name Jones," were *Alice, Katherine* and *Gwen,* minors in 1685.

CADWALADER MORGAN was residing in Gwernevel, or Gwernfell, Ismynydd tp., Penllyn parish, Merioneth, when he, with his wife and several children, removed to Pensylvania, coming over on the "Morning Star," with the Hugh Roberts party, in 1683.

He brought the usual certificate of membership and removal, from the Penllyn Men Friends' Meeting, dated 8. 5mo. 1683, and signed by Richard Price, Robert and Evan Owen, Evan Rees, Rees Evan, Roger Roberts, Hugh and Edward Griffith, Griffith John, William Morgan and David John. He was a minister among Friends, "though he held no great share of the ministry," was the estimate recorded of him by Eleanor Evans, of Gwynedd, a daughter of Rowland Ellis. But as he had greatly "suffered" in Wales, because of his prominence, and religious faith, he purchased 156 acres through Thomas & Jones, and permanently left Wales.

On arrival, he found part of his purchase laid out on the Schuylkill, and here he erected a dwelling house, near "Pencoid," and passed the remainder of his days. His will, signed 10 Sep. 1711, was proved at Philadelphia, on 10 Oct. following. In it he mentioned his brothers, "Morgan Lewis" and "John Morgan," of Radnor. Cadwalader was therefore a son of James Morgan, who in 1701, had 450 acres in Radnor tp., to which his son and heir, John Morgan, succeeded 1702.

By purchase, he greatly increased his holdings in Merion, originally only 76½ acres, which he had by deed, dated 1 April, 1682, recorded 13. 4. 1684. Witnessed by John Lloyd, Reece Evan, Griffith Evan, Robert Lloyd and William John. He bought by deeds, dated 18. 4mo. 1694, the Merion land, 76½ acres, of Rees John William, of "Rees Joans," and the 76½ acres which John Williams had from his father. William John, an original purchaser of Thomas & Jones, which lands lay on both sides of his, which was backed by the purchase of Gainor Robert, so he now had, by survey of 1701, 223½ acres in Merion, fronting on the river. And, by deed of conveyance, dated 19 Jan. 1707-8, he acquired 92 acres of land, from Hugh John Thomas, or "Hugh Jones," adjoining his last purchase, and this gave him 2,178, or more, feet on the river, near Roberts's "Pencoyd." By deed, 30 May 1709, he sold his last purchases, namely, 223 acres and 92 acres, to Robert Evans, and subsequently it became part of the "Roberts Estate."

The will of "Cadder Morgan, of Merion," signed 10 Sep. 1711, in the presence of Robert Roberts, Moses Roberts,*

---

*Moses Roberts was one of the children of Robert Ellis, who, with his wife, Ellin, and seven children, removed here in 1690, bringing their certificate from the Quarterly Meeting held at Tyddyn y Gareg, and Thomas Jones, was proved 10 Oct. 1711. Executors, sons-in-law Robert Evan and Abel Thomas. Names brother John Morgan (of Radnor), son-in-law Hugh Evans, Cadwalader, second son of son-in-law Robert Evan (of Gwynedd); Sarah, wife of Robert Evan; Elizabeth, daughter of son-in-law Abel Thomas; sister-in-law Elizabeth, wife of brother Lewis Morgan, and her child, not named. Appointed as overseers, Edward Jones, John Roberts, David Jones (of Blockley), and Thomas Jones.

Cadwalader Morgan married Jane, who d. before 1711, daughter of Richard Gryffyth (ap Rhys, or Rees, and Prees, or Price), of Llanfawr, Merioneth, who was of Royal Descent, and a sister of Rees Jones's wife, of Merion, and to Edward Price, of Merion, and had two sons and three daughters by her, who is recorded at the Merion Meeting as buried 7. 19. 1710, "Jane wife of Chadwalader Morgan," namely:

Morgan Cadwalader, b. 23. 6mo. 1679. He was a minister among Friends, and died young, and unmarried.

Edward Cadwalader, b. 22. 6mo. 1682. He died unmarried, before his father.

Sarah, m. Robert Evan, or Evans, of Gwynedd. *Issue.*

Daughter, m. Hugh Evan, or Evans, of Gwynedd.

Daughter, m. Abel Thomas, of Merion. *Issue.* The following entry at the Merion Meeting, 12. 23. 1807: Burial,

---

in Merionethshire, dated 5mo. 28. 1690. Their children named "Roberts" were Abel (*m.* Mary Price), Moses, Ellis, Aaron (*m.* Sarah Longworthy), Evan, Rachel, Jane, Mary, and Gainor. The will of Moses Roberts, of Merion, signed 16. 12. 1715-6, witnessed by John Roberts and David George, was proved 28 Feb. same year. He appoints brother Ellis Roberts, and friend Robert Roberts, executors. Names brothers Aaron, Evan, and Ellis, and sisters Jane, Rachel, Mary, and Gainor Roberts, nieces Katherine and Rachel Roberts, and Margaret Edwards, Elizabeth Roberts, Sarah Dickinson, Jane, daughter of Abel Thomas, John Kelly, and Thomas Bowen.

WELSH SETTLEMENT OF PENSYLVANIA

"Jacob Thomas, son of Abel, with the waggon Load of Stone run over his head."

HUGH JOHN AP THOMAS, Hugh John or Hugh Jones, was living at Nantlleidiog, in Llanvawr parish, Merioneth, and was a widower and a farmer and miller, when he bought 156¼ acres of land, deed dated 18 March, 1681, through Thomas & Jones, and decided to remove to it, and came over with Hugh Roberts's party, in 1683.

He lived several years on his Merion land, 76¼ acres, (the balance of his purchase being laid out in Goshen tp.), which on resurvey on order from the Commissioners, amounted to 92 acres. He paid for and retained the increased acreage, having patent for it, dated 8 Nov. 1703.

By deed, dated 19 Jan. 1707-8, he conveyed his Merion tract to Cadwalader Morgan, whose property then adjoined his, and his holdings in Goshen to John Roberts, of "Pencoid," and removed to the Welsh settlement at Plymouth, where he died in 1727, having had four wives.

He m. secondly, at the Merion Meeting, 16. 5mo. 1686, Margaret David, and m. thirdly, at the Radnor Meeting, 18. 11mo. 1693, and m. fourthly, at the Merion Meeting, 22. 9mo. 1703, Margaret Edwards. It is said that he had issue, and that one of his daughters married after his last marriage, and before 1708, Rowland Richard.

MERION ADVENTURERS

"JOHN AP. THOMAS, of Llaithgwm, Commott of Penllyn, in the County of Merioneth, gentleman," as contemporary manuscripts designated him, was a forefather of the Merion Meeting, and a partner in this, the first, and most notable, company of Welsh Friends that removed to the Welsh Tract, though not destined himself to come over.

He was a son of Thomas ap Hugh (ap Evan Rhys-Goch), a gentleman farmer, or country gentleman, of Wern Fawr, in Llandderfel parish, Merioneth, whose will was proved at St. Asaph registry, in 1682. His brothers and sisters were, Cadwalader Thomas, (mentioned in the will of John Thomas), who resided on a farm at Kiltalgarth, in Merioneth, and died before his father, and whose wife was a sister of Robert Owen, who became one of the most prominent residents of "Merion in the Welsh Tract," one of their sons, John Cadwalader. mentioned in the will of his uncle, John Thomas, was the founder of the well known family of Cadwalader, of Philadelphia and Trenton], Hugh Thomas, of Penllyn; Catherine, wife of Gawen Vaughn, of Hendre Mawr, and Elizabeth, wife of Maurice ap Edward, of Cae Mor.

John ap Thomas was of notable ancestry, according to his pedigree, complied before 1682, which is extant. The late Dr. Levick, of Philadelphia, owned this MS pedigree,* and reproduced it in full in the Pa. Mag. vol. IV. p. 471, but as it is a very extended one, in fact, showing the lineal descent of John ap Thomas from Noah, space for only the last seventeen generations can be given here, which runs: "John

---

*Now in the possession of Lewis J. Levick, Esqr., and loaned by him to the Historical Society of Pensylvania (July, 1910).

WELSH SETTLEMENT OF PENSYLVANIA

Thomas, of Llaithgwm, in the County of Merioneth, Gent., 1682|Thomas ap Hugh|Hugh ap Evan (of Wern Fawr)| Evan ap Rees Gôch|Rees Gôch ap Tyder|Tudor|Evan and county of Denbig|Evan ddu|David ap Eiynion|Eiynion ap Kynrig|Kynrig ap Llowarch|Heilin|Tyfid|Tagno| Ysdrwyth|Marchwysst|Marchweithian, one of the 15en tribes of North Wales, and Lord of Issallet," ap Llud, ap Llen, &c, &c. This Marchweileian, "who beareth guwls a Lyon Rampant Argent, Armed Langued Azure," was the eleventh of the fifteen tribes of North Wales (see "Cambrian Register," 1795, p. 151), who held their lands by Baron's service. He was called Lord of Is-Aled, and owned, or controlled many townships, about A. D. 720.

He was convinced by the Quaker apostle, John ap John, of the truth of the teachings of Fox, "God's Truths," and became a member of the religious Society of Friends, in 1672, and from then till his untimely death, he was a leader and minister amongst Welsh Friends. Hugh Roberts, his life-long friend and neighbor, in an extant sketch of him, tells of his conversion, "though it was a time of great suffering" among the Friends in Wales for being non-conformists.

The members of the Society were beset on every side by paid spies of the "established church," and informers working "on commission," so it could be expected that this prominent gentleman farmer of the neighborhood would be closely watched, and Mr. Roberts records: "The first two meetings he was at, he was fined fifteen pounds [by a magistrate, and refusing to pay] the informer took from him two oxen, and a horse that was valued to be worth eleven pounds, and returned nothing back!" "The appearance of Truth was so precious to him," continues Mr. Roberts, "that he did not only make profession of it, but was also made willing to suffer for its sake, which he did valiantly." This, however, could be said of Mr. Roberts, himself, and of almost every man and woman who fled finally from persecu-

COMPANY NUMBER ONE

tion to the Welsh Tracts in Pensylvania. "When this faithful man first came among us [in Wales], it was the hottest time of persecution that we ever underwent."

So active were informers working for percentage of the fines imposed, that the resourceful John Thomas, records Mr. Roberts, went to one of the county justices, "that was moderate," with strong indorsements, and got the appointment for himself to be the high constable for his district, the position being vacant.

It seems that the procedure against Quakers was for the spy, or informer, to find an alleged culprit, one who did not attend the services of the Established Church, after warning; one who declined to contribute towards the support of that church and its minister, upon assessment; for attending meetings of Quakers; having such meetings held in their homes, and a long list of more petty complaints, sware out a warrant against him before a committing magistrate, which would follow its usual course, be delivered to the high sheriff, who would issue an order to the county jailor to receive and take charge of the prisoner, arrested and brought in by the high constable.

There has been preserved among the papers of John Thomas one of the sheriff's orders to the jailor, and it is possible that it is one of those that came into John's hands when he was high constable, and which he "pigeon-holed."

"Merioneth, SS.

"To Lewis Morris, Keeper of his Majts goale for ye sd County, & to Richard Price and Joseph Hughes.

"Whereas, I have apprehended Cadwalader ap Thomas ap Hugh, Robert Owen, Hugh ap Robert, John David, John Robert David, & Jonett John, spinster.

"By virtue of his Ma'ties writt, issued out of the last great sessions, & unto me directed & delivered, I therefore do will and require you to receive into your custody the bodyes of the said Caddw'r ap Tho ap Hugh, Robert Owen, Hugh Roberts, Jo Robert David & Jonett John, and them safely to convey to the common geole of the sd County and them in a safe manner to be kept in ye sd geole whom I doe hereby commit, there to remain for the next great sessions to be held for ye sd county on Monday of ye sd sessions, then and there to answer such matters as shall be objected against them on his Ma'ties behalfe, this omitt you not at yr perill, given under my hand & seal of office, the fourth day of May, Anno R. Caroli (di) Angliæ & vicessimo sexto, Annoq dom 1674.

"Owen Wynne, Esq. Sheriff."

These apprehended Quakers were relatives and neighbors of John ap Thomas—one was his brother—so it may be imagined he did not carry out the order. It seems that in John Thomas's neighborhood, the most diligent of the informers, "a cunning, subtle man," was also an applicant for the position John captured,* and it was very evident to him why John sought it, and was glad to get it, so he set out to defeat him and have him impeached, in the following way, as told by Mr. Roberts:

"So the informer went on, and informed against Friends, and when he got a warrant, he brought it to the high constable, according to his orders" [from the magistrate], and John Thomas thereupon would tell him "to go about his business, that he was responsible for them" [the warrants]. So John simply pocketed the warrants, and did nothing. This was just as the informer hoped, for he knew that John was violating the Act of Parliament, and his office, and putting himself in the position to be heavily fined for every neglect. John certainly took great chances, for the informer had nine good cases against him, when fortunately "the King's Declaration came to put a stop to these wicked in-

---

*Among the papers of John Thomas is a letter, written about 1681, addressed to Richard Davies (one of the adventurers for Penn's land), by John ap David, a Friend, mentioned in the Sheriff's order, who also got the appointment of high constable to protect his brethren. It tells of the seizure of the chattels of Robert Evan.

formers," says Mr. Roberts. "Thus this faithful and valiant man hazarded his own estate to save his friends and brethren."

John Thomas wrote out, his notes still extant, many instances of his persecution and teasing, and those of his neighbors, wherein he tells of burdensome fines on the slightest provocations, and of scandalous tithing assessments and collections, all similiar to those related of others in Besse's "Sufferings of Friends." Probably the most disgraceful proceeding in John's experience was when the parish priest of the Established Church came one day to collect John's contribution towards his salary and support of the parish church. John's Mem.,

"In the year 1674, about the 20th day of the 4th month, Harry Parry, parson of Llanthervol, he and his men came to the ground of John ap Thomas, and demanded lambes tithes; and when the said John ap Thomas was not free to give him tithes, he sent his men abroad to hunt for the lambs, and at length they found them in one end of the barn, where they used to be every night, and they took out the best five out of 21 for tithes. And for the tithe corn, they took of the corn I cannot tell how much." John, like many Friends of the days of persecution, made memoranda of raids on his property, hoping a time would come when they could submit them, and be reimbursed.

Another interesting paper that has been preserved with the papers * of John ap Thomas, and which probably came into his hands when he was the high constable, is dated 20 May, 1675, and signed by Humphrey Hughes and John Wynne, justices of the peace, and addressed "To the high and pettie Constables" of Merionethshire, and to the church wardens, and the overseers of the poor in every parish in that county. It is the formal announcement, on informa-

---

*Nearly all of Mr. Thomas's papers are (1910) in possession of Mr. Lewis Jones Levick, of Bala, Pa.

tion from Owen David and Thomas John, of Penmaen, in Llanfawr parish, that certain persons in the county have met together on 16 May, "under colour of pretence of Religion," against the laws of the realm, "in a house called by the name of Ilwyn y Branar, in Penmaen, and orders distraints to be made against them. John ap Thomas is named in the list.

Volumes have been published telling of the persecutions of the Friends, yet the following letter, found among John Thomas' papers,** is interesting in that years after the aforesaid times, the Quakers were still being persecuted. And it was written just at the time the Welsh Friends were arranging to buy land from Penn, and remove to it.

"Dolgelley, ye 25th of the 4th mo., 1681.
"My dear friend John ap Thomas:

"These in haste may let thee understand that the persons undernamed are outlawed, and the Deputy Sheriffe hath writts against them.

"Many of them are dead, those that are alive (I) wish them to look to themselves, untill such time as friends shall come together to confer in their behalfe, that soe friends in their liberty may order some considerable gratuity to the Deputy Sheriffe for his kindness.

"Beside those undernamed, Elizabeth Williams is particularly to look to herself. There is a writt out of the Exchequer against her, as the Deputy Sheriffe informs me.

"Ye names are as followeth, vizt.:
William Prees, de Landervol.
Thomas ap Edward, de Llanvawr.
Litter Thomas, de eadem.
Thomas Williams, de ead.
John Davie, de ead.
Elizabeth Thomas, de ead, widdow.
Lodovicus ap Robt., de ead.

**Inherited by Mr. Lewis J. Levick and now in his possession.

Thomas ap Edward, de Llanvawr, Thomas Williams, de ead.
Robt. John Evan, de ead.
Griffith John, de Gwerevol, and Elizabeth his wife.
Hugh Griffith, of the same, & Mary his wife.
Maurice Humphrey Morgan, of the same.
This is att present from thy dear friend and desires to Excuse my brevity.   Lewis Owen."

This letter shows that the persecuted and outlawed Friends had at least one official interested in their welfare. The suggestion that the deputy sheriff be tipped to hold up the writs, has a modern look about it, yet it was a kindly meant suggestion.

Lewis Owen was a member of the Dolgelly Quarterly Meeting, Merionethshire, 2mo. 1684, with Rowland Owen, Humphrey Owen, Rowland Ellis, Ellin Ellis, Owen Lewis, Owen Humphrey, Hugh Rees, Reece Evan, Richard Jones, David Jones, Ellis Davies, Ellis Moris, John William, Kathrine Price, Jane Robert and Agnes Hugh.

"Elizabeth Williams is particularly to look to herself!" This most active preacher among Friends. What a terrible experience hers had been for a half century, and still she had "to look to herself"; stop getting up meetings and exhorting, else she would have to undergo further punishments, and this when she was nearly eighty years old. Nearly thirty years before this last warning, Elizabeth, when 50 years old, with the almost equally celebrated minister, Mary Fisher, nearly escaped execution of some sort in Cambridge, in 1653. Besse, the Quaker annalist, records that "the mayor ordered them to be whipped till the blood ran down their bodies, * * * * which was done far more cruelly than with worse malefactors, so that their flesh was miserably torn." They were then driven out of the city.

It has already been told that John ap Thomas was one of the party of Welsh Friends that went to London to interview William Penn, about the land in America, he was offering for sale. There is a letter extant, among his papers, from him to his wife, dated London, 28. 3mo. 1681, telling her that he is well, and that he arrived in London on 21st inst., "without any great difficulty," accompanied by Thomas Ellis, with whom he intended to return home "the next second day," and concludes:

"I lay it upon thee to mind my dear love to my friends, H. R. & his; Robt O. & his; E. Jo. & his; R. D. & his; H. G. & his; G. J. & his; Elizabeth John & hers; Elizabeth Wyn and hers, with all the rest as if named them one by one.

No more at present, but my dear love to thee, and soe I
      I am JOHN
      ap Thomas."

At this time John ap Thomas and Edward Jones secured rights to 5,000 acres of Penn's American land, and upon their return to Merioneth, after themselves subscribing for over 1,500 acres, they conveyed the balance among fifteen neighbors in Penllyn tp., as stated, the majority of whom removed to their purchases.

It was undoubtedly the intention of John Thomas also to remove with his family to his American land, as he was greatly interested in the plan for a refuge for the persecuted Welsh Quakers, and was a shareholder in the Society of Free Traders of Pensylvania, but a little time before the date, in July, 1682, set for the first departure of Welsh Friends, his partner and relative, Dr. Jones, and companions, he became too ill to travel, and never recovered. His old friend, Hugh Roberts, records the scenes of his deathbed, saying: "He took his leave of his friends, giving his hand to every one of us, and so in a sweet and heavenly praise, he departed the 3d day of 3mo. 1683." And of this event, his son, Thomas Jones, entered in the Family Bible, still preserved: "Our dear father, John ap Thomas, of Laithgwm, in the Commott of Penllyn, in the county of Merioneth, in North Wales, departed this life the 3d day of 3d month, 1683, being the 5th day of the week, and was buryed at Friends burying place at Havod-vadog in the said Commott and County, ye 5th of ye said month."

Although his health and strength was poor and failing, John Thomas looked forward to joining his friends in America, and to this end, "sent some effects [with them] and agreed with them to make some provision against his intended coming." This was certainly done, as John's portion of land was located on the Schuylkill, and in Goshen tp., the same as if he were present. In fact, there was an agreement, which is extant, signed by Edward Jones, per David Davies, while John Thomas was so ill, and before Dr. Jones sailed, saying: "And should John ap Thomas happen to die before ye said Edward Jones, that E. J. should take no benefit of survivorship," which probably referred to partnership in goods for sale in Pensylvania, which Dr. Jones took with him.

About four months after her husband's decease, "Katherine Robert," his relict, with her children, sailed from Chester, in the ship "Morning Star," for Philadelphia, with the parties of Hugh Roberts and John Bevan, and arrived 16 Nov., 1683, "and found one-half of the purchase taken up in the place since called Merion, and some small improvement made on the same where we then settled," as her son, Robert Jones, wrote to William Penn.

In a sketch of John Thomas and his wife, by the late Dr. James J. Levick, of Philadelphia, (in the IV Vol., of the magazine of the Historical Society of Pensylvania), he says: "From all that is left on record, Katharine Thomas was a woman of great force of character and of much Christian worth. * * * Great as was the sacrifice, she does not seem to have hesitated to leave her comfortable home for the distant and wild lands beyond the sea."

The certificate she brought from the Friends' Penllyn Monthly Meeting, of which she had been a member for ten years, dated 18. 5mo. 1683, was most flattering, and among others, bore the signatures of Robert Owen, Richard Price, Cadwalader Lewis and Edward Griffith.

Among the "Thomas Papers" there are letters from Robert Vaughan, "a learned man," to his "loving aunt," Katharine Thomas,—one written in 3mo. 1687, and a letter from her "loving nephew," Edward Maurice, dated "Eyton Parke, Denbigshire, 3 Sep. 1692," mentioning her kin, the Yales, of Plas yn Yale, and other "County Families" of Wales, all suggesting that Katharine was of gentle birth and refined breeding, which is borne out by Friends' endorsements, and the accounts of these families in Nicholas's "Annals and Antiquities of the County Families of Wales."

Many of the Welsh Friends, bound for Merion, came over on this voyage of the "Morning Star," as told before. Katharine's immediate party, her children and servants, numbered twenty. It was a long voyage, even at that time, and only the strongest survived it. Two of Katharine's children died and were buried at sea, namely, daughters Sydney, on 29. 7mo. and Mary, on 18. 8mo. as recorded in the Bible* of Thomas Jones, one of Katharine's sons.

As "some provision against" Katharine's coming had been made on her husband's land, her son records they went there at once, after landing, the place being called, he says, "Geilli yr Cochiaid," or "Grove of Red Partridges."

The "provision" was only a log cabin, and here the family resided till a small stone house was erected on another property she bought. Both of these remained till recently as landmarks near the village of Bala, on the property of Walter Jones. Her property here, as surveyed in 1684, was 612 acres of timber land, and was the furtherest located up the Schuylkill of the purchases through her husband and Dr. Jones, and extended back to north of the present village of Narberth. Adjoining her was her old

---

*This Bible, with its family data, has been presented to the Historical Society of Pensylvania by Lewis Jones Levick, Esqr.

friend, Hugh Roberts, who, with his family, had also, as said, come over in this voyage of the "Morning Star."

We can imagine Katharine Thomas to have been of good business acumen, as after getting her 612 acres here into working order, and made crop-yielding, she purchased the following summer 150 acres on the river, between the lands of Barnabas Wilcox and Joseph Harrison, adjoining her husband's land, on which there was "a dwelling house lately erected." On 10 Dec. 1689, took title for a tract of 500 acres north of her first land, on the river, called "Glanrason," from Joseph Wood, (son of William Wood, the first grantee, 30. 7mo. 1684), and adjoining the 500 acre tract, next above on the river of William Sharlow, called "Mount Ararat." * Besides these lands on the river, Katharine also had a tract in Goshen tp., on Chester Creek, being the balance of her husband's purchase for £25, and lots in the "city" and a questionable share of the "liberty land" which went with the original purchase.

About six years after their mother's death, the sons had all of her land that remained to them, surveyed, and it amounted to 679 acres in Merion, and 635 acres in Goshen, for the whole they received a patent dated 3. 11mo. 1703, The Merion land, in a general way, lay north of the town of Narberth, extending from Montgomery Ave. (the old Lancaster Road) to the river, and, from the Price property, west of and near the Merion Meeting House, westward to "St. Mary's" (the Wister, or Chichester property). East of the Ardmore toll-gate, on Montgomery Ave. A part of this Merion tract is still (1910) owned by descendants.

After coming over, Katharine, as executrix to her husband, had his will, a long one, dated 9 Feb., 1682, filed in Philadelphia, 10. 3mo. 1688. It was signed in the presence of Robert Vaughan, Rowland Owen and Thomas Vaughan.

---

*Sharlow's land was wrongly placed on Holme's Map. It was beyond Wood's property.

WELSH SETTLEMENT OF PENSYLVANIA

He desired his tract of 1,250 acres (mentioning the transaction between Penn, Dr. Jones and himself), to be divided equally between his four sons, and left £20 cash to each of his children, providing, of course, for his wife. He named as his overseers, John ap John, of Rhiwabon, or Ruabon, parish, Denbig; Thomas Ellis, of Cyfanedd, Merioneth; Thomas Wayne, "late of Bronvadog," Flintshire; Robert David, of Gwernevel, Merioneth; Hugh Roberts, of Kiltalgarth, Merioneth; Edward Jones, "late of Bala, Chirurgion"; Robert Vaughan, of Gwernevel; Edward Morris, of Lavodgyfaner, Denbig; Robert Owen, of Fron Gôch, and "my son-in-law, Rees Evans, of Fronween," Merioneth.

Katharine Thomas lived fourteen years in "New Merion" among her Welsh friends, and was a regular attendant of the Merion Meeting, her death being thus entered in her son's, Thomas Jones's, Bible: "Our dear Mother Katherin Thomas departed this Life ye 18th day of ye 11 month, 1697, about ye 2d or 3d hour in ye morning (as we thought), & she was buryed next day." Her will, not recorded, dated 7. 11mo. 1697, is mentioned in a deed, executed by her sons —Book G; V., pa. 496.

Her son *Evan* died unmarried a month after she died, in Feb. 1697, leaving a small money gift to the Merion Preparative Meeting.

Of her remaining children, who took "Jones" as their surname:

Thomas Jones, eldest son, was "through school" when he came over with his mother, and there is evidence that his education was a good one. He wrote a remarkably strong, clear hand, and kept a log of the voyage to America on the blank leaves of the Family Bible, and records of his kin. In 1709, he acted as clerk of the Haverford Monthly Meeting of ministers and elders, and was also their treasurer. He became an "approved minister" among the Friends, and was popular in his neighborhood as a guardian, and overseer.

He joined Dr. Jones, his father's co-trustee in the Pensylvania land, in conveying by deed, dated 27. 10. 1693, the 100 acres of liberty land due on account of their entire purchase, to William ap Edward.

He died 6. 8mo. 1727, at his home in Merion. His will, signed 31. 6. 1727, witnessed by Thomas Moore, Richard George and Robert Jones, trustees-"Cousins Robert Jones and Jonathan Jones," was proved on 5 Aug. 1728. He bequeathed lands in Merion adjoining Jonathan Jones, Sr., and in Goshen tp.

He married Anne, named in his will, daughter of Griffith ap John, or Jones, of Merion (a son of John ap Evan, of Penllyn, "old Merion," and a cousin of Robert Owen, of "New Merion"), who owned a 187 acre place northeast of Bala, Philadelphia County, and whose sons, John and Evan, and their descendants took the name "Griffith."

Thomas and Anne Jones had besides John and Catherine, both buried at Merion Meeting in 1706, Evan, Elizabeth, Ann, Mary, Sarah, who *m.* at Merion Meeting 8. 11mo. 1742, Jonathan Jones, (son of Jonathan Jones, and grandson of Dr. Edward Jones), and Katharine, who *m.* Lewis, son of David and Katharine Jones, aforesaid, of Blockley, Philadelphia County.

Robert Jones, named in his brother's will, second son of John ap Thomas, inherited the plantation called "Glanrason," 189 acres, and purchased from David Hugh, 20. 4. 1699, 150 acres (surveyed), 165 acres of Sharlow's "Mt. Ararat," confirmation deed, 12 Feb. 1704, and at one time owned 1,000 acres in Merion, and 426 acres in Goshen. "He was a useful member of both civil and religious society," having been a justice of the peace, and a member of the provincial assembly. He was buried at the Merion Meeting House.

He married 3. 11mo. 1693, at his mother's house, Ellen Jones, sister to David Jones, of Blockley tp., who with his wife, Katharine, had certificate from the Monthly Meeting at Hendrimawr, Wales, dated 24. 12mo. 1699, signed by Robert Vaughan, Ellis Lewis and Thomas Cadwalader.

Robert's will was dated 21. 7mo. 1746. Of the children of Robert Jones: Gerrad, eldest son, *b.* 28. 12, 1705-6; inherited "Glanrason," [he *m.* first, Sarah, daughter of Robert Lloyd and his wife, Lowry, daughter of Rees John William, of Merion, and *m.* secondly, Ann, (daughter of Benjamin Humphrey, of Merion?) and had eight children, of these Ellen, *m.* Robert Roberts and Isaac Lewis, and Paul, *m.* Phoebe Roberts]; Elizabeth, *b.* 1695, first child, Katherine, *b.* 1700, *m.* Thomas Evans; Ann, *b.* 1702, *m.* James Paul, of Abington tp., and Robert, *b.* 3. 6mo. 1709, who received land from his father.

Cadwalader Jones was a shipping merchant in Philadelphia. The Land Commissioners on 23 Feb. 1702, granted him and his brother Thomas, executors to their mother's will, power to take up 100 acres of land (being part of 200 acres sold by the Commissioners to Hugh Roberts "for their mother's use"), which they had laid out in Merion tp., in 11mo. 1712-13, adjoining the lands of Mordecai Moore, John Havid (Havard), James Atkinson, and Owen Roberts.

Cadwalader, and his brothers, Thomas Jones, procured grant and survey of a 34 foot lot in 2d street, and a 20 foot lot in 3d street, in place of one "whole lot" of 51 feet, in 2d street, "of which they have been disappointed."

Katherine Jones m. Robert Roberts, son of Hugh Roberts, of Merion, the eminent minister among Friends, and next neighbor to Katharine Thomas.

Elizabeth Jones, m. before 1662, Rees Evan, of Fonween, in Penmaen, Penllyn, Merioneth. Their son, Evan Rees, came to Pensylvania and his daughter Sydney *m.* Robert Roberts, of "Pencoyd," Merion.

John Thomas had reserved to himself 1,250 acres, of which 1,225 were in the City Liberties, and 612½ acres in Merion, and the same number in Goshen. On re-survey, it was discovered that his Merion tract contained 679 acres, while that in Goshen came out right. On 19. 2mo. 1703, the Land Commissioners confirmed the land to the brothers, Thomas, Robert, and Cadwalader Jones, the joint heirs under their father's will. It may be noticed all through these notices of Welsh families, that primogeniture was not the custom amongst them. Equal division of the land was made between the sons, and possession given without livery of seizine, that is, immediately. Since it was the practice to divide the land amongst the heirs, especially the improved parts, which they had helped to till, small farms prevailed, and they also became more numerous because they were easier worked.

A SECTION FROM HOLME'S MAP.

MERION ADVENTURERS

GAINOR ROBERTS, a spinster, was about 30 years old, a daughter of Robert ap Hugh, or Pugh, of Llyndeddwydd, near Bala, in Merioneth, (by his wife Elizabeth, daughter of William Owen, of Llanvawr), and a sister of the Friends' minister, Hugh Roberts, when she bought on her own account 156½ acres of the Thomas & Jones tract, and came over to Pensylvania with her celebrated brother, with whom she lived in Kiltalgarth, on the ship "Morning Star," in 1683. Part of her purchase, 76½ acres, was laid out in Merion, back of Calwalader Morgan's land, and the remainder in Goshen tp., and these lands she took to her husband as a marriage portion.

She *m.* at Merion Meeting, 20. 1mo. 1683-4, whether in the traditional log Meeting House, the predecessor of the present stone one, or at her brother's home, is not known, John Roberts, who came over also on this trip of the "Morning Star." She *d.* 20. 12mo. 1722, aged 69 years, and was buried with her husband at the Merion Meeting House.

They were the founders of the Roberts family of "Pencoyd," Merion, and theirs was the first marriage in the Welsh tract of record.

John Roberts, of "Pencoyd," though not one of the original purchasers in Thomas & Jones tract, should be noticed here, with the other first settlers of this land, as he was the earliest of Welsh purchasers of the adjoining land, on the river, and became a noted man in the settlement.

In the days of this John there were three, or more, men in the Welsh tract named "John Roberts," and, to distinguish them from the subject of this sketch, their occupation or place of residence, was given with their names in early deeds, as later there was "John Roberts, Skuilkill," buried at Merion Meeting 7. 28. 1747, and "John Roberts, millwright," buried here 11. 10. 1803.

John Roberts, of "Pencoyd," as he named his seat, and as it is still called, born about 1648, was the son of Richard Robert (ap Thomas Morris), of Cowyn, Llaneingan parish, in Carnarvonshire, and his wife, Margaret, daughter of Richard Evan, of the same parish. He was about 29 years of age when he became a Quaker, in 1677. John Roberts's account of himself, filed with the Merion Meeting:

"John Roberts, formerly of Llyn, being son of Richard Roberts and grandson of Robert Thomas Morris, who lived at Cowyn, in the Parish of Llaneigan and County of Carnarvon; my mother being Margaret Evans, daughter of Richard Evans, of Llangian and county aforesaid.

"Being convinced of God's everlasting worth about the year one thousand six hundred and seventy seven, not by man nor through man, but by the Revelation of Jesus Christ, in my owne heart, Being about thirty miles from any Friends' Meeting in that time when I was convinced but coming into acquaintance with Friends near Dalgelle and near Bala in Merionethshire, I frequented their Meetings while I abode in those parts, but by the Province of God in the year One thousand six hundred and eighty three, I transported Myself with many of my Friends for Pensylvania where I and they arrived the sixteenth day of the Ninth month One thousand six hundred and Eighty three being then Thirty five years old, and settled myself in the place where afterwards I called Pwencoid, in the Township of Merion, which was afterwards called by them being the first settlers of it, having brought with me one servant man from my Native Land, and fixed my settling here. I took to Wife Gainor Roberts, Daughter of Robert Pugh from Llwyndedwydd near Bala in Merionethshire, her Mother being Elizabeth William Owen one of the first that was convinced of the Truth in that Neighborhood. So leaving this account for our ofspring and others that desire to know

COMPANY NUMBER ONE

from whence we came and who we descend from and when we came to settle unto this place where we now abide being then a Wilderness, but now by God's Blessing upon our endeavours is become a fruitful field. To God's name be the Praise, Honour and Glory who is worthy of it for ever and for ever more."

As apparently Mr. Roberts had a good home, and had not "suffered" much, it must be supposed that he only came over to Pensylvania because his lady-love, Gainor Roberts, did. Theirs was probably a long drawn-out courtship, as he was 35, as he states, and she 30, when they came over together, with her brother.

He was living near Dolgelly, and near where Gainor lived, when he set out for America, taking with him only one indentured servant, and his certificate of membership from the Men's Meeting, in Penllyn, dated 18. 5mo. 1683, which described him as of Llun, in Carnarvonshire. On the same date this Meeting issued Certificates to many others bound for Pensylvania, among them Cadwalader Morgan, and Hugh John Thomas, of Gwernfell, Robert David, of Tuyn y nant, Katharine Roberts, of Llaethgwn, widow, and Gaynor Roberts, of Kiltalgarth. All were signed by nearly the same men. Both John and Gainor were members in good standing of the Penllyn Monthly Meeting, as may be seen. It is presumed that John's brother Richard and sister Ann, who came in the Hugh Roberts party, both had issue.

John Roberts probably stayed close to Hugh Roberts and helped put up his house in Merion, in the winter of 1683-4, for in the early spring of 1683-4, he married Gainor Robert. Theirs was the first wedding in the Merion Meeting.

"John Roberts the maltster," as he was known from his occupation, had bought from Richard Davies (Company No. 7), 150 acres by deed dated 30 July, 1682, and this right he had surveyed and laid out to him in "the city liberty" on the Schuylkill, and next east of the land of Evan Rees, in the Thomas & Jones tract. This land he named "Pencoyd," which it has ever since been so called. With the land he had by Gainor, both in Merion and in Goshen, as the marriage portion, this gave him, "on paper," 306½ acres, but on resurvey, (by report of 12. 2mo. 1703), it turned out that he had 108 acres in Merion, and 262 acres in Goshen, which was 25 acres too much in Merion, and 8½ acres too much in Goshen, this over-plus he bought. And on resurvey of another parcel of 150 acres in Merion, this was found 20 acres short, and a resurvey of 60 acres (which had been part of Swan Lum's grant of 400 acres, in 1677, he bought in 1699 of Andrew Wheeler, a Swede, in the "liberties," and Merion tp., "on the westerly side of the Schilckul by the falls," showed 47 acres over, and thus, between the over-plus and shortage, he had to pay for a balance of 60½ acres.

John Roberts bought, by a joint deed dated 8. 6mo. 1702, the land due as head-rights for a lot of servants and others, who had come over about 1683-4, amounting altogether to 750 acres, laid out at his first purchase, among the Swedes, which his son Robert inherited. By deed of 7. 7mo. 1687, he bought from Cadwalader Morgan and Hugh John, 156 acres, in Goshen tp., on Chester Creek. At one time, with his wife's lands, John Roberts owned about 1,250 acres.

1704, 11mo. 5th., according to desire of the Merion Preparative Meeting, extended to all its members, he filed "an account of his place of abode in his native country, his convincement, his removal to this country, his marriage, and other remarkable passages of his life." A copy of this statement is extant in the family of a descendant, and an extract is given above.

He was from the first a prominent man among the Pensylvania Welsh, and was a justice of the peace in the Welsh Tract, and a representative for it in the Assembly, and owned a very large landed estate. He died at his residence in Merion, which now forms a portion of the "Roberts mansion," on the City Line, on 6. 4mo. 1724, aged 76 years, and was buried with his wife, Gainor, in the ground of the Merion Meeting. The record of their burials at the Merion Meeting being "Gainor Roberts, wife of John Roberts, maltster, 12. 23. 1721," and "John Roberts, maltster, 1724, 4mo."

His will, signed 3. 7mo. 1722, witnessed by Edward George, Gainor Jones, and Thomas Jones, was proved at Philadelphia, 31 Aug. 1724. He named "brother Richard and his daughter Margaret," his niece Margaret, daughter of his own sister Ann: grandsons John, Alban, Rees and Phineas. Overseers appointed—Robert Jones, Robert Evans, and Thomas Jones: Owen Roberts mentioned. He bequeathed five pounds to the trustees of the Merion Meeting, for relief of the poor of Merion Meeting.

John Roberts, of "Pencoyd," had only two children, by his only wife, Gainor Roberts, who were named in his will, namely:

Elizabeth Roberts, b. 21. 1mo. 1692, d. unm., 9. 7mo. 1746 She received by her father's will £200, and half of his personal estate.

Robert Roberts, of "Pencoyd," first child, and only son and heir, b. 15. 12mo. 1685. He inherited from his father, the homestead and all his lands, and half of his personalty. He was a member of the Merion Peculiar Meeting, and the Haverford Monthly Meeting, and he and his wife were buried at the Merion Meeting House. He d. 17 March, 1768, leaving a will signed when "antient and Infirm of Body," 4. 7mo. 1764, in the presence of Richard George, Jr., David Lloyd and John Roberts, Jr., proved at Philadelphia 26 March, 1768.

He m. at the Merion Meeting, on 17. 4mo. 1709, Sidney Rees, daughter of Rees Evan, of Penmaen, in Merionethshire (whose mother was a daughter of John ap Thomas, of Llaethgwm, who d. in 1683), and had by her, who d. 29 June, 1764, aged 74 years, the following children named in his will:—

WELSH SETTLEMENT OF PENSYLVANIA

John Roberts, eldest son and heir, b. 26. 4mo. 1710, inherited the homestead farm, about 180 acres, on the City Line, where he d. 31 Jan. 1776. It adjoined land of Robert Evans, on the north, John Griffith on the west, and south, "tp. line road to the Ford road," and land of Rudolph Latch and John Garrett. His will, signed in Oct., 1775, in the presence of John Robert, miller, Rees Price, and Hugh Cully, was proved 7 Feb. 1776. He named all of his children then living. To son Algernon, 50 acres in Blockley, bought of Joseph Abraham, south of the City Line, and north of lands of David George, and the homestead, then 100 acres, laying above and west of the "new road," and adjoining the lands of Thomas Norris, John Leacock, Jacob Bealer, and William Stadleman. To son Jonathan, 27 acres on the river, in Blockley, and money to sons Benjamin, John, Robert, and daughters Elizabeth, wife of Thomas Palmer, and Tacy, wife of John Palmer. Trustees, "loving brothers Owen Jones, Jacob Jones, and kinsman James Lewis Jones, Jr.

He m. at Merion Meeting, on 4. 3mo. 1733, Rebecca, daughter of Jonathan Jones (son of Dr. Edward Jones), of Merion, and had twelve children by her, who d. 8 Dec., 1779. His son Algernon also was the father of twelve children.

Algernon Roberts, who was a lieut. col. of Philadelphia militia, lived and died at the old Roberts homestead. He m. at the Swedes Church, in Philadelphia, 18 Jan. 1781, Tacy, daughter of Isaac Warner, of Blockley, colonel of Philadelphia militia. Of their many children, John 1787-1837, was the ancestor of B. Frank Clapp, of Phila., Isaac, 1789-1859, was the ancestor of the late George B. Roberts, who resided in the old homestead; Algernon Sidney, 1798-1865, was the ancestor of George T., Dr. A. Sidney and Percival Roberts, of Philadelphia, Edward, 1800-1872, was the ancestor of Edward Browning, and Mrs. Arthur V. Meigs, of Philadelphia.

COMPANY NUMBER ONE

Phineas Roberts, *b.* 13. 3mo. 1722. He inherited 30 acres on the river, adjoining the homestead that had been Wheeler's land in Blockley. His wife Ann, aged 80 years, was killed by their insane son, Titus Roberts, in 11mo. 1803.

Sidney Roberts, *b.* 9. 3mo. 1729; *m.* John Paul, who received a portion of the personalty of his father-in-law.

Alban, 1712-1727; Reese, 1715-1755.

"REES JOHN WILLIAM, of Llanglynin," yeoman, or "Rees Joans," or Jones, was one of the seventeen original purchasers, by deed of 1 April, 1682, through Thomas & Jones, but he did not come over till in 1684, when the land on the river was partly cleared and planted, and the "first come-overs," the parties of Dr. Jones, and Hugh Roberts, were well housed on their purchases, He found the land (his deed being recorded at Philadelphia 21. 4. 1684), allotted to him the worst proportioned in the tract, it being a narrow strip, only about 66 feet on the river, extending the full length of the other lots, to the Charles Lloyd land, where it was only about 264 feet wide, in all, here, 76½ acres, and remainder in Goshen tp.

"Rees Jones," as he was generally known, was a son of John ap William, a farmer in Llangelynin parish, Merioneth, who "suffered" considerable with the other Quakers in his neighborhood, 1661, &c. Rees came over with a large party of Welsh settlers in the ship "Vine, of Liverpool," sailing from Dolyserre, near Dolgules, in Merionethshire, which is a maritime county, and arrived at Philadelphia on 17. 7mo. 1684. He was accompanied by his wife and three children.

His sister, "Margaret John William, of Llangyllynin, widow," had preceded him, coming over in the party of Hugh Roberts, bringing a certificate of membership from the Quarterly Meeting, near Dolgelly, dated 27. 5mo. 1683, recorded at the Haverford (or Radnor) Monthly Meeting. As Margaret John she had patent, 18. 1mo. 1717-8, for 400 acres of land on a branch of French Creek.

His brother, Evan John William, or Evan Jones, also came over at that time, with his son, Robert Jones (who resided at Gwynedd), and died soon after, being buried in the ground of the Merion Meeting, in 11mo. 1683. He bequeathed some land in Goshen tp. to his nephews, Richard and Evan Jones. Evan Jones, and Hannah, his wife, and Mary Ellis, his mother-in-law, and Gemima, her other daughter, brought certificate, undated, from the Meeting held at Tyddier y Gareg, in Garthgunfawr, near Dolegelle, Merioneth, to the Haverford Monthly Meeting, signed by Humphrey, John, Robert, and Rowland Owen, Owen, Robert, and Howell Lewis, and Hugh Rowland.

Rees Jones, and his wife, Hannah, also brought the usual certificate of membership and removal, from the Quarterly Meeting, near Dolgelly, dated 4. 2mo. 1684. Rees was described as "of Llwyn Grevill, Clynn parish, Merioneth."

Before coming over, he purchased, by deed dated 16 July, 1684, the original right of Thomas ap Richard, or Prichard, of Nant Lleidiog, to his share 156¼ acres, of the Thomas & Jones tract. The 76½ acres of which that lay in Merion adjoined the back part of Rees's land, and this gave him 153 acres in Merion. The present settlement of Merion, or Merion Station, on Pensylvania Railroad, is on his land, and Rees's dwelling house was near it. By deed of 8. 4mo. 1694, he sold his 76½ acres on the river end, or his original purchase, to his brother-in-law, Cadwalader Morgan, whose land adjoined.

Rees Jones died 26. 11mo. 1697-8, and was buried at the Merion Meeting House. His will, which he signed with his mark, dated 24. 11mo. 1697-8, witnessed by Griffith John and Abel Thomas, was proved at Philadelphia, 4 March, 1702-3. He named his sons, Richard, Evan, and John; and overseers: Cadwalader Morgan, Abel Thomas, Edward Jones, Griffith John and John Roberts.

He *m.* about 1678, Hannah Richards, or Price, *b.* in 1656, sister to Jane, wife of Cadwalader Morgan, of Merion, and to Edward Price, who came to Pensylvania before 1685-6, and daughter of Richard Gryffyth ap Rhys, or Prees, and Price, of Llanvawr, or Lanfor parish, in Merioneth, a member of the Friends' Penylln Monthly Meeting, near Bala, whose will, dated 26. 11mo. 1685, was filed at St. Asaph registry in 1686. His will describes him as of Glanlloidiogin, Llanfor parish. Witnesses were Edward Nicholas, Thomas ap Robert, Lowry v. Thomas Rees Evans, and Cadwalader Ellis. To Edward Prees, alias Price, (of Merion), eldest son; (after he came over here, he sent to Wales for "some intelligence of his Pedigree," which he received about 1700, and is extant); Jane, eldest daughter, wife of Cadwalader Morgan; daughter Hannah, wife of Rees John William; grandchildren William John, and Catherine John, children of John William; and son Thomas ap Richard, the executor, who received all of the estate of his father. Thomas renounced the trust, when the Court gave the administration to Edward Nicholas, of Cynlas.

After Rees's death, Hannah, his relict, m. secondly, at the Merion Meeting, on 22. 2mo. 1703, Ellis David, of Goshen tp., a widower, who was buried, s. p. 17. 1mo. 1720, and m. thirdly, 14. 1mo. 1722. Thomas Evans, of Gwynedd tp.

Rees Jones,* had by his wife, Hannah Price, who was of

---

*Among the present-day people, descendants of Rees John William and Hannah Price, are:

Frank Foulke.
Samuel Marshall.
Hugh Jones Brooke.
Mrs. Charles Richardson.
Mrs. George B. Roberts.
Mrs. Henry K. Dillard.
Miss Mary William Perot.
Mrs. J. Howard Lewis, Jr.
Mrs. Hunter Brooke.
Mrs. George H. Colket.
William T. Brooke.
John W. Townsend.

Mrs. Harrison K. Caner.
William P. Troth.
Henry T. Coates.
William M. Coates.
Joseph H. Coates.
George M. Coates.
Edward H. Coates.
Mrs. Charles Ridgway.
Mrs. Henry S. Harper.
Mrs. John R. Drexel.
Mrs. Edward Y. Townsend.
Henry Troth Townsend.

WELSH SETTLEMENT OF PENSYLVANIA

Royal Descent, the following issue, besides *Margaret*, *b.* 20. 6. 1697, *Edward*, and *Catharine*, who *d. unm.*

Richard Jones, b. about 1679. He came over with his parents, and according to the records, filed with the Merion Preparative Meeting, of which he was a member, an account of their ancestry, and life in the Old Country, on 2. 12mo. 1704-5.

He inherited from his father the home-farm of about 100 acres, which he increased to 156¼ acres, and with some land he owned in Goshen, he had 293¾ acres altogether, in 1703. By deed of 8 Nov. 1720, he bought of John Roberts (the nephew of Thomas Lloyd, of Llangower, one of the original purchasers through Thomas & Jones), 39½ acres, adjoining his Merion land.

By deed, dated 26 June, 1729, Richard Jones conveyed all of his Merion land, then 156¼ acres, to Hugh Evans, and removed to his land in Goshen tp. which he had increased by purchase. He and his brother, Evan Jones, bought there a tract of 153¼ acres, which on resurvey was 178 acres. He *d.* aged 92 years, in Goshen tp., on 16. 7mo. 1771, having been twice married. He had three children by each wife. He *m.* first, 6. 4mo. 1705, Jane Evans, who *d.* 27. 2mo. 1711, and was buried at the Merion Meeting House, and *m.* secondly, in 1718, Rebecca Vernon, widow of Thomas Garrett. She *d.* 23. 12mo. 1748.

Lowry Jones, d. in Philadelphia, 25. 11mo. 1762, aged 80 years. She *m.* first, at Merion Meeting, 11. 8mo. 1698, Robert ffloid, or Lloyd, who came over with Hugh Roberts, in 1683, and bought land, some 400 acres, north of Rowland Ellis's seat, "Bryn Mawr," where he *d.* 29. 3mo. 1714, aged 45 years and was buried at the Merion Meeting House, being the father of eight children. Of these Hannah, 1699-1763, *m.* first, 1720, John Roberts, (son of John Roberts and Elizabeth Owen v. Owen Humphrey); *d.* 1721; Sarah,

1703-1730, *m.* 1729, at Merion Meeting, Garrad Jones, *d.* 1765; Gainor, 1705-1728, *m.* 1727, at Merion Meeting, Mordecai James, *d.* 1776; Rees, 1709-1753; Robert, 1711-1786; and Richard, 1713-1755. Lowry Jones *m.* secondly, at the Merion Meeting, 13. 12mo. 1716-7, Hugh Evans, and had three children by him. Of them Ann, *m.* 1745, (?Samuel Howell); Susanna *m.* 1740, Owen Jones, *d.* 1793.

Evan Jones, b. about 1682-3. He and his brother John inherited from their father 153½ acres of land in Goshen tp. on Chester Creek, which was resurveyed in pursuance of the order of 27. 10mo. 1701. He was also a partner with his brother Richard in some Goshen land. He never married, and was buried at the Merion Meeting, 7. 2mo. 1708. His will, signed 28. 7. 1708, witnessed by Rowland Ellis, Richard Jones, and Robert Lloyd, was proved 1. 25. 1708 He mentions his mother and brothers and sisters, Lowry Lloyd, Richard, John, Edward, Jane, Sarah and Margaret Jones; overseers, Cadwalader Morgan and Abel Thomas.

Janne, or *Jane Jones, b.* in Merion, 15. 9mo. 1635, *d.* 27. 8mo. 1764, and was buried at the Goshen Meeting. She *m.* David Davis, and had nine children by him, four of whom married into the Ashbridge family.

John Jones, b. in Merion, 6. 4mo. 1688, *d.* in Goshen tp., 30. 12mo. 1774. He *m.* at the Gwynedd Meeting, 9. 4mo. 1713, Jane Edward, and had ten children. He and brother Evan shared the lands of their father.

Sarah Jones, b. 25. 7mo. 1690, *d.* 28. 3mo. 1758. She *m.* first, at Merion Meeting, 2. 8mo. 1712, Jacob Edge, 1690-1720, and had four children, and *m.* secondly, 10. 11mo. 1721, Caleb Cowpland, *d.* at Chester, 1757, and had five children by him.

Margaret Jones, b. 20. 6mo. 1697, *m.* first, at Merion Meeting, 16. 10. 1716, Thomas Paschall (and had Margaret,

WELSH SETTLEMENT OF PENSYLVANIA

m. first, Samuel Mather, and Hannah, *m.* Isaac Roberts), *m.* secondly, 6. 1mo. 1729, George Ashbridge, *d.* 1748.

These following Welsh Friends, of Penllyn parish, Merioneth, purchased portions of Thomas & Jones's 5,000 acres, but sold out, and did not come over.

EVAN AP REES, or Evan Price, a grocer, of Penmaen, bought 312½ acres of this tract, for £6. 5s., by deed dated 18 March, 1681, recorded 13. 4. 1684, witnessed by John Lloyd, Griffith Evan, Reece Evan and William Jones. He did not come over, but his son, Rees Evan, did.

By deeds dated 28. 5mo. 1683, Evan Rees conveyed away his Merion land, 153¼ acres, (which on a resurvey amounted to 178 acres) as follows—100 acres to Robert David, one of the original purchasers through Thomas & Jones, and about 54 acres to Griffith John (ap Evan), who also bought the Goshen portion. This Griffith Jones was a cousin of Jane Owen, Hugh Roberts's wife, and came over with them in 1683, and resided in Merion. He was one of the subscribing witnesses to Penn's "Conditions and Concessions to Adventurers for Land," 11 July 1681. His will, signed 26. 4. 1707, witnessed by John Roberts and Robert Jones, was proved 31 Jan. 1707-8, named his sons John and Evan, and son-in-law Thomas Jones, to be executors. Griffith John also bought from John Roberts (nephew of Thomas Lloyd), 37½ acres, and had patent for all, dated 8 Nov. 1703. This land, surveyed 194 acres, lay along the old Lancaster Road, and the City Line, and included, besides the land from Rees, 76¼ acres from each Thomas Lloyd and John Watkin.

THOMAS AP RICHARD, or Prichard, a farmer, of Nantlleidiog, bought 156¼ acres of the tract, of which 76¼ acres were laid out in Merion, and balance in Goshen tp. He did not come over. By deed, dated 16. 5mo. 1684, he conveyed all his lands to Rees John William, or Rees Jones, of Merion.

COMPANY NUMBER ONE

THOMAS LLOYD, a yeoman, (son of John Lloyd), of Llangower, bought 156¼ acres, of this tract, paying £3. 2. 6., but did not come to Pensylvania. It was his intention to come over, but he died suddenly, and by his will, bequeathed his land to his nephew, John Roberts, (his brother Robert Lloyd's son), who came over, and by deeds, conveyed of the part in Merion, the east end, 37½ acres, to Griffith John (ap Evan) in 1700, and dated 8. 9mo. 1720, the west end, 39½ acres, to Richard Jones.

John Roberts also had, with what he received from his uncle, and what he bought subsequently from Evan John William (a part of the Richard Davies tract), 153 acres in Goshen tp.

JOHN WATKIN, who was described as a bachelor, when he purchased, by deed of 1 April, 1682, witnessed by John Lloyd, Griffith Evan, Robert Lloyd and Reece Evan, of Thomas & Jones, 156¼ acres, and a yeoman, of Gwernevel, or Gwernsfel, did not come over, but sold his land. By deed, dated 23. 4mo. 1684, he conveyed all of rights to land, to Hugh Roberts, who sold his Merion portion, 76¼ acres, by deed of 26. 5mo. 1688, to Abel Thomas (who married Cadwalader Morgan's daughter), which land was resurveyed and patented to said Abel, 16 Feb. 1701-2.

This concludes the sketches of the original seventeen partners, purchasers through Thomas & Jones, of 5,000 acres, 2,500 of which were at the Falls of the Schuylkill, and who had the land laid out to them in Merion, on and near the river. It may be seen that four were first settlers, in 1682, one came over in 1682-3; seven were settlers in 1683, and one in 1684, and that four did not come over, but sold their land to the other original purchasers from Thomas & Jones.

It is also worthy of notice that these early settlers were nearly all in some way related to each other. For instance, John Thomas's son married Griffith John's daughter, and a daughter married a son of Hugh Roberts; Dr. Jones's son married a daughter of Robert Owen; Dr. Jones married Dr. Wynn's daughter; Hugh Robert's son married a daughter of John Bevan; Rees Jones married a sister of Cadwalader Morgan's wife; William Edward married a sister of Hugh Roberts; Edward Rees was brother-in-law to Cadwalader Morgan and Rees Jones; John Roberts married a sister of Hugh Roberts; Robert Owen and Hugh Roberts were brothers-in-law; Robert Owen was a brother-in-law to Cadwalader Thomas; John Cadwalader was a nephew of John Thomas, and of Robert Owen, and a son-in-law of Dr. Jones; both Rees Thomas and his wife were related to John Bevan, and his son married a daughter of Dr. Jones; Hugh Roberts's first wife was sister to Robert Owen, and his son married John Bevan's daughter; Robert Lloyd's wife was daughter of Rees Jones; Thomas Lloyd's wife was daughter to William Edward, and a niece of Hugh Roberts; Griffith John was a cousin to Hugh Roberts's wife, and so on. All of these intermarriages among the leading Welsh families, however, did not establish a long-lived Welsh community, for it has for many years been only a tradition.

Having thus seen the pioneers of the Welsh tract settled, and taken account of these men and women, good Welsh Quakers all, who first ventured into the wilderness, west of the Schuylkill, and discovered the localities of their landed estates, we will take a glance at the people and their lands of the other Welsh companies who followed, many of whom were closely allied by intermarriages and blood with the pioneers.

ADVENTURERS FOR LANDS
IN MERION AND HAVERFORD

LLOYD & DAVIES' LAND PATENT

Company No. 2. The grantees, under the patent for 5,000 acres in the Welsh tract, to Charles Lloyd, gent., and Margaret Davies, widow, both of Dolobran, Meifod parish, Montgomeryshire, to whom, as trustees, they conveyed the land by deeds dated in April and June, 1683, were, in part, as follows:

Joseph Harris, "late of Wallbrook, Middlesex Co."	1,250 acres
And these, all of Montgomeryshire, Wales:—	
Thomas Jones, of Llanwthin parish, yeoman..	156¼ "
Edward Thomas, of Llanwthin parish, yeoman	312½ "
Margaret Thomas, of Garthlwlch parish, widow	156¼ "
John Humphrey, of Llanwthin parish, gent..	312½ "
John Rhytherch, of Hirnant parish, yeoman..	156¼ "
Thomas Morris, of Marchnant Issa parish, gent	156¼ "
	2,500 acres

It appears that Mr. Lloyd and Margaret Davies each had a half interest in this patent, and that it was her 2,500 acres which were conveyed to the aforesaid grantees, for Mr. Lloyd conveyed his share, 2,500 acres, by deed dated 6. 4mo. 1683, to his brother, Thomas Lloyd, some time the deputy-governor of Pensylvania, much of which was laid out in Merion tp., some north of Haverford,* and some northeast of Ardmore.

---

*"Dolobran," the seat of the Griscom family, is on a part of it. Mr. Clement A. Griscom, though a descendant of Gov. Lloyd, acquired the property by purchase. His wife is a collateral descendant with these Humphrey grantees.

WELSH SETTLEMENT OF PENSYLVANIA

About 1694, the following accounting of the "Lloyd & Davis grant" was filed with the Land Commissioners, showing a difference from the above statement:

"Sales of Charles Lloyd and Margaret Davis":—

"To Benj. Humphries	312½	acres
To Edw'd Thomas	312½	"
To Tho. Jones	156¼	"
To Marg't Thomas	156¼	"
To Tho. Jones & Jno. Rhoderick	312½	"
By Tho. Lloyd to Ev. Owen &c.	340	"
	1,590	acres"

"A new patent was requested for 2,215 acres, making in all 3,805 acres granted."

CHARLES LLOYD, gentleman, the grantee and grantor, of this Welsh Tract land, was born 9 Dec. 1637. He was a son of Charles Lloyd, gent., of Dolobran Hall, in Montgomeryshire, where he was a magistrate, and whose will, signed 17 June 1651, was proved in 1657.

Charles Lloyd was educated at Jesus College, Oxford, became a magistrate and was nominated for the shrievalty in Montgomeryshire. He joined the Society of Friends, about 1662, and erected a public Meeting House near his residence. He and his wife were imprisoned for ten years in the Welshpool jail, on account of their religious principles. He died at Dolobran Hall, which subsequently degenerated into a tenant's house, 26. 11mo. 1698. He married twice. He *m.* first, 11 Nov. 1661, Elizabeth, *b.* 2 Nov. 1633, *d.* 7 Feb. 1685, daughter of Sampson Lort, of Eastmoor (or East Meare), and Stackpole, in Pembrokeshire, high sheriff in 1649, brother to Sir Roger Lort, first Baronet, and *m.* secondly, 8 Feb. 1686, Ann Lawrence, of Lea, in Herefordshire, who *d. s. p.*, 2 March 1708. By his first wife, Charles Lloyd had two sons and one daughter. Two of these were born in jail. They married, and had descendants, but none came to Pensylvania.

COMPANY NUMBER TWO

Charles Lloyd's sister, Elizabeth, married Henry Parry, of Llanfillyn, and his brother, John Lloyd, also educated at Jesus College, Oxon, became "clerk of the petty bag in chancery," 1683-95, and his other and youngest brother,

THOMAS LLOYD, *b.* 17 Feb. 1640-1, *d.* in Pensylvania 10 Sept. 1694. Like his brothers, he was educated at Jesus College, and became a lawyer, and "a Quaker," and "a minister among Friends." In 1681, he and Charles, and other Friends had a celebrated debate, at Llanfillyn, with the Rt. Rev. the Bishop of St. Asaph, about religion, and religious questions, by request of the Bishop, who wished to learn their reasons for becoming non-conformists, and Quakers.

The life and services of Thomas Lloyd as the deputy of William Penn in his Province, and presiding officer of the council, have been frequently printed.

He first, it might be said, came into prominent notice in the Province when he bitterly opposed the Cromwellian soldier, and non-Quaker, Blackwell, whom Penn sent over as another of his experiments, as his Deputy-Governor, having so appointed him on Christmas Day, 1688. At this time, Lloyd had general authority over Penn's affairs, and it hurt him that an outsider superceded him, but Penn continued him as the keeper of the Great Seal, which still, in some things, made him a power Blackwell had always to reckon with, because the royal charter required that to make any law valid it must pass under the Great Seal, which meant Lloyd's consent.

So soon as Blackwell entered upon the duties of his office, Lloyd inaugurated his campaign of opposition by flatly refusing to affix the Great Seal to Blackwell's first commissions, and when declining to do so, sent him a rather insulting note. Only Penn could remove Lloyd from his office, so Blackwell brought charges against him and waited.

While waiting Penn's decision, the election for councillors came off, and Mr. Lloyd was returned as a member. When he went to take his seat, Blackwell ordered him not to enter the room, because he could not be seated while he was charged by him "with high crime and misdemeanors."

Thereupon, Mr. Lloyd, and two others, also elected but refused their seats by the Governor, forced their way into the Council Chamber, and took their seats. Blackwell, presiding, asked them by what right they presumed to do so, and Lloyd, replying for himself, answered insolently, "by special appointment by letter of the proprietor, which was as good as the Governor's commission."

This occasioned great confusion in the Chamber, the Quakers being in the majority, and supporting Lloyd, bitterly denounced Blackwell to his face, "so that he had to flee from the room, nearly all the members yelling at him," and telling him what they thought of him, and, the report says, that "Lloyd being the most clamorous was heard in the street."

Those who supported the Governor, did so from conviction, holding that Lloyd was not altogether within his rights in the matter of the Great Seal, because not one of the engrossed laws then in force, excepting it be the Frame of Government, had passed under the Great Seal. They had been considered "instructions from the proprietor." If Penn had not recalled Blackwell so promptly, on learning what was taking place in his far-off Province, there would certainly soon have been chaos in it. That Penn was "somewhat unsteady in his principles of government, as well as in his matters of carrying them out," was apparent to the thoughtful, so when Mr. Lloyd received the appointment, succeeding Blackwell, there was a great sigh of relief, for everybody was tired of continual misunderstandings, and contentions over the laws and positions. It required the strong will, with his gentle manner, of Governor Lloyd to prevent Penn himself from violating his own laws, which was a cause for "his people" losing confidence in him as a ruler, and of being prejudiced against him.

COMPANY NUMBER TWO

Although Gov. Lloyd never resided in the Welsh Tract, he was strongly in sympathy with the Welsh Quakers in it in their "little unpleasantness" with William Penn and his agents. He was frequently at their meetings as a minister, and they were loyal to him in his difficulties with the Proprietary, for the Welsh stood together, and were always helpful to one another. For years, Gov. Lloyd's was one of the great families of the city, and his sons-in-law were among the most prominent and influential citizens, being mayors and provincial councillors.

He arrived in Philadelphia, in the ship America, 20. 6mo. 1683. His most intimate fellow passenger was the German gentleman and scholar, Fra. Dan. Pastorius, who was coming to settle here, "in this uncouth land, and howling wilderness," as the German described the Province, and of the city, he said, "then Philadelphia consisted of 3 or 4 little cottages, all the residue being only woods, underwoods, timber and trees." Mr. Lloyd's daughters, Rachel Preston, Deborah Moore and Mary Norris, came with him. To them Pastorius dedicated, in 1718, a poem, and in a note told that he could only converse with Mr. Lloyd in Latin, the only language in common between them.

Charles Lloyd, the grantee of Penn, conveyed, as mentioned, the balance of his interests in Pensylvania to his brother, Thomas Lloyd, by deed dated 6. 4mo. 1683.

As above, Charles Lloyd and Margaret Davies jointly, by deed dated 29 June, 1683, conveyed 1250 acres of Margaret's land, for £25, to Joseph Harris, of Wallbrook, near London. Mr. Harris, by deed of 23 May, 1688, conveyed the rights to this tract of Pensylvania land to Francis Smith, "plaisterer," who sold it to Gov. Thomas Lloyd, but he died before the deed was executed, or the papers made out. But his son, William Smith, on 21 Oct. 1693, conveyed it by deed to Gov. Lloyd, and this brought his holding up to 3,750 acres.

WELSH SETTLEMENT OF PENSYLVANIA

Of these lands, Gov. Lloyd sold 1,000 acres, in one tract, to William Cuarton, 200 acres to David Pugh, 118 acres on the Liberty Lands line, to David Prees, or Price, but deed not made till 4. 10mo. 1694, 548 acres to Robert Owen, by deed of 5. 6mo. 1691, and 125 acres to E. Rees. The Governor also owned land in the City Liberties, and sold two lots, 100 acres and 145 acres to B. Chambers, a Philadelphia tavern keeper, and also sold 100 acres, above Merion to Thomas Davies.

After his decease, Thomas Lloyd's* executors, Judge Isaac Norris, of Philadelphia, and Judge David Lloyd, of Chester, had considerable and endless trouble trying to settle his land interests. On 28. 4mo. 1703, they asked of the

---

*Thomas Lloyd of Philadelphia, m. first, in Wales, 9 Sep. 1665, Mary, daughter of Roger Jones, of Welsh Pool, Montgomeryshire, and had ten children by her. His will, signed 10. 7mo. 1694, proved 22 Oct. 1694. He left his estate to his second wife, Patience, and his own children named Thomas, Hannah, Rachel, Mary, Elizabeth and Deborah: appointed Executors, his wife, "son Mordecay," son-in-law, Isaac Norris, and "kinsman David Lloyd." Witnessed by Samuel Carpenter, Alexander Beardsley, and John Jones. He names wife's children: Enoch and Marcy Story. His wife Patience's will, signed 14 Aug. 1720, proved 30 June, 1724,. "son-in-law Richard Hill," Executor: her son Enoch, deceased; names granddaughters, "Deborah Moor and Patience Story": desired to be buried by the side of her husband, Thomas Lloyd. Signature witnessed by John Weaver (marked), and Charles Osborne. Of his children:

Thomas Lloyd, Jr., 1675-171—; m. Sarah Young, who d. in Philadelphia, and had issue from which descended the Pensylvania families of Moore, Willing, Wharton, Ridgway, etc.

Deborah Lloyd, 1682-172—; m. 12 Sep. 1704, Dr. Mordecai Moore, of Md. (second wife), and had issue, from which descend the Pensylvania families of Morris, Ellis, Collins, Lightner, Waln, Vaux, etc.

Rachel Lloyd, 1668-172—; m. 6 July, 1688, Samuel Preston, mayor of Philadelphia, 1711 (first wife), and had issue, from which descended the Pensylvania families of Carpenter, Ellett, Shoemaker, Moore, Wainwright, Preston, Roberts, etc.

Mary Lloyd, m. Judge Isaac Norris, of "Fairhill," d. 1735, and had issue from which descended the Pensylvania families of Harrison, McClenachan, Vaux, Logan, Dickinson, Emlen, Norris, etc.

Land Commissioners that 500 acres in the Welsh Tract, any way, anywhere, be confirmed to his estate, and that his purchase from his brother, and his sales and leases may be adjusted somehow, (and they never were), for this reason it is impossible to adjust this land account now; but it would seem that Gov. Lloyd got more than his original purchase, and that his estate had 2,215 acres for sale.

These Lloyd lands lay next, and west of the tract taken up by the Thomas & Jones Company, which is quite as interesting a section of the "Main Line." After Gov. Lloyd's death, there are many transfers of his Merion, and other lands, by his executors.

"My Respected friend,

James Logan: I hould my self obledged to give thee an account of those Lands belonging to the purches of Thomas Lloyd where David Lloyd is conecirned, and Likwise of Richard ap Thomas, that is how much is taken up and subdevided to them and sould by them, and what Remaines not disposed of by the sd Thomas Lloyd and the sd Richard Thomas.

	Accres.
Thomas Lloyd had a Richt by his Brother Charles to.	2,500
took up between Mirion and Harford..............	1,100
And one 100 accres he ordered in his Richt to Thomas David the wich was Laid out unto him......	100
	1,200
Remaining	1,300
he allso Bought of ffrancis Smith the Sheare of Margaret Davise to herself being 1250 accres.......	1,250
	2,550
there is I think 100 accres of Liberty Land Laid out to him	100

WELSH SETTLEMENT OF PENSYLVANIA

The Rest is to be yeat setled, and war'ts to be granted for the subdeviding of it within the Welsh tract.

allso Richard ap Thomas his purchus is	5,000
out of wich he sould to Philip Howell	700
and 100 of Liberty Land to Hugh Robarts	100
and to Robart William	300
and I think to Edward Joanes	200
	1,300

Remaining to him to have War'ts to himself for...... 3,700

as to David Lloyd part, there is an Imaginary Survey made one about 1,800, accres but not perfected.

When thou art pleased to order war'ts for them or any others of the said Welsh purches'es I think there ought to be a Recitall of the first war'ts by wich the Land was first bounded by, and the time of the survey, Likwise comanding a Return of the Respective Subdivisions within the bounds of the said tract when not allready subdivided to any other Company, the wich Survey was done on the 28th of ye 8th Mo. 1684, and finished the   day of the 11th Mo. Ensuing.

I Request thee allso to put an end to Philip Howell's business to Ease both myself and the Rest of ye Comiss'rs of his Continuall Importuning, and I think it were best to Let him have that Lott on Thomas Joanes account and Let him pay the money to Joanes, Least the Warr't granted by the Gover'r to Nealson take hould of it, and the Gover'r forced to pay the 35 pounds of Joanes out of his own pocett.

these things I Refer to thy Consideration Leaving it wholy to thee to order it as thou think best and desire thy favor in Leting me have and End to my one business that my most Cordiall freind and Governor Left with thee to do for me Ells I am afraid I shall Suffer for want of it, who am thy Real freind.   D. Powell."

"Dat 5th 12th Mo. 1701."

COMPANY NUMBER TWO

Evan Owen, to whom Thomas Lloyd seems to have sold 340 acres, was a brother of Robert Owen, of Merion. As I do not find Evan was in possession of such a tract in Merion, and the Lloyd land covered the tract Robert Owen subsequently owned, it is probable that Evan only engaged this 340 acres for his brother Robert, as by deed, dated 5. 6mo. 1691, Thomas Lloyd conveyed to said Robert this amount of land, which, with a piece he bought later, on resurvey, 30. 3. 1703, amounted to 450 acres.

Another sale made by Thomas Lloyd, which may have been out of his new patent land, was, by deed of 3. 6mo. 1693, to Richard Cuarton, 200 acres in Merion, with one bushel of good winter wheat as the annual rental. His son, William Cuarton, assumed this land by agreement that he would pay his sister, then the wife of John Moore, seventy pounds, two years after his father's death.

Of the grantees of Margaret Davis, or of her and Charles Lloyd, gent., as they joined in the deeds, when the land was conveyed, all dated 24 April, 1683, and having the same witnesses:— Thomas Lloyd, Richard Davies, Richard Owen, Amos Davies, Rowland Ellis, David Davies, and Solomon Jones, and all recorded at Philadelphia 15. 5. 1684.

Margaret Thomas, of Garthlwlch, Montgomeryshire, widow, who bought 156¼ acres, by deed from Charles Lloyd, appointed, on 14 Aug. 1683, Thomas Jones, of Lanwithin, yeoman, who was also a purchaser of the same number of acres, her attorney to take possession of her grant, and look after the land. He had certificate, dated 31. 5mo. 1683, from the Quarterly Meeting at Dolobran, signed by John ap John, Charles Lloyd, Richard and Evan Davies and Sampson Lloyd. After her death, the Commissioners released him, as his interest in the matter had ceased.

Thomas Morris, of Marchnantissa, Montgomery, yeoman, also a purchaser of 156¼ acres, also gave the like power to him, and on Morris's death, he was also released from this stewardship.

WELSH SETTLEMENT OF PENSYLVANIA

David Rhoderick, or Roderic, succeeded to his brother's, John Rhydd's, land. "John Rhydderch, of Hirnant" parish, Montgomeryshire, yeoman, brought certificate, dated 31. 5mo. 1683, from the Quarterly Meeting at Dolobran, which he filed with the Haverford Monthly Meeting. It was signed by John ap John, Charles Lloyd, and Richard and Evan Davies.

Edward Thomas, of Lanwithin parish, Montgomery, yeoman, appointed John Humphrey, of Lanwithin, yeoman, to be his attorney, in the matter of his 312½ acres, after his decease, and the guardian of his children. Subsequently, Samuel Humphrey, and then his son Benjamin Humphrey, succeeded in this trust. Catherine, wife of Edward Thomas, was buried at the Merion Meeting, 10. 21. 1716.

John Humphrey sold, by deed of 1. 7mo. 1697, 100 acres of his own 312½ acres, to his nephew, Joshua Owen, and gave the balance by will to his nephew, Benjamin Humphrey, whose son, John Humphrey, succeeded to it.

The various Humphreys families, descendants of the first settlers, have always been noted in what was the Welsh Tract, residing on farms about the modern villages of Ardmore, Haverford and Bryn Mawr, and much of their original purchases remain in descendants' hands.

Two brothers, JOHN HUMPHREY, of Llanwddyn, and SAMUEL HUMPHREY, were Haverford land owners, and their cousin, RICHARD HUMPHREY, a purchaser from "Richard Davis Co., No. 7." John and Richard, came over in the "Morning Star," with Hugh Roberts, in 1683, as mentioned.

John and Samuel were sons of Humphrey ap Hugh, of Llwyngrill (1662), and "late of Llwyn du," in Merioneth, d. about 1664-5, by his wife, Elizabeth Powel, daughter of John ap Howel (or Powel, who was buried in the parish church of Llanwddyn, in Montgomeryshire, 24 July, 1636), and his wife, Sibill v. Hugh Gwyn, of Penarth.

They were uncles of Rowland Ellis, of "Bryn Mawr," Merion, (whose land adjoined Benjamin Humphrey's land),

and also of Robert Owen's wife, Rebecca, (whose farm lay to the eastward on both sides of Montgomery avenue, between Ardmore and Wynnewood), and of John Owen and Joshua Owen, of Merion (1683), (whose property adjoined that of Humphrey), and of Elizabeth, wife of "John Roberts, of the Mill," and "of Wayn Mill," who came from Pen y Chyd, in Denbighshire (whose estate was northward of Humphrey). They were brothers to Owen Humphrey, of Llwyn du, 1625-1695, a J. P. in Merioneth, and a prominent Friend, who was the father of Rebecca, wife of Robert Owen, of Merion, and Elizabeth, wife of John Roberts, aforesaid.

"JOHN HUMPHREY, of Llanwddyn, gent," purchased 312½ acres of the Lloyd & Davies land, by deed dated 24 April, 1683, and witnessed by Thomas Lloyd, Richard Davies, Richard Owen, Amos Davies, Rowland Ellis, David Davies, and Solomon Jones. By deed dated 1. 7mo. 1697, John conveyed 100 acres of this tract to his nephew, Joshua Owen, and by will bequeathed the balance to his nephew, Benjamin Humphrey. He married his cousin, Jane Humphrey (sister to Richard Humphrey, aforesaid).

In 1698-9, John Humphrey was one of the attorneys for Richard Davies, one of the purchasers of Welsh Tract land. His will, signed 22. 7mo. 1699, witnessed by John Roberts and David Llewellyn, was proved at Philadelphia 31 Aug. 1700. He named as executors his nephew, Benjamin Humphrey, his wife Mary, and son John; named friends Rowland Ellis, Sr., and his daughter Jane, Joshua Owen, John Owen, John Robert's children, Robert Owen's son John; cousin Tabitha, Ann, and Joseph Humphrey.

He said, "I give and bequeathe £10 towards putting in the Press the Testimony of the Twelve Patriarchs, in the Welsh tongue, if conveniences can be had for the same in these America pts." Otherwise, he desired this money should be used for the charities of the Haverford Monthly Meeting. This English work, which was to be a reprint in

Welsh, was probably never so printed, as the money was still in the hands of the Quarterly Meeting, in 1702, when Daniel Humphrey and David Lewis tried to have it appropriated for furnishing of the Haverford Meeting House. If the book was printed in the Province about this time, it was the first book printed in the Welsh tongue in America, as Pugh's "Annerch ir Cymru" was not printed till in 1721, by Andrew Bradford, Philadelphia.

John Humphrey, "of Llwundu," and his wife, Joan, brought their certificate, filed with the Haverford, or Radnor Monthly Meeting, from the Quarterly Meeting at Dolyserrey, dated 27. 5mo. 1683, signed by Robert Humphrey and Richard Owen, Griffith and Owen Lewis, John Evans, Hugh Reese, Amos Davies, William Thomas, William, Evan and Rowland Ellis, Ellis Morris, Evan Harry, and Evan Rees.

Richard Humphrey, "of Llanbynin, Merioneth, bachelor," also had certificate of same date from the same Meeting, and signed by the same Friends, with the addition of Humphrey Reinald.

Elizabeth Humphrey, "of Llanegrin, Merioneth, widow," "whose son Daniel is in Pensylvania, the 12 months past," brought certificate, dated 27. 5mo. 1683, from the Merioneth Quarterly Meeting. Her children, Charles, Benjamin, Lidia, Ann, and Gobeithia Humphrey, came over with her to Pensylvania and filed certificate with the Haverford Monthly Meeting. Signers, Owen Humphreys, Hugh and Evan Rees, Humphrey, Robert, Lewis and Rowland Owen, Griffith and Owen Lewis, Rowland Ellis, Evan Will Powel, John and David Evans, Amos and Ellis Davies.

SAMUEL HUMPHREY, the other brother, died in Wales. He was married to Elizabeth Rees, on 20. 2mo. 1658, by Morris Wynne and Robert Owen, both justices of the peace, by Friends' ceremony, and it is believed that this was the first marriage of this kind. They had 8 children. His relict and children removed to Haverford. Of these,

COMPANY NUMBER TWO

Benjamin Humphrey inherited 212 acres of land in Haverford from his uncle, John Humphrey, about where the village of Bryn Mawr, formerly called Humphreyville, stands, and adjacent to Rowland Ellis's land, and resided near the present Bryn Mawr College grounds. He *d.* 4 Nov. 1738, age 76 years. He *m.* (1694), Mary, daughter of Morris Llewellyn, of Haverford. Of their children, Ann *m.* 23. 10mo. 1742, Garrad Jones (son of Robert Jones, a first settler of Merion); Elizabeth, *m.* John Scarlett; Owen Humphrey *m.* 29. 7mo. 1738, Sarah, widow of John Hughs, of Merion. The will of John Hughs, of Merion, was signed 2 Jan. 1736, witnesses Griffith and Morris Llewellyn, and William Lloyd, was proved by wife Sarah, 12 Feb. 1736, mentions father-in-law Morgan Herbert, but no children. Trustees, John Roberts and Griffith Llewellyn. Benjamin Humphreys succeeded Rees Price as landlord of the Blue Anchor tavern, on Dock Creek landing, in Philadelphia.

Through Thomas John Thomas, he also had a tract of land, lying east of his other plot, and north of the present Montgomery avenue, at Haverford R. R. Station.

Daniel Humphrey in 12mo. 1701, received warrant for 200 acres of land, which was also located in Haverford, about the present Haverford College grounds, and on resurvey found to be 41 acres "overplus," which he bought, paying 8 shillings an acre. This land was in the right of "T. Ellis, L. David, & J. Poyer," who were grantees of Richard Davies. He also bought, 5. 3mo. 1694, 50 acres "due several purchasers," of the same Davies lands. He lived and died in Haverford, and was appointed to adjust the estates of Thomas Ellis and wife. His will, dated 26. 9mo. 1734, was proved at Philadelphia, 7 April, 1735.

He had thirteen children by his wife (*m.* about 1695) Hannah, daughter of Thomas Wynne, who survived him, named Samuel, *b.* 3. 6mo. 1696, first child; Joshua, Edward, Charles, Jonathan, Solomon, Thomas, Benjamin, Hannah, Elizabeth, Martha, Mary and Rebecca, *b.* 2. 10mo. 1716, last

WELSH SETTLEMENT OF PENSYLVANIA

child, all of record at Haverford Monthly Meeting. His cousins John and David Humphrey, with his first three named sons, were trustees under his will.

Anne, m. (1699), Edward Roberts, son of Hugh Roberts, of Merion.

Lydia, m. (1706), Ellis Ellis, son of Thomas Ellis, of Haverford.

Rebecca, m. (1713, second wife), Edward Rees, of Merion.

Elizabeth, m. (1693), Thomas Abel, of Haverford.

ROBERT OWEN, mentioned above as one of the purchasers of "548 acres" of Lloyd's land, by deed 5. 6mo. 1691, was a minister among the Friends. The Pensylvania historian, Proud, says of him, "he was an eminent preacher, and a very serviceable and worthy person among the Quakers, being a man endowed with many excellent qualities, a skilful peacemaker, and of much service and utility in various respects."

From 1674, he was much persecuted in Wales for being a Quaker, and removed with his wife Rebecca, "and their dear and tender children" to Pensylvania in 1690, bringing a flattering certificate from the Quarterly Meeting at Tyddyn y Garreg, in Merionethshire,* dated 8. 6mo. 1690; which is

---

*The members of the Tyddyn y Garreg Quart. Mtg., signers of the Certificate of Removal:

Evan Owen.	Rees Evan.
Rowland Owen.	Hugh Rees.
Lewis Owen.	Evan Rees.
Griffitt Robert.	Robert Vaughan.
Jane Robert.	Rees Thomas.
Margaret Robert.	David Jones.
Ellis Morris.	Elizabeth Jones.
Hugh David.	Gainor Jones.
Margaret David.	Jonett Johnes.
Rowland Ellis.	Regnald Humphrey.
Ellin Ellis.	Ann Rowland.
John Evan.	Owen Lewis.

COMPANY NUMBER TWO

preserved in the archives of the Haverford (Radnor) Monthly Meeting.

It may be seen he was not one of the original purchasers of land, in the Welsh Tract from the "Adventuring Companies," and it is not known why, nor is the reason apparent why he did not seek refuge from his "sufferings" sooner, since he was nearly related to many of the original settlers.

Robert Owen was born about the year 1657, and was the eldest son of Owen ap Evan Robert Lewis, of Rhiwlas, who resided on the "Fron Gôch" plantation, or farm, near Bala, in Merioneth, and who died before 1678-9 (by his wife, Gainor John), and brother to Jane, wife of the minister, Hugh Roberts, and to Ellin, wife of Cadwalader Thomas, and to Evan Owen, of Merion, b. 1665-6, and nearly related to John and Samuel Humphrey, of Haverford, and others here.

Mr. Owen was one of the signers of the certificate of removal for John ap Thomas, the partner of Dr. Edward Jones, who was fated not to remove here, and was an overseer of his will by appointment, 9 Feb. 1682.

After his arrival, Robert Owen purchased, by deed dated 5. 6mo. 1691, for one hundred pounds, the lands from Thomas Lloyd, variously estimated, according to surveys, at 442, 450, or 548 acres. This land lay west of the present settlement of Wynnewood, towards the village of Ardmore, north of the P. R. R., and was the plantation, which was confirmed to his eldest son and heir, Evan Owen, by the Commissioners, on 8. 12mo. 1704, who conveyed it, by deed dated 31 Dec. 1707, to his brother-in-law, Jonathan Jones.

The original farm of Robert Owen, which is now being sub-divided into little lots for picturesque little country houses, lay in a general way between Thompson avenue, in Ardmore, and the west boundry of Narberth, and north from the P. R. R. to the Mill Creek Road, on both sides of Glenn Road, and Cherry Lane. He left it to his son, Evan Owen, in 1697, who sold it to his brother-in-law, Jonathan

WELSH SETTLEMENT OF PENSYLVANIA

Jones, in 1707, whose son, Owen Jones, 1711-1793, had all of it, three lots, 350, 101 and 20 acres. His sons, Owen Jones, Jr., and Jonathan Jones, next had the property, Owen 350 acres, and Jonathan 101 and 20. Owen devised half of the 350 (on which the stone house stands) to Col. Owen Jones, who also had from his father his 121 acres, and the other half to his sister's son, John Wister, which portion is called "St. Mary's," and was inherited by his grandchildren, two daughters of the late Col. Lewis Wister, and Col. Owen Jones's property, "Wynnewood," went to his son and heir, Awbrey Jones, who, dying without issue, left the place to collateral heirs.

Immediately after he had possession, Robert Owen began the erection of a stone dwelling, which, as the date-stone tells, was completed in 1695. This house, which was built about the same time, apparently of similar materials, and possibly by the same contractor, as the Merion Meeting House, not far away, still stands, somewhat altered, on Montgomery avenue, east of Church road, a noted landmark. Here Mr. Owen resided at the time of his decease, on 8. 10mo. 1697,

Mr. Owen was a justice in Merion and twice chosen as a member of the Assembly, 1695-1697, and was a trustee of the Merion Meeting, in whose ground both he and his wife were buried.

His will, signed 2. 10mo. 1697; witnessed by John Owens, Rowland Ellis and Robert Jones, was proved at Philadelphia, 16 May, 1705. He left his plantation to his eldest son, Evan Owen, only child named, and named as overseers, Messrs. Hugh Roberts, John Humphreys, John Roberts, Griffith John, Robert Jones, Robert Roberts, Robert Lloyd and Rowland Ellis, the foremost men of Merion, and appointed his cousin, Griffith John, sole executor.

The inventory of the personal estate of Mr. Robert Owen was made "ye last day of ye eleventh month, 1697," by John Roberts and John Owen. It is preserved at the Historical

Society of Pensylvania. He had seven cows, valued at £3. 10, per head, two steers at £2. 10, per head, seven young cattle "at £1. 05, ye head," five horses and mares at £4. 10 ye head, twenty sheep valued at £7, twelve swine, £9, and wheat, barley, implements for farming, "books, £3," "bedding, and apparel, £47. 09. 6," "brass, pewter, and other household stuff, £12. 16. 0." Total valuation of the personalty £188. 18. 06. (This John Owen was "ye 2nd son of Owen Humphreys, of Llwyn du," and brother to Joshua Owen).

Mr. Owen married Rebecca Owen, daughter of Owen Humphrey, gent., of Llwynddu, in Llangelynin parish, Merioneth. The marriage agreement, still extant, dated 6. 1mo. 1678-9, was between Robert's mother, Gainor John, his father being dead, and Owen Humphrey. It was signed, as witnesses, by Rowland Ellis, Edward Vaughan, John ap Thomas, and Cadwalader Thomas. The marriage certificate, also extant, is dated 11. 1mo. 1678-9.

Robert Owen had by his wife, Rebecca, who died 23. 8mo. 1697, the following eight children (*sic*) Pa. Mag. vol. xiii, p. 168, etc.), four, born in Wales, between 1697-1690, coming over with them.

Evan Owen, eldest son, born probably at Fron Gôch, about 1682-3; died intestate in Philadelphia, and power to administer on his estate was granted to his widow and relict. 27 Oct. 1727.

On his request, 3. 3mo. 1703, a resurvey was made of all the lands he inherited from his father, and it was found he had 450 acres in Merion, and 100 acres in Goshen tp. He had no desire to be only a country gentleman, and sold his farms to his brother in-law, as above, and removed into the city, after his marriage.

Like his father, Evan Owen was a man of affairs. He removed into Philadelphia and was a member of the City Council, 1717, a Justice in Philadelphia county, 1723, &c, the treasurer of the city, 1724-27, a member of the Provin-

WELSH SETTLEMENT OF PENSYLVANIA

cial Assembly, 1725, and of the Provincial Council, 1726, and a trustee of the Society of Free Traders in Pensylvania, etc.

He was a member of the Philadelphia Monthly Meeting, where he was married to Mary, daughter of Dr. Richard Hoskins, (then deceased), 1. 10mo. 1711, (53 Friends signed their certificate), and had four children by her, of record at the Arch Street Meeting. One, Esther, *m.* 1743, William Davis, at Christ Church, Philadelphia.

Elizabeth Owen, *b.* in Wales, in 168-, *d.* in Philadelphia 22. 10mo. 1753. She *m.* David Evans, of Philadelphia, a deputy sheriff, 1714-21, will signed 27 Sept. 1745, and had six children. Of these, Evan Evans *m.* and had issue, and Sidney, second wife of Joseph Howell, of Chester, Pa.*

Jane Owen, *b.* in Wales, in 168—. Probably died young.

Gainor Owen, *b.* in Wales, 26. 8mo. 1688, *d.* ———. She *m.* at the Merion Meeting, 4. 8mo. 1706, Jonathan Jones, 1680-1770 (son of Dr. Edward Jones, of Merion), and had ten, or more, children, of these, Mary, *b.* 14. 5mo. 1707, *m.* at Merion Meeting, Benjamin Hayes, (a son of Richard Hayes, of Haverford) ; Rebecca, *b.* 20. 12mo. 1709, *m.* at Merion Meeting, 4 June, 1733, John Roberts, 1710-1776 (son of Robert Roberts, of Merion), and had twelve children; Owen Jones, 1711-1793, the last provincial treasurer, *m.* 30 May, 1740, Susanna Evans, 1719-1801, a daughter of Hugh Evans, of Merion, 1682-1772, (their daughter, Hannah Jones, *m.* Amos Foulke, 1740-1791) ; Jacob Jones, *b.* 1713, *m.* Mary Lawrence; Jonathan Jones, Jr., *b.* 1715, *m.* at Merion Meeting, 8. 11mo. 1742, Sarah, daughter of Thomas Jones, of Merion, a son of John ap Thomas, (their daughter, Katherine, *m.* Lewis Jones, of Blockley), and Elizabeth *m.* about 1758, Jesse George, of Blockley.

---

*See "Howell Family," in the American Historical Register, Jan. 1896.

COMPANY NUMBER TWO

Owen Owen, second son, b. Merion, 21. 12mo. 1690-91, d. Philadelphia 5. 8mo. 1741; will dated 4. 5mo. 1741, proved 11 August. He resided in the city and was high sheriff of Philadelphia Co., 1726, and city coroner, 1729-41. He m. 23. 3mo. 1714, Ann Wood, d. 4. 2mo. 1743, and had five children. Of these, Jane, d. s. p., wife of Dr. Cadwalader Evans; Sarah, m. 3 March 1736, John Biddle, (and had, besides others, Col. Clement Biddle, 1740-1814, who had 13 children), and Tacy, m. Daniel Morris, of Upper Dublin tp.

John Owen, third son, b. 26. 12mo. 1692, d. in Chester Co., Pa., will proved 23 Jan. 1752. He was high sheriff of Chester Co. 1729-51, assemblyman, 1733-43, collector of the port of Chester, 1733-37. He m. at Chester Monthly Meeting, 22. 8mo. 1719, (48 Friends signed their certificate), Hannah, b. 17. 12mo. 1698, d. 1752, daughter of George Maris, of Chester, a provincial councillor, and had five children. Of these, Jane, m. Joseph West; Elizabeth, m. James Rhoads; Rebecca was the first wife of Jesse Maris, 1727-1811, and Susanna, m. Josiah Hibbard.

Robert Owen, Jr., who, with his brother, Evan, was admitted a freeman of Philadelphia in 1717, was b. 27. 7mo. 1695, and d. about 1730. He m. at the Philadelphia Monthly Meeting 11. 10mo. 1716-17, (sixty-one Friends signed their certificate), Susanna Hudson, (she m. secondly, John Burr, of Burlington, and d. 4. 3mo. 1757), daughter of William Hudson, mayor of Philadelphia, 1726 (by his first wife, Mary, daughter of Samuel Richardson, a provincial councillor), and had three children. Of these, Hannah Owen, 1720-1791, (will proved), m. first, 23. 8mo. 1740, at Arch Street Meeting, Philadelphia, John Ogden, widower, of Philadelphia, d. 6 Feb. 1742, will dated 31 Jan. proved 12 Feb. 1742, and had William Ogden,* d. in Camden, N. J., 13. May, 1818,

---

*See "Owen of Merion," Pen. Mag. vol. XIII, Glenn's "Merion in the Welsh Tract," Browning's "Colonial Dames of Royal Descent," Pedigree XXXVII, Browning's "Americans of Royal Descent, 4th edition, pp. 592-596, and Browning's "Magna Charta Barons and their American Descendants," pp. 373-380.

aged 77 years; *m.* first, 1. 11mo. 1769, Marie Pinniard, and had by her, who *d.* 14. 7mo. 1775, Hannah, 1770-1827, who *m.* first at Christ Church, Philadelphia, 10 April, 1795, Capt. William Duer, drowned in 1800-1, and had Mary Ann, *m.* 5 May, 1825, Lewis W. Glenn, and had Edward, late of Ardmore, Pa., deceased, who *m.* secondly, Sarah Catherine Allen, and had Thomas Allen Glenn, author of "Merion in the Welsh Tract." Hannah Owen *m.* secondly, in 1754, his second wife, Joseph Wharton,* of "Walnut Grove," in Southwark, Philadelphia Co., *d.* 1776, and had issue.

Rebecca Owen, b. 14. 1mo. 1697; buried at the Merion Meeting House, on 21. 9mo. 1697, surviving her mother only one month.

The aforesaid Robert Owen should not be confounded with a contemporary Welshman of the same name. This other Robert Owen, of Dolserau, came over in the ship Vine, of Liverpool, sailing from Dolyserre, near Dolgules, Merioneth, with his wife, Jane, son Lewis, and a servant boy and four maid servants, and arrived at Philadelphia in Sep. 1684. He had been a Justice of the Peace at Dolserau, near Dolgelly, (and near Bala), where he was incarcerated five years in the jail because he was a Quaker. He had been the Governor of Beaumaris, and became a Quaker about 1660. When he came over here, he settled on Duck Creek, in New Castle Co., where his son, Edward Owen, who had come over earlier, in Hugh Roberts's party, in Nov. 1683, was then settled. Both Robert Owen and Jane, his wife, died in the next year. They had altogether nine sons, and all were of age before 1684. Their son Lewis Owen returned to Wales to reside, but their son Dr. Griffith Owen, who bought his brother Edward Owen's land, in the Thomas & Jones tract, Merion, remained here, and became prominent in the Province. The mother of this large family, was Jane, daughter of Robert Vaughan, of Heng Wert, or

---

*See Pa. Mag. Vol. II, "Wharton Family."

COMPANY NUMBER TWO

Hendri Mawr, near Bala, and of Nannau, Merionethshire, and a relative of the John ap Thomas family.

The late Dr. Levick recorded that the Pensylvania historian, Dr. George Smith, was a descendant of the Merion settlers, Dr. Edward Jones, and Dr. Wynne, and also of "Robert and Jane Owen, that brave pair, who, whether as lord and lady of Beaumaris Castle, or for conscience sake, within the gates of Dolgelly jail, commanded the admiration and respect of all about them."

In the ship Vine, of Liverpool, William Preeson master, which sailed from Dolyserre, and arrived at Philadelphia on 17. 7mo. 1684, there were, besides Rees John William, or Rees Jones, one of the purchasers of "Thomas & Jones," or "Company No. 1," and the aforesaid Robert Owen and Jeane, his wife, the following other passengers:

David Davis, and his sister Katharine, and her daughter, Mary Tidey, and one man servant, named Charles Hughes, who had three years to serve. They were from Denbighshire.

Hugh Harris, and Daniel Harris. They were from Macchinleth, or Manhinteth, in Montgomeryshire, as were also the following:

John Richards, Susan, his wife, and daughters Hannah and Bridget, and one servant, named Susan Griffith, to serve six years.

Margaret, the wife of Alexander Edwards, and her daughters, Margaret and Martha, and two sons, Alexander and Thomas.

Rees Prees, and wife Ann, and daughters Mary, Sarah and Phebe, and two sons, Richard and John. From Radnorshire.

Jane Evans, widow, and four daughters, Mary, Alice, Sarah and Elizabeth, and a man servant, named Joseph.

Anne Jones, and her daughter, Ann Jones. From Carmarthenshire.

Griffith Owen, (the physician), his wife Sarah, and children, and servants, from Prescoe, in Lancashire.

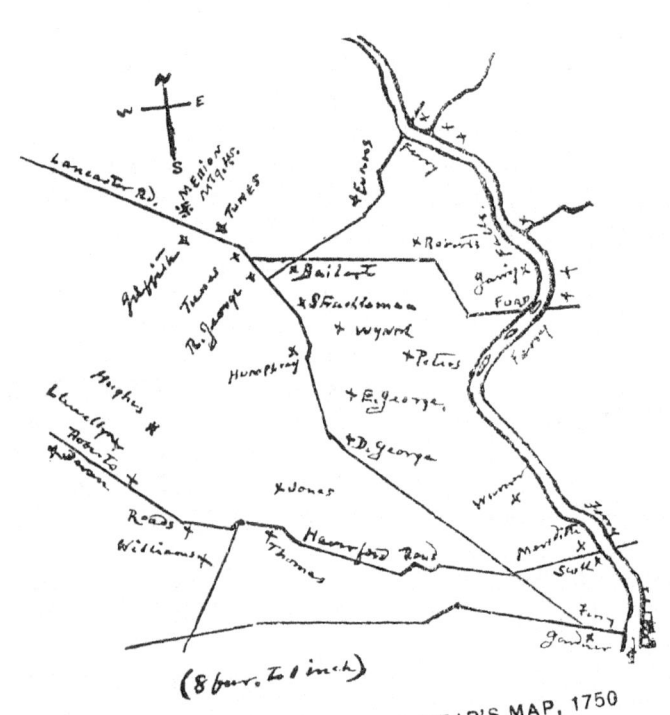

A SECTION OF SCULL & HEAP'S MAP, 1750

JOHN BEVAN'S LAND PATENT

Company No. 3.—The deeds to grantees, who all resided in Glamorganshire, under the patent for 2,000 acres to John ab Evan, yeoman, (or John Bevan), of Trefyrhig, or Trevorrigge, Llantrissent parish, Glamorganshire, were dated after 16 Sept. 1681, and the grantees were, in part, as follows:

Charles ab Evan, (Bevan), of Trevorrigg, and Llantwit Vardre parish, Glamorganshire, brother to John.

John Richard, of Trevorrigg, tailor.

Elizabeth Prichard and Katharine Prichard, of Telcha, Llantrissent, spinsters, whose deed for 250 acres, dated 8 May 1682, was witnessed by Barbara Awbrey, John ab Evan, Jun'r, Evan John, and John Richard.

Matthew Jones, of Carmarthen, Carmarthenshire, Mercer, whose deed, dated 1 Aug. 1682, for 125 acres, was witnessed by Will Broadber, Ch Evans, Ebenezer David, and Jane Miller.

David Jones, of Carmarthen town.

Ralph Lewis, of Eglwysilan.

Eventually John Bevan bought back the lands taken by John Richard, and the Prichards, and Ralph Lewis.

The Commissioners' minutes relating to Welsh purchasers, however, give the following details. After getting deeds for their grant from Penn in Sept. 1681, John and Charles Bevan had laid out to themselves, 980 acres, in three tracts, 750 acres in Marple tp., and 170 and 60 acres in Haverford tp., on warrants, dated 23. 5mo. 1688. By deed of 1 March, 1698, Charles Bevan conveyed all his rights to his brother, John Bevan. Shortly, John sold the 170 acres in Haverford to Evan Williams, and to John Hayes, 275 acres of the

WELSH SETTLEMENT OF PENSYLVANIA

Marple tract, and his "liberty land" to Benjamin Chambers, of Philadelphia, and then had 535 acres left. He then bought, in 1697, 250 acres in Haverford, the purchase of Katherine and Elizabeth Prichard, or Prichit (ap Richard), and about 200 acres in Haverford which he had sold to John Richard, from said John's heir, Lewis Richard, or Richards, in Haverford, and 168½ acres also in Haverford, from "William Howel, and his wife, Mary, relict and administrator of Evan Thomas, who by deed, dated 10 May, 1683, purchased 250 acres of Lewis David." This gave John Bevan three tracts in Haverford tp., or in all 678 acres there, this, with his balance of 475 acres in Marple tp., made him holder of 1,153 acres in Haverford and Marple tps., at one time,— when he sold to the Welsh.

By deed of 16. 5mo. 1684, John Bevan bought of Thomas Wynne 300 acres in Merion, at Wynnewood, which was confirmed to him by patent from the Commissioners, dated 9. 5mo. 1688, and then owned 1,453 acres.

The brothers, Ralph Lewis and William Lewis, relatives of John Bevan, came with their families from Eglwysilan, in Glamorganshire.

Ralph Lewis came over with Mr. Bevan, in 1683, having bought from him 250 acres, which were laid out in Haverford, next to the land of Thomas Rees. He sold part of it back to Mr. Bevan, and a part to David Lewis. He had several children by his wife, Mary. Hugh David, of Haverford, in his will, signed 27 April 1709, present Daniel Lawrence, Thomas James, Robert Jones, and Henry Lawrence, proved by wife Martha, 9 June, 1709, names children David, Ruth, Mary, Jonathan, Caleb, and Samuel, and to be overseers, father-in-law, Ralph Lewis, cousins David Lewis and William Lewis, and Lewis David.

William Lewis, the other brother, arrived in Philadelphia on 11. 5mo. 1686. He purchased, by deed dated 13. 10mo. 1692, a plantation of 120 acres, adjoining his brother Ralph's land, but which had been a portion of the Lewis David

COMPANY NUMBER THREE

("Company No. 5") tract of 3,000 acres. It lay in Haverford, to the south of the present settlement of Wynnewood, and near the old Haverford Road. Subsequently, he bought 50 acres in Radnor, and, by deed, 10. 10. 1698, he bought 300 acres in New Town tp., Chester Co.

William Lewis died in New Town, 9. 12mo. 1707-8. His will, signed 16 Jan. 1707-8, was proved at Philadelphia 12 March following. He had five children by his wife, Ann, namely: David, Lewis, Evan, William and Nathan Lewis, whose son Levi had a son Jesse, father of Levi Lewis, who was a practical farmer in Radnor tp. The latter's son, Tryon Lewis, born in 1839, was of the fourth generation of sons only born at the old Lewis home, and his daughter, Lydia T., was the first girl child born in this branch of the family in five generations.

William Lewis's son, David Lewis, was the father of Amos, who owned the farm near Bryn Mawr, purchased by the late George W. Childs, of Philadelphia, for a country seat. The will of David Lewis, of Haverford, signed 9 Sep. 1723, in the presence of Richard Hayes, John Parry, and John Jones, was proved 23 Sept. 1723, by wife Ann and eldest son William, executors. Other children named, James, Edmond, Amos, Enoch, Elizabeth and Ellen Ann. "To the Quaker Meeting at Haveford." Brothers Lewis, Evan, and William Lewis, and Robert Jones to assist the executors.

The wills of the other two men, in Haverford, having his name, give the following data. "David Lewis, late of Landewi, Pembroke, now of Haverford," marked in the presence of Abraham Hardiman, David Lawrence, and David Lloyd, 26. 3mo. 1697; will proved 22 Jan. 1708. Appoints son James Lewis executor, names son-in-law Peregrine Lewis, and his three children. Codicil 26 Feb. 1707, witnessed by John Maris and David Jones. The will of the other "David Lewis, of Haverford, yeoman," marked 24. 1mo. 1714-5, in the presence of Lewis David (marked), Henry Lewis, Richard Hayes, and Henry Lawrence, proved

WELSH SETTLEMENT OF PENSYLVANIA

28 Jan. 1715, by wife Katherine. Children, Joseph, Susanna, Hannah, James, and Sarah Lewis. Trustees, Lewis David, of Darby, Richard Hayes, Henry and Daniel Lawrence all of Haverford.

JOHN BEVAN, or John ab Evan, who was the trustee for this small company of settlers, was one of the early converts to Quakerism, and became an accepted minister among Friends. He apparently was a well educated man, and belonged to the landed gentry of Wales. He was the son of Evan ap John Evan, of Treverigg, Llantrisant parish, in Glamorganshire, and his wife, Jane, daughter of Richard ap Evan, of Collena, in the same parish.

He and his first wife, Barbara, and their children, "their tender family," and some other relatives, removed to Pensylvania, coming over in the ship "Morning Star," with Hugh Roberts and party bound for the Thomas and Jones land, arrived at Philadelphia in Nov. 1683. He and his wife brought the usual certificates of membership and removal from the Treverigg Friends' Meeting, and the Men's Meeting of Cardiff and Trefrig, dated 10. 7mo. 1683. Among the many signers, William Lewis; Howell, William, Watkins, and James Thomas; Thomas, Edward, Jenkin, and Mireck Howell, John David, John Mays, and his uncle, (his mother's brother), Thomas Richard (or Prichard) ap Evan, of Collena, for whose daughters, Elizabeth and Catherine, John Bevan bought some Haverford land, which he bought back from them as above.

John Bevan left a copy (still extant) of the written account of himself and family, which, at the request of the Merion Preparative Meeting, or the Haverford Mo. Mtg. he had filed with it in 1704, beginning:—"Sometime before the year 1683, we had heard that our esteemed friend, William Penn, had a patent from King Charles the Second for that Province in America, called Pencilvania, and my wife had a great intention to go thither, and thought it might be a good place to train up children amongst sober people, and to prevent the corruption of them here,.... She acquainted me therewith, but I then thought it not likely to take effect, for several reasons." It further tells how he found the way clear to remove; of his voyage; of his experience here; of his travels as a minister into New England, in 1701; and of his final return to his home in Wales in 1704, with his second wife and young daughter, Barbara, as "the aim intended by my wife was in a good measure answered," where they lived the balance of their lives.

Though he lived here, off and on, only about twenty years, or till in 1704, John Bevan was a prominent man of affairs in the Welsh tract. He was chosen one of their representatives, in the Provincial Assembly, by the Welsh, in the years of 1687, 1693, and 1700, and was appointed a justice in Haverford tp., Philadelphia Co., in 1685, and for the same in Chester Co., in 1689.

He visited Wales on private matters, in 1694-5, and married his second wife. An extant letter, dated 29. 2mo. 1695, from Rees Thomas, of Merion to his father-in-law, William Awbrey, says "my unkle John Bevan came over very well, and a good voyage he had." In 1698, he went to his old home again, where he still owned property, and in 1704, went there to remain, as the Quakers were no longer persecuted in Wales, and there was too much unpleasantness in Penn's country.

After John Bevan had made several sales in right to these 2,000 acres he bought from Penn, as explained above, he had remaining, besides 25 acres of the liberty land that went with his purchase, for which he had warrant dated 5. 8mo. 1702, the farm of 300 acres in Merion, and 90 acres adjoining, located in Haverford, constituted his homestead here. This land lay to the south of the present Wynnewood R. R. station, and South of the modern Lancaster Ave., across the old "Haverford Street," and along the lines of

WELSH SETTLEMENT OF PENSYLVANIA

Haverford tp., and of the present Philadelphia Co. Some of this tract belonged to his descendants for about one hundred years,—not after 1810.

John Bevan lived to be about 80 years old, and died at his home, called "Treveyrig," or Treverigg, where he resided after his final return in 1704. His will, dated 1mo. 1724-5, was a very long, and full one, and was witnessed by his brother, Charles Bevan, and was proved at Llandaff Registry, in Glamorganshire, 21 Oct. 1726. Charles Bevan, William Awbrey, of Pencoed, and others, named as the overseers.

To his grandson, John Bevan, he bequeathed his messuage, called "Treveyrig," and a gristmill on this property, and mentions said John's children, his own great-grandchildren, to wit, Richard, Thomas, and Barbara Bevan. He mentioned his 90 acres in Haverford, and his 300 acres in Merion, and two other pieces of land that he had given to his son Evan Bevan.

John Bevan, when a young man, married Barbara, daughter of William Awbrey, of Pencoed, or Pencoyd. She came over with him in 1683, and they returned to the old home in 1704, as he relates in his journal, as follows: "We landed at Shields in Northumberland, and staid over the meeting on first-day, next day we set forward toward our habitation in Wales, having near 300 miles to travel. We had several good meetings in our way, and about the beginning of the Eighth month, 1704, we came to our home at Treveyricke." Telling of his wife's last illness six years later, "in her last sickness she was sensible, she was not likely to recover out of it, she said, 'I take it as a great mercy that I am to go before thee, we are upwards of forty-five years married, and our love is rather more now towards one another than at the beginning,' she quietly departed this life the 26th of the Eleventh month, 1710, aged 73 years, and about 4 months." It has been said that he had two wives, both named Barbara, but this wife was certainly the wife of his youth, as they were married in 1665, he being only 19 and she 28 years old. Of their children:

John Bevan, the eldest. He came to Pensylvania with his parents. He may have been the bachelor of this name, buried at the Merion Meeting 11mo. 13. 1715-6. It is also supposed that he returned to "Treveyrig" with his father, married and died there, before his father, having a son John, who was a gentleman farmer and miller, enjoying the land of his inheritance, and whose children in 1724 were, (named in will of John Bevan, 1725), Richard, Thomas, and Barbara. The father of these children is also placed as a son of Evan, named below.

Jane Bevan, b. about 1667, d. 12. 10mo. 1703; m. at the home of William Howell, in Haverford, 1. 10mo. 1687, John Wood, of Darby, a member of Pensylvania Assembly 1704-1717, a son of George Wood, a J. P., and Assemblyman, 1682-1683, and had seven children, A descendant is John W. Jordan, LL.D., of Philadelphia.

Evan Bevan, from whom all of this surname in Merion descended, was born about 1672. He visited his father at "Treveyrig," and from the Friends' Meeting there brought his certificate, dated 10. 5mo. 1707. He m. at the Darby Monthly Meeting, on 9. 11mo. 1693, Eleanor Wood, who administered on Evan's estate, 13 Aug. 1720, and had eight children. She was a minister among Friends, and d. 28. 11. 1744, and was buried at the Haverford Meeting House.

Evan Bevan resided on his father's Merion land, and died intestate before his father. His father bequeathed his Merion-Haverford plantation to his daughter-in-law in trust for his grandson, Evan Bevan, Jr., 1698-1746, and should he not live to enjoy it, then it was to go to Awbrey Bevan, 1705-1761, or Charles Bevan, other grandchildren of the testator, children of this Evan Bevan. Evan Bevan, Jr., was the father of Charles, who inherited the home farm, but generally resided in Philadelphia. His estate was administered in Jan. 1800, his wife dead, and two children minors. One of these, Charles, Jr., *m.* Mary Lippincott, and died intestate, in 1809, in Merion, also leaving two children minors, named John L. and Henry C., who inherited the John Bevan property.

Ann Bevan, b. about 1676-7; *m.* at the Merion Meeting, 23. 1mo. 1696-7, Owen Roberts, of Merion, (son of the Friends' minister, Hugh Roberts), and had six children.

Elizabeth Bevan, b. about 1678; *d.* 1739; *m.* at Merion Meeting 30. 4mo. 1696, Joseph Richardson, *d.* 1752, son of Samuel Richardson, a Provincial Councillor, and had eight children. Descendants were Mrs. Arthur D. Cross, of San Francisco, and Judge Samuel W. Pennypacker, of Philadelphia, former Governor of Pensylvania.

Barbara Bevan, b. in Pensylvania 5. 7mo. 1696. "She was the only child by his second wife," and went to Wales with her parents in 1704, where she *m.* William Musgrove.

Charles Bevan, of Lantwit Vardre, had a son Evan Bevan, or "Evan Bevan alias Jeuans," as he signed his name, oorn in 1678, educated at Oxford, and became a lawyer, and a minister and elder among Friends, and *d.* in 1745. Testimony as to his good character made in the Monmouthshire Meeting, 17. 2mo. 1746. (See Memoir of him in the "Friends' Library," vol. XIII.)*

---

* The following item concerns another branch of this family.

A Mrs. Catherine Bevan was sentenced by the Court of New Castle Co. (Delaware), to be burned alive at New Castle, in 1731, for the murder of her husband. It was the intention of the kind-hearted sheriff to hang her by the neck over the pile of fagots, in the hope she would strangle to death before being burned. But some accident happened to the rope—it broke, slipped, or was cut, after the fire was well under way, when she dropped, bound hand and foot, into the blaze. Struggling to free herself from her bindings, she nearly escaped from the pyre, and had to be pushed back into the flames, and held there by the sheriff and the crowd, while she died a lingering and horrible death, in conformity with the sentence of the Court.

COMPANY NUMBER THREE

REES THOMAS, who came over with John Bevan, in 1683, was then a young and unmarried man. Nothing certain is known of his ancestry, but it is presumed he had lived in Glamorganshire, and was a relative of Mr. Bevan. In time, he became a prominent man in the Welsh Tract, a justice of the peace, and an Assemblyman, and a successful farmer.

About two months after his marriage, he bought his first land, some 300 acres in Merion, from Sarah, the relict and widow of John Eckley, by deed dated 15. 6mo. 1692, which land adjoined that of Ellis Hugh, of Merion. Later, he bought 170 acres adjoining this first purchase, from Edward Prichard. These two tracts of land lay about where the village of Rosemont stands, and north and west of the P. R. R. station. From the Land Commissioners' minutes, it appears that "Rees Thomas, of Haverford," by deed dated 4 May, 1713, acquired 500 acres, with the usual bonus of a city lot, and liberty land, from John Clark, of Devizes, Wiltshire, and on 12. 1mo. 1715, he desired warrant of survey to lay out this claim, but it is not evident that this was granted, or that he entered upon this land.

About this time, Rees Thomas and Anthony Morris, Jr., bought from William Awbrey, of London, (a relative of Rees's wife), executor to Richard Whitpain, the right of Whitpain to 7,000 acres "in the country," city lots and liberty land. This tract lay in West Town, Chester Co., in the "Welsh Tract," of that county, a distinct purchase from that of which I write. In 1717, when they applied to have this land laid out to them, they had considerable trouble over it with the relict and heirs of Whitpain, and had to compromise, and on 30. 3mo. 1718, received warrant of survey for only a part, but subsequently were allowed another selection, and had 2,000 acres in Chester Co., and 4,500 acres in Philadelphia Co., and for all this land, they asked for a re-survey, 19. 3mo. 1726.

There is a copy of the following note from James Steel, who was one of the great land-grabbers of the time in the

Lower Counties (Delaware). It is dated 17. 9mo. 1722, "To Rees Thomas, upon his brother's illness: I hereby certify that I did agree with Rees Thomas, on behalf of his brother, William Thomas, for 200 acres of land in Radnor, formerly held by Rees Prees on Rent." The purchase price was £40 for the whole, in consideration that William Thomas also purchase the right in the land of Rees Thomas.

Rees Thomas's will, signed 10 Sept. 1742, was proved 12 Feb. 1742-3. He left the homestead farm, and 200 acres of the "Rosemont" land, bought of Eckley, to his son Rees, and the other tract there to son William.

Rees Thomas married at the Haverford Meeting, 18. 4mo. 1692, Martha Awbrey, who also came over in Mr. Bevan's party, in 1683. She died 7. 12mo. 1726. She was one of the ten children of William Awbrey, who was buried at Llanelyw parish church, in Brecknock, in 1716, aged 90 years, and his wife, and cousin, Elizabeth, a daughter of William Awbrey, eldest son of Thomas Awbrey, gent., of Llanslyw.

In an extant letter, dated 29. 2mo. 1695, Rees Thomas and his wife wrote a joint letter to her father in Wales, telling him about their two children, their farm life, and asked the date of Martha's birth. Mr. Thomas concluded with:—
"I doe understand yt thou were not well pleased yt my oldest son was not caled an Aubrey. I will answer thee I was not against it, but my neibors wood have him be caled my name, being [as] I brought ye Land and I so beloved amongst them, I doe admite to what thee sayes in thy letter yt an Aubrey was better known than I, though I am hear very well acquainted with most in these parts. He is ye first Aubrey in Pensilvania and a stout boy he is of his age being now a quarter."

Of the six children of Rees and Martha Thomas:—

Rees Thomas, Jr., b. 22. 2mo. 1693, who is referred to in the above letter. He *m.* Elizabeth, daughter of Dr. Edward Jones, of Merion.

COMPANY NUMBER THREE

Awbrey Thomas, b. 30. 11mo. 1694, d. s. p. He m. Guleima, only daughter of William Penn, the younger. His mother was a sister of William Awbrey, the son-in-law of William Penn, the Founder.

Herbert Thomas, b. 3. 9mo. 1696, d. s. p. He m. Mary, daughter of John Havard.*

William Thomas, who died at "Rosemont" before 1787. He married and had seven children.

---

*In the will of Lewis John, of Haverford, signed 2. 9mo. 1704, in the presence of Nathan Thomas, John Havard, William Sinkler (marked), and David Powell, proved by wife, Elizabeth, and daughter, Margaret Lewis, the executors, 2 Dec. 1704, he mentions daughter, Elizabeth, wife of John Rees, and "my kinsmen John Havard and Nathan Thomas."

Will of Margaret Thomas, of Merion, widow, marked 23 April, 1719, in presence of James John (marked), Griffith and Mary Llewellyn, names son Owen Thomas, (and his children, William and Hester), daughter Katherine, wife of Robert Pearson, (and their children, Thomas and Mary), and "grandson John, son of James Thomas, and his uncle Nathan Thomas."

Will of Edward Thomas, of Merion, signed 21 Dec. 1729, witnessed by Robert Jones, Hugh Evans, John Bowen, and Owen Roberts (marked). Proved 26 March, 1733, by Thomas Thomas, his son. Other children, Evan, Elizabeth, and Margaret Thomas. Legacy "to the Grave Yard at Merion Meeting." Overseers, Hugh Evans, Robert Roberts, Jonathan Jones, and Robert Jones.

Will of John Thomas Thomas, of Merion, yeoman, marked 25 May, 1721, witnesses Henry Lewis, Jenkin David, Llewellyn (marked), and Evan David. Proved 16 Sep. 1723. Names Margaret, wife of James Mortimer, nephews Thomas Edwards, Morris Thomas, and John Thomas. Cousin Benjamin Humphreys, of Merion, to be executor.

[173]

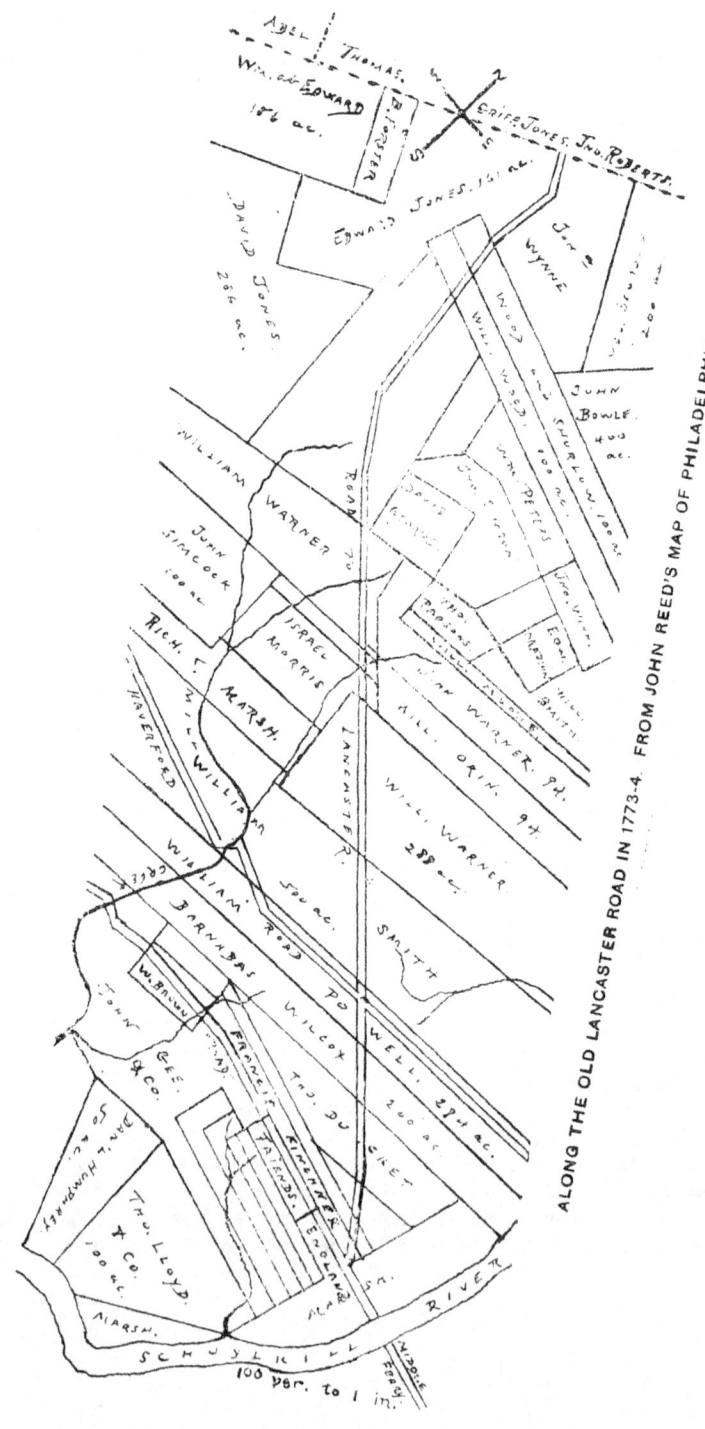

JOHN & WYNNE'S LAND PATENT

Company No. 4. The grantees under the patent, dated 14. 7mo. 1681, for 5,000 acres, issued to John ap John, the founder, probably of the Welsh Tract idea and indirectly of the Merion Meeting, and Dr. Wynne, were Denbighshire people, and in part, as follows: It seems that each of these "trustees," John and Thomas, took 2,500 acres of their joint purchase to keep, or to sell, as they thought best.

John ap John, according to a memorandum, in his own writing, says:

"Here is An Account of what I John ap John have sould out of my part of this deed and what remains still in my hands. First, I paid William Penn, by ye hands of Richard Davies and his sonn David Davies, ye sum of Fifty pounds Stl., and for which I have their recets, and I have disposed of ye land as followeth:—

"To Thomas Taylor I sold .... 500 acres
"To John Roberts I sold 500   "
"To Treial Reider I sold 400   "
"To Mary Fouk I sold 200   "
"To Richard Davies 250   "
"To Owen Parry 150   "
"reserved for myself 500   "

"Be it remembered also yt I rebought from Trial Reder aforsd 400 acres.

"So wt remains for me unsold is 900 acres."

But Dr. Wynne left no memorandum of the disposition of his share, but he soon got rid of it.

Some of John ap John's land seems to have passed to the following:

WELSH SETTLEMENT OF PENSYLVANIA

Howel and Philip James, of Philadelphia.

Isaac Wheeldon, of Llanroost, Denbighshire, a glover. His is a very long deed, dated 20 Mar. 1681, for "1 2-30 part, or share of 5,000 acres of land." He assigned his rights, 13. 10. 1695, to Samuel Lewis, of Darby, whose son Samuel, Jr., inherited it.

"Lucien Sixsinth," bought 200 acres.

Owen ffoulke, of Bettws y Coed, Caernarvonshire, a tanner.

Mary Southworth (ffouk?) was also a purchaser from John ap John of 200 acres. Afterwards, she married Henry Molineaux, and the right to this land was sold to John Parker, of Philadelphia, with her right for 300 acres more of her land, bought from Dr. Wynne, for all of which Parker had deeds and warrants, which were accidentally destroyed by fire and he could not locate the purchases.

The dates of the various deeds conveying these lands by John ap John, were, between the first one of 25. 5mo. 1681, and 7. 5mo. 1682.

By deed dated 20. 7mo. 1691, John ap John sold his remainder of 900 acres to Hugh Roberts, of Merion, who had 200 acres of the purchase laid out in Merion, which he sold to Robert Owen, and Robert, by deed of 30. 3mo. 1696, conveyed 100 acres of same to Daniel Thomas, of Merion, and after Robert's decease, 100 acres to Thomas Rees, by deed of 27. 7mo. 1700.

John ap John further sold, of this balance, 482 acres, laid out in Goshen and had about 200 acres left, for which a warrant was issued to him.

"Tryall Rider," never came to Pensylvania. In 1695, with John ap John, he attended a meeting at Tregaron, in Radnorshire. He was a flax dresser, at Wrexham, in Denbighshire.

These further items as to the disposition of the lands of John & Wynne are also of interest.

COMPANY NUMBER FOUR

"Owen Pusey," or "Owen Parry, of Dynullo, Issa, Denbigh, yeoman," named as a purchaser from him by John ap John. It was claimed to the Land Commissioners that he bought 150 acres, by deed dated 17. 5mo. 1682, "of John ap John and Jon (sic) Wynne," and it was wished to have same located. No deed, however, could be produced, and said Owen was then dead, yet it appeared that his son had sold the right to this land in 1707, to Owen Roberts, whose executor sold it to John Walter. Jonathan Wynne confirmed this sale, 23 March, 1727. Owen Roberts, and his wife Ann, had certificate from the "Harford," i. e. Haverford Monthly Meeting, "held at Merion," addressed to the Philadelphia Monthly Meeting, dated 9. 12mo. 1709-10.

After John & Wynne's purchasers were put into possession of their lands, scattered in the townships of Merion, Haverford, Radnor, Goshen, New Town, Middletown, and in the Great Valley, it was discovered by Jonathan Wynne that 100 acres of their joint transactions were not accounted for. Their land operations were complicated.

When Jonathan Wynne made his application, elsewhere mentioned, and was granted 400 acres on his father's own account, in the "Great Valley," or Chester Valley, it was on condition that he surrender the right to those 100 acres, if such an amount was needed to make up the full acreage of any of John & Wynne's sales to original purchasers; he had to surrender these 100 acres subsequently to one James Steel, who also bought from Jonathan another 100 acres in the Great Valley, paying him £15. 10, and on 14. 7mo. 1736, the Commissioners issued patent to said Steel for 200 acres, as "in old right of John & Wynne."

"Richard Davis," or Davies, had his 250 acres (less 5 acres of Liberty land) laid out in Goshen tp., adjoining the land of Griffith Owen, who subsequently bought it. He had also 312½ acres, laid out "above Newton" (in Chester Co.), which he sold to David Evan, who had bought of "Howel James and son" 232 acres, also "out of the John & Wynne

WELSH SETTLEMENT OF PENSYLVANIA

tract," and two lots of 150 acres and 50 acres from William Davies, also of same tract, and supposed he had 744½ acres altogether, but these tracts, upon resurveys, after he had paid for 20 acres over-plus, on an earlier survey, came out only 662½ acres.

Richard Orme (or Orms), who owned 150 acres in the "Letitia Penn Tract," in Goshen tp., above Merion, bought 150 acres in Radnor tp., of "the John & Wynne land," which Jonathan Wynne gave him a deed for, 2. 4mo. 1704. Richard Orme also bought 125 acres of the land in the Welsh Tract, from "Humphrey Bettally," or Bettly, who had 250 acres from John & Wynne, (Jonathan Wynne bought the other 125 acres), and sold the same to "Jonathan Height." It seems that Orme had "located" this land, but someone else also got hold of the same land, for when the Height heirs, (Richard Maris and Elizabeth, his wife, and Evan Lewis, and wife Mary), wanted to sell the land it could not be found. Thereupon, on petition, in 2mo. 1720, the Commissioners granted 120 acres to Lewis Lewis, of Chester Co., to be "located back in the country," and was laid out near New Town.

Thomas Taylor's (he was a resident of Denbighshire), land, 500 acres, which he acquired by deed of 8. 1mo. 1683, was laid out to him in Middletown, Chester Co., next to land of Richard Crosby. His ten acres bonus in the Liberties he sold to William Edwards. Thomas Taylor, Jr., inherited the Chester Co. tract.

The John Roberts, of "Pennyckland," Penytklawe, or Pen y Clwyd, in Denbighshire, yeoman and millwright, to whom John ap John states he sold, for ten pounds, 500 acres, by deed dated 7. 5mo. 1682, when he came to Pensylvania, was known as "John Roberts, the miller," and "of the Wayne Mill," in Merion, where he had a grist mill.

This deed was recorded at Philadelphia 11mo. 16. 1683-4, the grantors being "John ap John, of Ruaben parish, Denbigh, yeoman, and Thomas Gynn, of Cairwis, Flint, Chirurgeon," Dr. Wynne's signature was witnessed by Richard Davis, Tryall Ryder, Richard Orms, and Mary Southworth, and John's by Richard Davis, and ———— Rogers. The deed recites that the 500 acres conveyed was a part of 5,000 acres purchased from William Penn, and that John ap John and "Thomas Gynn" were co-trustees, and only contributed some part of the £100 to pay for the 5,000 acres, or, quoting the deed, "though the sd John ap John and Thomas Gynn were entitled to take up ye sd conveyances of all ye sd 5,000 acres, yet they onely intended to have their separate shares and proportion of the sd 5,000 acres according to the sume they laid out as part of ye sd 100 pds, and are onely trustees as to ye rest of ye sd 5,000 acres," and that "the said John Roberts hath contributed some part of the said £100 consideracon money towards the purchase of the sd 5,000 acres, that is to say, the sd John Roberts hath laid out Tenn Pounds." This clause in Penn's, and his "first purchasers"'s deeds, was the cause of considerable misunderstanding subsequently, when first purchasers asked to have bonus lands conveyed to them, because it defined them as only "trustees," as may be seen hereafter.

Of his 500 acres, which lay along the "Mill Creek Road" (and ten acres of liberty land he received as bonus, which lot he sold to William Edwards), he sold 100 acres, lying in the upper part of Merion, adjoining the land of Edward Griffith, to Thomas David. He retained two parcels of 250 acres and 140 acres, in the same locality, and these were laid out to him, 12. 2mo. 1685, and 12. 2mo. 1696. In 4mo. 1703, he had trouble with Martha Keite, or Kite, a neighbor, about division lines. The matter was laid before the Commissioners, who ordered a jury on the case, and a resurvey, and after all the miller lost his suit.

This John Roberts married here a few years after coming over, it is said, Elizabeth Owen, a niece of Owen Humphreys (ap Hugh), of Llwyn du, in Merionethshire, and it has been printed that he was then 60 years old, and the bride was only 16. His will, signed 18. 12mo. 1703-4, witnessed by James Thomas, Nathan Thomas and John Roberts, Jr., was proved at Philadelphia 13 March following. He names sons John and Matthew Roberts, and daughter Rebecca; nephews Robert, Joseph and Edward Roberts, brothers Edward and Matthew Roberts, and John Owen, his brother-in-law, to be executors, and appointed friends Thomas, John and Benjamin Humphrey, and brother-in-law Joshua Owen,* overseers of his will.

"John Roberts, of the Mill," who was buried at the Merion Meeting House, 27. 2mo. 1721, was his son. His will, "John Roberts, of Merion, wheelwright," was signed 22. 2. 1721, witnesses, John Vaughan, Owen Roberts (marked), and Robert Jones, was proved by his relict, (who was "possibly with child"), Hannah, 17 May, 1721, names aunt Ann Roberts, cousin Robert Roberts and sister Rebecca, overseers, brothers Matthew and Joseph, and step-father, Hugh Evans, and Robert Jones. It has been printed, but without proof, that the "John Roberts, of Merion, miller," who was hung, in Philadelphia, by the order of the President of Pensylvania, for being a traitor to apparently both the British and the Americans, was a grandson of the aforesaid immigrant, John Roberts. Owen Roberts, a blacksmith, of Merion, was of this family. His will, signed 23 July, 1732, witnessed by Joseph Humphrey, John Bowen, and Robert Jones, was proved 26 March, 1733. Names brothers Edward, Robert, Joseph, William, and John; cousin Ann Roberts, but no children; a legacy to the Merion Meeting. His brothers executors.

Ann Humphrey, sister to Owen Humphrey aforesaid, married Ellis Rees ap Lewis, of Bryn Mawr, and was the mother of Rowland Ellis, of "Bryn Mawr," Merion, 1686. Her

---

*Joshua Owen, of Llwyndu parish, Merioneth, bachelor, had certificate, dated 27. 5mo. 1683, from the Quarterly Mtg. at Dolyserry, which he filed with the Haverford (or Radnor) Mo. Mtg., signed by Robert, Humphrey, and Richard Owen, Griffith and Owen Lewis, Rowland Ellis, Humphrey Reinald, etc.

COMPANY NUMBER FOUR

brother Samuel Humphrey was the father of Daniel and Benjamin Humphrey, and three daughters.

JOHN AP JOHN, of Plas Ifa, in Ruabon parish, Denbighshire, as has already been told, did not come to Pensylvania, and died 16. 9mo. 1697, at Whitehough Manor, in Staffordshire, having long before disposed of all his Pensylvania lands.

THOMAS WYNNE (or Gynn, fair haired), was called a "practitioner of physick" in an early mention of him. Watson, in his "Annals of Philadelphia," states that "Dr. Wynne was an eminent Welsh physician," who had "practiced medicine several years with high reputation in London," and that his brother, also a physician, came over with him in 1682, but this brother is not clearly identified, unless he was the John Wynne, a lawyer in Sussex Co. (Del.), in 1687, or was the "John Wynn, chyrurgeon," whose will was proved at Annapolis, Md., in 1684. But the latter may have been the son, or of the family, of Thomas Wynn (son of Gruffydd Wynn, of Bryn yr Owen (ap Richard John Wynn), of Trefechan, near Wrexham, in Denbighshire, who was in Maryland as early as in 1671, and was a sub-sheriff, in 1678, and doorkeeper of the House of Assembly, of Maryland.

In a pamphlet issued by Dr. Wynne, in 8mo. 1679, replying to the attack, entitled "Work for a Cooper," by one William Jones, on his defense of the antiquity of the Quakers, who challenged the claim of Dr. Wynne having any knowledge of the practice of medicine and surgery, saying he was only a cooper by trade, and also "The Ale-Man, the Quack, and the Speaking Quaker," Dr. Wynne tells of his youth, and how he came to be called a physician and surgeon. He says, "my genius from a child had lead me to surgery, insomuch that before I was ten years old I several times overran my school and home when I heard of any one's being wounded, or hurt, and used all my endeavours then to set the fractures and dislocations reduced and wounds dressed."

[181]

WELSH SETTLEMENT OF PENSYLVANIA

He says his father died before he was eleven years old, (therefore, the Doctor could not have been identical with Thomas, baptised 1 Feb. 1636, who had a brother John, both living in 1665, when their father, William Wynne's, a son of Sir John Wynne, of Gwydis, Bart., will was proved, as has been suggested), and left his family poor, and "mother not being able to produce so great a sum as to set me to Chyrurgery, I betook myself to this honest and necessary calling he upbraids me with," referring to his having learned the occupation and trade of cooper. "Yet, during all this time (while a cooper's apprentice), I left no opportunity to inform myself in the practice of Chyrurgery, and continued this untill I became acquainted with an honest Friend and good Artist in Chyrurgery, whose name was Richard Moore, of Salop, who, seeing my forwardness to Chyrurgery, did further me in it, and brought me to Defecations in Salop, the Anatomists being men of known worth in practice, whose names are Dr. Needham and Dr. Hallins."

Continuing, he says, after he had learned enough and was able, with the assistance of Dr. Moore, "to set up a Skelliton of a man's bones," the afore-mentioned doctors "thought me fit to be licensed the practice of Chyrurgery, and this is near 20 years ago."

Shortly after being licensed to practice medicine and surgery, Dr. Wynne became too prominent in Quaker affairs, and was arrested and imprisoned for six years in Denbighshire, and when released, he continues: "I betook myself wholly to the practice of Chyrurgery," and says he became a remarkable expert "in the use of the Plaister Box and Salvatory, the Trafine and Head Saw, the Amputation Saw, and the Catling, the Cautery, Sirring and Catheter," . . . "to the great comfort of many, some of them desperately wounded by Gun Shots, others pierced thorow with Rapiers."

Coming over in the "Welcome" he must have been a busy doctor, as nearly all the passengers and the crew were taken ill with the smallpox, and thirty were buried at sea en route for Pensylvania. One of the passengers executed his will, signed 19 Sept. 1682, which was proved at Philadelphia, and with its germs, is preserved in the office of the Register of Wills. It was witnessed by Dr. Wynne, who sealed with a coat of arms, "gules; a three-turreted castle, argent," which arms were his own, but only in American fashion, by adoption, as they were the arms of the first husband of his third wife, Joshua Maud.

In connection with Dr. Wynne's professional life, we have from the minutes of the Quarterly Meeting of Merionethshire, Montgomeryshire, and Shropshire, which met "under the care of Charles Lloyd, Richard Davies, Thomas Lloyd, and Richard Moore," (familiar names in the Welsh Tract), at Dolobran, in 1668, that the said Richard Moore, of Shrewsbury, (who had been the instructor of Dr. Wynne), died in this year, leaving a son, Mordecai Moore, a minor and without money. For the love the Friends had for the lad's father, the Quarterly Meeting appointed a committee to learn what occupation would be suitable for him, and what he "had a taste for." The result was the committee found the "poor boy" had the desire to be a "chirurgeon Barber," so a collection was taken up at the Quarterly Meeting "to bind him as an apprentice to some reliable barber-surgeon." It was decided to send him as an apprentice for seven years to Thomas Wynne, of Caerwys, in Flintshire, and John ap John was instructed to see the arrangement was made, and the boy delivered to Mr. Wynne. Subsequently, this boy came to Maryland, and married Deborah, a daughter of Gov. Thomas Lloyd, of Pensylvania.

From this minute, we learn that Thomas Wynne, in 1668, was a barber-surgeon, or a barber who practiced surgery, and cupping and bleeding, with some knowledge of the use and effect of herbs, and from his own statement, that he never acquired the degree of M.D. from a university.

WELSH SETTLEMENT OF PENSYLVANIA

The place of the birth of Dr. Wynne, and his parentage is unknown, though it may possibly have been in Flintshire, where he resided, in 1682, at Bronvadog, near Caerwys.* The minutes of the Merion Preparative Meeting 5. 11mo. 1704, record that Dr. Edward Jones filed an account of Dr. Wynne, his parentage, home life, conversion, etc., but it has disappeared, otherwise we could know more of him. Dr. Wynne was probably one of John ap John's earliest converts to Quakerism, about 165—, and became himself an accepted minister among the Welsh Friends. He published in 1677, when living at "Caerwys," near the palace of the Lord Bishop, a pamphlet, "The Antiquity of the Quakers," defending Friends' teachings.

The full titles of this pamphlet, and that containing the abusive attack on it, both extant, are quaint, and of the manner of the time:— *The Antiquity of the Quakers, Proved out of the Scriptures of Truth. Published in Love to the Papists, Protestants, Presbyterians, Independents, and Anabaptists. With a Salutation of Pure Love to All the Tenderhearted Welshmen. But more especially to Flintshire, Denbighshire, Caernarvonshire, and Anglesea. By their Countryman and Friend, Thomas Wynne.* Part of it is in Welsh, and "your real friend, Thomas Wynne," wrote it at "Carwys y mis yr ail dydd 1677."

The title of Mr. Jones' effusion:— *Work for a Cooper. Being an Answer to a Libel written by Tho Wynne the Coop-*

---

*If it is any suggestion as to the Doctor's ancestry, his son Jonathan named his seat in Blockley, "Wynnstay," or "Wynnestay," (*i.e.*, Wynne's Field), and there was an estate by this designation near Ruabon and Wrexham, in Denbighshire, in the Doctor's time, in which vicinity he resided prior to removal to Pensylvania. The late Howard Williams Lloyd had the parish Registers, and all the Wynne wills in Flintshire, that would possibly give a clue to the Doctor's ancestry, examined, but got only the information that at that period Wynne, sometimes Gwin, was a common name in North Wales. The most prominent family of the surname was that of Gwydir House, of which there is a printed history, and it was to this family that "Wynnstay" belonged.

COMPANY NUMBER FOUR

er, the Ale-Man, the Quack, and the Speaking Quaker. With a brief Account how that Dissembling People differ at this Day from what at first they were. By one who abundantly pities their Ignorance and Folly.. London. Printed by J. C. for S. C., at the Prince of Wales Arms near the Royal Exchange. MDCLXXIX. The writer thought the Doctor "is ignorant in his very trade of Quack * * * Chyrurgery," and that "he's much fitter to mind his Ax and saw, the Joynter, and the Adz, the Crisle, and the Head knife, the Spoak & the Round Shreve, the Dowling, and the Tapir Bitts, the Tap and Bungbore." This brought out a reply from the Doctor entitled:— *An Anti-Christian Conspiracy Detected, and Satan's Champion Defeated.*

In 1682, he and Charles Lloyd (Co. No. 2), and Richard Davies, (Co. No. 7), who were subsequently also grantees, and "trustees" for large tracts of Pensylvania land, went to Whitehall, London, to see the Secretary of State, and intercede for the Friends of Bristol, who were being badly treated, and received a "fair promise." They themselves had known what it was to "suffer." Joseph Besse, in his book of "The Sufferings of the People Called Quakers," tells that Nathaniel Buttall, Bryan Sixsmith (draper), and Thomas Gwin, and others, "being met together in their own hired house at Wrexham [were] taken to the Common Goal at Writhen," in Dec. 1661. And at another time, when Thomas Wynn and 23 others "were on their way to the Meeting House at White Hart Court, [in London], they were arrested in Angel Court, and sent to prison." On 8. 10mo. they were tried at Guildhall, charged with "being guilty of a riotous assembly, with force and arms," in White Hart Court. All pleaded not guilty, as they had not yet been in White Hart Court, and were only passing through Angel Court. However, as both places were in the same ward, and a woman had preached in the street, they were all confined in Newgate till they raised the money to pay the fines.

WELSH SETTLEMENT OF PENSYLVANIA

He joined the Welshmen who went to London, in May, 1681, to interview William Penn about his Pensylvania lands, and becoming interested himself, became a co-trustee, as said, with John ap John, for 5,000 acres, and from this time he was an intimate of the Proprietary for several years, and came over with him on the ship "Welcome," which sailed 30. 6mo. 1682, and arrived here in the 8mo. following, which was a memorable voyage for many reasons. There were upwards of 100 Quaker immigrants from Penn's home county, Sussex, on the ship.

As to this voyage of ship "Welcome," the *London Gazette*, (No. 1752), in the issue of 31 Aug.—4 Sept. 1682, printed this dispatch:— "Deal. Aug. 30th. [1682]. There are now in the downs, outward bound, two or three merchantships for Pensylvania." And, in issue of 4 Sept.—7 Sept. 1682.— "Deal, Sept. 2d. Two days since sailed out of the downs three ships bound for Pensilvania, on board of which was Mr. Pen, with a great many Quakers, who go to settle there."

Here is an extract from a fictitious letter addressed to John Higginson, written in Oct. 1682, it was said, by the reputedly pious, Rev. Dr. Cotton Mather, of Boston: "There is now at sea a shipp (for our friend Elias Holcroft, of London, did advise me by the last packet that it would leave some time in August), called the Welcome, which has aboard it a hundred or more of the hereticks and malignants called Quakers, with William Penn, the scamp, at the head of them. The General Court has accordingly given instructions to Master Michael Haxett, of the brig Porpoise, to waylay said Welcome as near the end of Cod [Cape Cod, Mass.], as may be, and make capture of Penn and his ungodly crew, so that the Lord may be glorified and not mocked on the soil of this new country with the heathen worshipps of these people. Much spoil may be made by selling the whole lot to Barbadoes, where slaves fetch good prices in rumme and sugar." Signed: "Yours in the bonds of Christ, Cotton Mather."

COMPANY NUMBER FOUR

This alleged "extract" created considerable of a sensation when it was started on the rounds of the newspapers. It was thought it would not have been beneath this devine to take such a fling at the Quakers, therefore the letter, which was addressed to Rev. Mr. Higginson, "at New Port," (Rhode Island), was believed to be genuine. But, after investigators failed to see, or locate such a letter, and on making the discovery that Mr. Higginson was not then living at Newport, but was then established as the minister at Salem, Mass., and knowing that Mather was then only 19 years old, the story of the attempt to kidnap Mr. Penn was pronounced a fake, when several people had the assurance to come forward and each claim, for the fame there was in it, to have been the perpetrator of the "joke on the historians."

It may be presumed that Dr. Wynne passed his first winter here with Penn, at Upland and at New Castle, looking after the small-pox patients, and accompanied him to New York and to Baltimore, on business trips, taking as many of the germs along as possible.

He was chosen by Penn as a member, and his representative possibly, in the first preliminary assembly of delegates from the settlements on the Delaware and Schuylkill, held at Upland, 4. 10mo. 1682, and was appointed a member of the committee to "petition" Penn for a constitution for his Province. And when the first organized Assembly was held in Philadelphia 12. 1mo. 1682-3, he was chosen one of the members to represent Philadelphia Co. in it, possibly by the Welsh, and was selected speaker at the first meeting.

He was present at the first Monthly Meeting of Friends, held in Philadelphia, on 9. 11mo. 1682-3, and was appointed of the committee to select and secure the site for the Philadelphia Meeting House, in Second street, and was a member of the building committee.

It is claimed that his brick dwelling in the west side of Front Street, above Chestnut Street, was the first brick house erected in the town. The street now called Chestnut was originally called Wynne.

In the 6mo. of 1684, he went to England on a business matter, probably with William Penn, in the ketch "Endeavour," sailing from Philadelphia 12. 6mo. 1684, and, on his return, went to Lewes to reside, which then was a more desirable place than Philadelphia for a residence. Here he became a justice of Sussex County, in 3mo. 1687, and a representative of that county in the Assembly, 3mo. 1688.

He died while attending a meeting of the Assembly, in Philadelphia, on 16. 1mo. 1692, and was buried the next day in the Friends' ground, Philadelphia. His will, dated 16. 1mo. 1691-2, was proved at Philadelphia 20. 2mo. 1692, the overseers named being Thomas Lloyd, the Dep. Gov., and Dr. Griffith Owen, the Provincial Councillor. He named his wife, Elizabeth, his brother-in-law, Samuel Buttall, (to whom he owed £25), and his children as below. The only land he mentioned was what he owned at Lewes, valued at £80, which went to his wife and then to son Jonathan, to whom he also gave 200 acres on Cedar Creek, Sussex Co., valued at £20. His personalty amounted to £430. 1. 3., including 3 negroes, valued at £60, and one "servant."

According to the Minutes of the Provincial Council, 6 Oct. 1693, Charles Pickering (who had been convicted of passing counterfeit money in Philadelphia, by the first Court, see Minute of 28. 8. 1683), "in behalf of the widdow Wynne, having preferred a pe'tion to the Leivt. Governor and Council, setting forth that her Husband, Thomas Wynne, Late of Sussex Countie, deceased, had been Sumoned to the Court of New Castle, to ans'r the Complaint of Adam Short and others. But falling sick, dyed 3 or 4 hours befor Judgm't past ag't him, att the said Court, and that the originall proces ag't her husband was by a wrong name, and therefore requested that the execu'on be stopt, and that the pe'tionr have a fair tryall." The clerk's record of the New Castle Court being produced, and it was found the petitioner's husband's name

COMPANY NUMBER FOUR

was written "Thomas Guin." The Council ordered the matter before the next Provincial Court to be held for Sussex Co., and that in the meantime execution be suspended.

Dr. Thomas Wynne* was married three times. He married first, possibly at Wrexham, Denbighshire, Martha Buttall, about 1655-57, by Morgan Lloyd, who sent John ap John to "try out" Fox's teaching. She was the sister of Jonathan Buttall, sugar baker, of the Surry side of the Thames, and was named, with her brother Samuel, in his will, signed 26 Aug. 1695. Her issue was to be his heirs on failure of his own. She died about 1670, and is presumed to have been the mother of all of Dr. Wynne's children.

Dr. Wynne married secondly, a widow named Rowden, who by her first husband was the mother of Elizabeth, who m. in Philadelphia Monthly Meeting, 5. 6mo. 1684, John Brock, of Philadelphia. She died in 1675-6.

Dr. Wynne married thirdly, 20. 5mo. 1676 (record of Monthly Meeting of Hardshaw East, in Lancashire), Elizabeth Parr, widow of Joshua Maud, who survived him. When he married her, who came to Pensylvania with him, he was living at Caerwys, Flintshire. Her daughter, Margery Maud, married at Lewes, Thomas Fisher, *a quibus* Fisher family of Philadelphia.

He married Elizabeth Maud, or Mode, of Rainhill, Lancashire, at the dwelling of John Chorley, and among the signers of their certificates were John and Alice Barnes; Bruen, William, and Ester Sixmith; Samuel, Alice, and Margaret Dunbabin; John, Alice, and Mary Southworth.

But his wife, Elizabeth, did not come in the same ship with the Doctor. According to the extant log, 6. 7mo. to 21. 8mo. 1682, of the "Submission," one of the vessels which sailed with the "Welcome," she was a passenger on that ship, and was accompanied by her daughters, Jane and Margery, whose surnames appears as "Mode," and the Doctor's daughter, Rebecca Wynne.

---

*See further as to Dr. Wynne, in the *Philadelphia Friend*, vol. XXVII, p. 228.

WELSH SETTLEMENT OF PENSYLVANIA

By deed of 3. 3mo. 1688, Dr. Wynne bought for his wife, an island in "the Broad Kill Marshes," in the Schuylkill, near its mouth. After his death, his relict, by deed of gift dated 1. 12mo. 1693, conveyed this island, which, on survey of 5mo. 1701, contained 175 acres, to her daughter, Margery, and husband, Thomas Fisher, and then it became known as Fisher's Island, but subsequently was called Province Island, and was the location of hospitals.

Of the children of Dr. Wynne* by his first wife,

Jonathan Wynne, only son and heir. It is not known when, nor where he was born, nor how old he was when he came to Pensylvania, and it is only presumed he was the youngest child, and that he came with his father, either on his first trip in the "Welcome," or his subsequent trip.

We have seen that Jonathan was to receive, after his stepmother's death, the homestead near the town of Lewes, and 200 acres on Cedar Creek, in Sussex Co., (Del.). After his father's death, he began investigating both the land transactions of "John & Wynne," and his father's personal operations in the Welsh Tract.

He made it out that only 1,850 acres of the 2,500 acres of his father's land had been located and sold by him, and that

---

*These are some of the many present-day descendants of Dr. Thomas Wynne:

Mrs. Stevenson Crothers. Mrs. Thomas Stewardson.
Mrs. Henry Kuhl Dillard. Frank Foulke.
Mrs. Henry B. Robb. Abraham L. Smith.
Mrs. Charles F. Hulse. Benj. Hayes Smith.
Miss Elizabeth Moser Jones. Joseph A. Steinmetz.
Mrs. Jawood Lukens. Charles Williams.
Mrs. Arthur V. Meigs. J. Randall Williams.
Mrs. Charles Richardson. Rodman Wister.
Mrs. George B. Roberts. Alexander W. Wister.
Mrs. S. Bowman Wheeler. Miss Martha Morris Brown.
Mrs. Howard Comfort. Mrs. Robert R. Corson.
William Penn Humphreys. Mary Hollingsworth Stewardson.

All of the descendants of John Cadwalader, 1677-1734, are descendants of Dr. Wynne:

COMPANY NUMBER FOUR

there was thus 650 acres due him, besides 50 acres of the Liberty lands, as bonus; this besides the 100 acres due on the joint account, mentioned above. He went before the Land Commissioners, Edward Shippen, Griffith Owen and James Logan, 18. 4mo. 1705, and presented his claim, as he understood it.

The decision of the Commission as to the 100 acres was made as above, and from the Surveyor General's office it found that 2,125 acres of Dr. Wynne's 2,500 acres could be accounted for. That is, he had sold to Thomas Taylor 500 acres, to John Bevan 300 acres, to Richard Orme 150 acres, to Humphrey Bettly 125 acres, to Richard Crosby 500 acres, and to Cary Southworth 300 acres, and had retained for himself 250 acres in Radnor. The Commission also found some evidence that the Doctor had sold some land to Roger Andrews and to Trial Rider, but not the amount.

Of the Doctor's 250 acres, in Radnor, the Commission learned that it was confirmed to him by patent, dated 29. 5mo. 1684, and that, of this land, he had sold 200 acres to Howel James, of Radnor, by deed of 9. 10mo. 1687 (who sold 100 acres out of the tract to David Evan, and 100 acres to his son, William James, who also sold to David Evan, by deed, dated 26. 11mo. 1689), and had conveyed the balance, 50 acres, to Hugh Williams.

The Commissioners decided to throw out the possible sales to Andrews and Rider, after investigating for two years, and in 7mo. 1707, and granted a warrant to Jonathan for 400 acres even, which he was authorized to lay out in the Welsh Tract if possible, that is, if he could find so much untaken land therein. "The Commission considered that Dr. Wynne's son had all, and more, that was coming to him from his father's grant," was its recorded opinion. This land, 400 acres, was finally laid out in the Chester Valley.

As to the 50 acres of Liberty land, claimed due by Jonathan to complete his father's purchase, the Commission found out that his brother-in-law, Dr. Edward Jones, of Merion, had acquired, in some way not revealed, 10 acres of it, so a warrant for 40 acres only of this choice land was given him, which was laid out to him in the Liberty lands, or Blockley tp., southeast of the present settlement of Bala, just without the township of Merion. Here Jonathan erected a stone house, which he named "Wynnestay," after the Welsh seat mentioned, or, as is also said, "Wynne Stay," for he proposed to stay here till he died, which he did. The property remained in the possession of this Wynne family till after the close of the Revolutionary War. Since that time it has passed through the hands of several owners, and several years ago was completely "remodelled." In September, 1910, it was leased for Miss Hannah Smedley to Mr. Alvin Ehret.

Jonathan also was granted a lot, 60 by 300 feet, in High (Market) street, in the city, due also on account of his father. This he devised to two of his daughters, Hannah and Mary, to be equally divided between them. He devised to his other three daughters, minors, 400 acres in The Great Valley, "Great Meadows," or Chester Valley, where he had also acquired by purchase 500 acres which he divided between his sons, Thomas and John.

The will of "Jonathan Wynne, of Blockley, yeoman," dated 29 Jan. 1719, was proved 17 May, 1721, by his wife, Sarah. Overseers appointed, "brother-in-law Edward Jones and Daniel Humphreys"; if they died before him, then John Cadwalader and Jon. Jones. The witnesses were Rowland Ellis, Thomas Jones, and Edward Jones. He was buried at the Merion Meeting House, 28. 12mo. (Feb.) 1720-1. His widow, Sarah, was also buried here, 27. 2mo. 1744. He had by his wife, Sarah, whose surname has not been preserved, (unless it was Graves, or Greave, as there is reason to believe), married possibly at Lewes, about 1700-1, eight children mentioned in his will, and a son James, who was buried at the Merion Meeting House, 24. 8mo. 1714, namely, Thomas, his heir, who was to have the homestead (near Bala) after his mother's death, John, Jonathan, Hannah, Mary, Sidney, Martha and Elizabeth.

COMPANY NUMBER FOUR

Mary Wynne, who *m*. Dr. Edward Jones, of Merion. *Issue*.

Rebecca Wynne, who *m*. first, at the Third Haven Friends' Meeting, in Talbot Co., Md., in 3mo. 1685, Solomon Thomas who *d. s. p.*. She *m*. secondly, 23. 7mo. 1692, John Dickinson, of Talbot Co., an uncle of Samuel Dickinson, son-in-law of John Cadwalader.

Sidney Wynne, who *m*. in Anne Arundel Co., Md., 20. 10mo. 1690, William Chew, son of Samuel Chew, of this county.

Hannah Wynne, who *m*. at the Merion Meeting, 25. 8mo. 1695, Daniel Humphreys, son of Samuel and Elizabeth Humphreys, of Merion.

Tibitha Wynne, who never came over here, but died in England, after 1692.

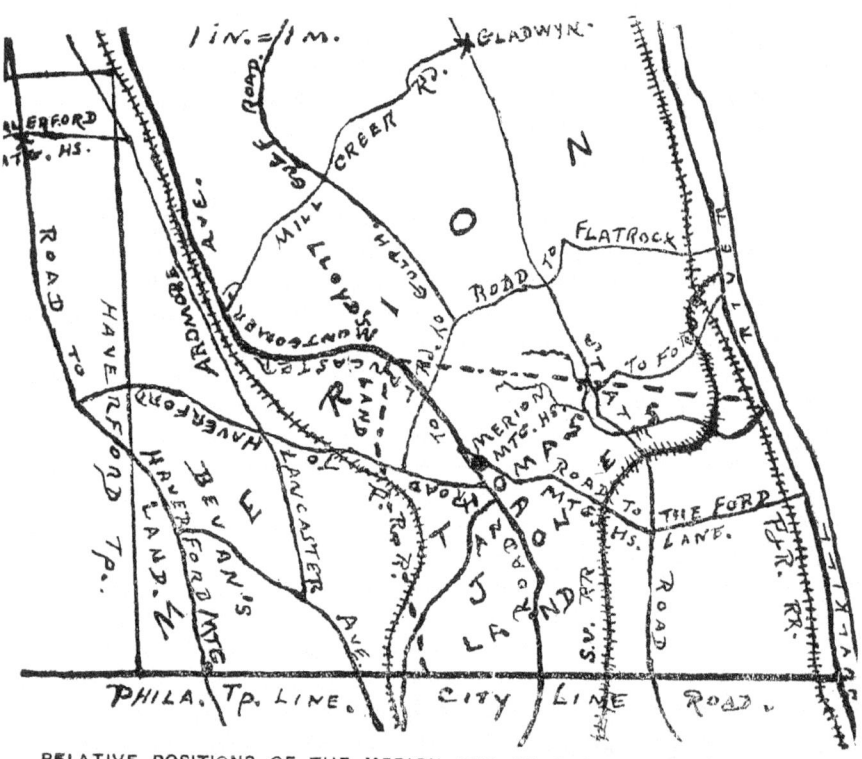

RELATIVE POSITIONS OF THE MERION AND HAVERFORD MEETING HOUSES, AND THE THOMAS AND JONES LAND.

LEWIS DAVID'S LAND PATENT

Company No. 5. The 3,000 acres of land subscribed for by "Lewis David, husbandman, of Llandewy Velfry," in Pembrokeshire, and conveyed to him by deeds, dated 2 March, 1681, for which he paid £60, were taken, under deeds, dated in May, 1682, by the following:

William Howell, Castlebigch, Pembroke, yeoman, 500 acres.

Henry Lewis, Narbeth, Pembroke, yeoman, 1,000 acres.

Rees Rothers (Rotheroe), Lanwenog, Cardigan, yeoman, 500 acres.

Evan Thomas, Lanykeaven, Pembroke, yeoman, 250 acres.

Lewis David retained 750 acres for himself. (24 Oct. 1681.)

His deed from Penn was similar to those of the other "adventurers for land;"—land was to be set out "as provided for in the Concessions, or Constitucons, bearing date of 11th July last past," 1681, "to be holden in free and common socage of him, the said William Penn, as of the signory of Windsore," etc. His deeds to his sundry purchasers, or co-partners, were also, as those of the other adventurers, very explicit as to the tenure, citing the grant of King Charles to Penn, and the latter to Lewis David. In these, he was described as "gentleman." Lewis David was buried at the Merion Meeting, 2. 1mo. 1707-8.

On 16. 12mo. 1701, the following, being grantees, "in the right of Lewis David," of the original company, had their purchases resurveyed and confirmed to them:

Henry Thomas, 400 acres, and 180 acres, in Haverford tp.
John Lewis, Sen., 350 acres in Haverford tp.
John Lewis, Jr., 100 acres in Haverford tp.
Richard Hayes, 260 acres in Haverford tp.

John David Thomas, 210 acres in "Duffein Mawr" tp.
Maurice Llewellyn, 420 acres in Haverford.
David Rees, 260 acres in Haverford.
David Hugh, 220 acres in Haverford.
Nathan Thomas, 81 acres in Haverford, and "100 acres in the upper end of the Welsh Tract."

These further details of Lewis David's purchase are from the "Welsh Minutes" of the Commissioners of Pensylvania land.

He took for himself 750 acres, but by deed of 10 May, 1682, he sold 250 to "Maurice Skurfield," or "Scourfield," who by deed 22 April, 1699, sold the same to Owen Thomas, who by deed, 15. 11mo. 1701, sold same to Ralph Lewis.

William Howel, had deed, dated 10 May, 1682, witnessed by Daniel Humphrey, Rees Henten, and Humphrey Ellis, for 500 acres, which he had laid out in Haverford tp. and Marple tp. He sold 200 acres in Marple to Jonathan Hayes, and by deed of 29. 3. 1697, sold 220 acres in Haverford, to David Hugh. On his own right, and on account of Evan Thomas, whose widow he married, he had 15 acres of the Liberty land, in 1702. Howel sold his 10 acres Liberty land to Benj. Chambers.

Henry Lewis bought by deed, dated 10 May, 1682, 1,000 acres, for which he paid £25. Witnessed by the above witnesses, and William Howell. Part of the tract was laid out in Haverford. His 20 acres of Liberty land, or bonus, he sold to John Ball. He sold, by deed of 6. 12mo. 1684, 250 acres in Haverford to John Lewis, who also had 100 acres, bought of William Rowe, who had same from Thomas Ellis, in Haverford. His son, Henry Lewis, Jr., by deed, 8. 1mo. 1694-5, conveyed 100 acres to John Lewis, Jr. Henry, Jr., also conveyed by deed of 12. 1mo. 1694-5, to Richard Hayes, Sr., 50 acres, who had 50 acres, bought of William Howel, and 160 acres from John Burge.*

---

*Filed with the Haverford (or Radnor) Mo. Mtg. about 1684-5, is the certificate, undated, of "Allice Lewis, daughter of James Lewis,

COMPANY NUMBER FIVE

Henry Lewis, Jr., having right to 180 acres in the Welsh Tract, on his father's account, and 79 acres, bought of John Burge, had same laid out in the Great Valley. On resurvey, this 259 acres was found to be 352 acres, or allowing 25 acres, he had 248 acres there, 68 acres being over-plus. He also had 50 acres over-plus in Haverford, on his 400 acres. He bought the "overs."

Henry Lewis, is probably the best known of this company. He resided at "Maencoch," as he called his seat, or plantation, 250 acres in Haverford. He and his wife, Margaret, removed from Narberth, in Pembroke, in 1682. "As a member of the Religious Society of Friends, he was strict in the performances of his duties, and, during the short period in which he lived after reaching his new home, he devoted much of his time to civil affairs, and acts of benevolence." Before the establishment of the Haverford Monthly Meeting, in 1684, he belonged to the Monthly Meeting of Philadelphia, and was by that Meeting appointed one of a committee "to visit the poor and sick, and administer what they should judge convenient, at the expense of the Meeting." He held the office of "peace maker" for the county of Philadelphia, and was foreman of the first Grand Jury for that county. His will, signed 6. 14. 1688, witnessed by Lewis David, Griffith Owen, and Thomas Ellis, all well known gentlemen, was proved in Philadelphia on 8. 8. 1705.

He was a carpenter by trade, and owned a house and two lots in Philadelphia. He left his homestead to his wife, Margaret, and desired that, after her death, their sons, Henry Lewis, Jr., and Lewis Lewis, should have it. He provided for his son Samuel, and daughter Elizabeth, who married, in 3mo. 1697, Richard Hayes, Jr., of Haverford.

---

of Llardevy, Pembrokeshire," saying she "is clear from all men on ye acc't of Marriage." Signed by Alice, Margaret and Lewis Musgrave, Mary Morce, Mary Bowen, Mary and Henry Smith, Deborah Weston, Margaret and James Skone, Henry and Jone Hilling, Letice Pardo, James, Mary, and James Lewis, Jr., Anthony Tounson, Thomas Marchant, William Garret, John Perrot, and David Morgan.

His father, Richard Hays, Sr., mentioned above, made his will 4. 8mo. 1697, which was witnessed by William Jenkins, Adam Roades, William Howell, Henry and Samuel Lewis, and proved 30 Oct. 1697, leaving his estate to his wife Issat, and then after her decease to his son and heir, Richard Hayes, Jr. He gave legacies to his son John, and "cousin Sarah James," and to the Haverford Meeting. Trustees named: David Lawrence and Rowland Powell. Richard and Isatt were "aged Friends," when they removed from Pembrokeshire, to Haverford, in 1687. Their son, Richard, Jr., resided on the farm first taken. "Having received a better education than was usual among the early emigrants, and being withal a man of excellent business qualifications, he was almost constantly kept in some public employment, yet he managed his pecuniary affairs to great profit and advantage." In company with David Morris and Samuel Lewis, Richard Hayes, Jr., erected, about 1707, a mill on Darby Creek, which for a long time was known as "Haverford New Mill," but now called Leedom's Mill. He conducted the mill at the time of his death, and for many years before, on his own account. He was a justice of the Courts of Chester Co., a member of the Assembly for seven years, and for years was one of the commissioners of the Loan Office. His children were Joseph, Mary, Hannah, Richard 3d and Benjamin.

The daughter Hannah Hayes *m.* at Haverford Meeting, 10. 8mo. 1727, James Jones, *b.* in Wales, 31. 3mo. 1699, a son of David and Katherine Jones, who came over in 1700, and settled on their purchase, 350 acres, in Blockley, bringing certificate from the Monthly Meeting at Hendri Mawr, dated 24. 12mo. 1699, signed by Robert Vaughan, Cadwalader Ellis, Evan Rees, Thomas Richards, Rowland Owen, Edward David, Owen Lewis, Thomas Cadwalader and John Robert, and a certificate from the Men's Meeting, in Haverford West, dated 4. 1mo. 1699-00. David Jones was one of the first that was appointed an Elder in the Haverford

COMPANY NUMBER FIVE

Meeting, "He conducted faithfull, and was approved of, in good esteem to his dying day, which was the 27. 6mo. 1725, and was buried at Merion." His wife, Katherine, appears from the minutes of the Haverford Monthly Meeting to have been called into active service in the Meeting almost immediately after arrival in this country.

Richard, Jr.'s son Benjamin Hayes, *m.* at the Merion Meeting, 2. 10mo. 1737, Mary, *b.* 14. 5mo. 1707, daughter of Jonathan Jones (son of Dr. Edward Jones, of Merion), and Gainor Owen, and had Elizabeth, *b.* 16. 7mo. 1738.

Evan Thomas, who bought by deed, witnessed by Hannah Hardiman, Mary Phillpin, and Henry Lewis, 10 May, 1682, 250 acres, died and left his rights to his children, Daniel Evan, or Evans, and Mary, and his widow, Mary, (who remarried William Howel), who sold it. By deed, 22 Aug. 1700, they sold 75 acres to Nathan Thomas, and 170 acres to John Bevan.

Rees Rothers, or Rytharch, Rutrach and Rotheroe, who bought for £10, by deed, dated 10. 3mo. 1682, witnessed by Samuel Rees, Tho. Ellis, David Lawrence, George Painter, John Humphrey and Morris Llewellyn, 500 acres in Haverford tp., sold 120 acres, by deed, dated 12. 10mo. 1692, to Thomas Rees. Next day, he transferred the same to William Lewis, who, by deed of gift, 6 Jan. 1700-1, gave the same, with 125 acres he had bought of John Bevan, to his son, David Lewis, who subsequently bought 100 acres from Morris Llewellyn, in Haverford. Rytharch also sold 100 acres to George Painter, and, by deed, 6. 8mo. 1695, he conveyed 30 acres to Maurice Llewellyn (who held 390 acres more in Merion, being part of his father's original 500 acres), bought by deed dated 20 Jan. 1681, (100 acres had been sold to David Lewis). The balance of Rytharch's land lay in Dyffrin Mawr tp., and of this, he sold 210 acres to John David Thomas.

Of Lewis David's balance of 500 acres, and 10 acres of liberty land, ("sold to B. Chambers"), he sold 260 acres

WELSH SETTLEMENT OF PENSYLVANIA

in Haverford to "Peregr. Musgrove," who by deed, 14 Nov. 1699, sold the same to Samuel Lewis, who by deed, 21 March, 1699-1700, sold same to David ap Rees (Prees, or Price), whose son, John Price, inherited it. (Burials at Merion Meeting, Gwenllen, wife of David Price, 6. 20. 1715, and Hannah, wife of David Price, 10. 13. 1727).

Lewis David also sold 30 acres in Haverford, by deed 28 Feb. 1691-2, to William Jenkins, (on account of 250 acres William Jenkins bought of John Poyer,—the Lewis David lands,—he had 5 acres of Liberty land in 1702), who by deed, 24. 6mo. 1698-9, conveyed the same to William Rowe, together with 30 acres he had from John Poyer, out of his 250 acre tract he bought of John & Wynne. William Rowe's executors, Rowland Ellis and Thomas Paschall, by deed of 8. 9mo. 1700, conveyed two lots of 30 acres each to Daniel Humphreys. The will of William Rowe, marked 8. 3mo. 1699, in the presence of John Roberts, Daniel Humphreys, and Lewis Waker, was proved 1 July, 1699. His wife, un-named, was living. He bequeathed his estate to his daughter, Grace Rowe, and legacies to the Haverford Meeting, to David Lawrence and Rowland Howell. Names guardians for daughter, John Lewis, David Maurice, and Henry Lewis.

By the usual deeds of lease and release, dated 24. and 25. Oct. 1681, William Penn conveyed to William Jenkin, or Jenkins, "a Friend who had suffered," of Tenby, in Pembroke, 1,000 acres of land. Of this grant, Jenkins conveyed 500 acres to Francis Howell, of Llancilio, in Caermarthen, by deed of 1 Sept. 1686, which tract was laid out to him in Duffryn Mawr, or Whiteland tp., in Chester Co. The balance of the grant was also located in Duffryn Mawr and laid out to Jenkins, who conveyed 250 acres of it, by deed of 30 Sep. 1686, to James Thomas. But when Jenkins removed to Pensylvania, about 1686, he settled on the 250 acres which he bought of John Poyer, 13 July, 1686, in Haverford. About 1698, William Jenkins removed into Abington tp., then in

COMPANY NUMBER FIVE

Philadelphia Co., and Jenkintown was named for him. In 1691, he was a justice in Chester Co., and in 1690 and 1695, a member of the Assembly. He died 7. 4mo. 1712, aged 54 years, having married, 2. 7mo. 1673, at Tenby, Elizabeth Lewis, died 14. 9mo. 1711, daughter of Lewis Griffith. The births of their four children are recorded at the South Wales Monthly Meeting. Of these, Margaret, *b.* 23. 3mo. 1674, *m.* at Haverford Meeting, 15. 9mo. 1692 (first wife), Thomas Paschall, Jr., of Chester Co., and had eleven children, *d.* 17. 11mo. 1728; and Stephen Jenkins, 1690-1761, *m.* at the Abington Meeting, 14. 9mo. 1704, Abigail, a minister among the Friends, who *d.* 2. 9mo. 1750, daughter of Phineas Pemberton, of Bucks Co., Pa., and had seven children.

Lewis David also sold, 5. 9mo. 1691, 10 acres, and 30. 3mo. 1700, a lot and grist mill, in Haverford tp., which he held with Humphrey Ellis, to William Howel.

Lewis David also held about 190 acres in Dyffrin Mawr tp.

Morris Llewellyn, of Haverford, mentioned above, bought by deed dated 1. 1. 1697-8, for £100, a tract of 500 acres, in Haverford, from the estate of Nathaniel Pennock, (who died 15. 10mo. 1697), the heir to George Collet, of Philadelphia, a glover, who had bequeathed this right, in 10mo. 1686, to Nathaniel, a minor. The said Nathaniel died unmarried, and his father, Christopher Pennock, administered his estate, and conveyed the right to the 500 acres to Llewellyn. This land was a portion of 5,000 acres Penn had sold, 14. 6mo. 1682, to Joshua Holland, of Chattam, Kent, mariner, whose son, John Holland, of same place, a shipwright, had power of attorney to sell 1,000 acres, and therefore sold 500 acres "on West side of river Schuylkil," for £25, by deed of 13. 3mo. 1685, to said George Collet.

The oldest land corner-stone extant, (discovered by Samuel M. Garrigues, surveyor, of Bryn Mawr, in 1889), is on the line of Hannah Llewellyn, to whom descended some of this land, and land of Haverford College, on the north side of Cobb's Creek. This stone, set up in 1683, probably by

Morris Llewellyn, as a deputy surveyor, approximates the date of ownership of land here by the Llewellyns, and marked the corner of the land of Thomas Ellis, on the south, David Llewellyn, on the west, and Morris Llewellyn, on the east, as on the east face of the stone is cut C—D M L, and on the west face C — M D L L — T E — 1683.

Morris Llewellyn's 420 acres in Haverford were surveyed to 490 acres, before 16. 12mo. 1701, when he requested of the Commissioners warrant for the usual bonus of 10 acres of the Liberty land, which was granted, and ordered surveyed to him.

Before the Land Commissioners, 27. 8mo. 1712, "Maurice Llewellyn" produced a deed from James Thomas, of Merion, conveying to him 100 acres in Merion, whereon the said James and his father had been seated. On official survey it was learned there were 137 acres in this place. But when his brother David Llewellyn, surveyed it, he found only 30 acres over, so Morris, taking benefit of all doubt, agreed to pay £15, "at the next Spring Fair of Philadelphia," for 27 acres. The chain of title for this land starts with Penn's sale to Davies, and his conveyance by deed, 10. 6mo. 1686, to one Steel, of Llancillis parish, in Caermarthanshire, and Ellis Ellis, of Haverford, for 410 acres in Merion,

Of this there were conveyed 10 acres to Thomas Ellis, 100 to Francis Howel, 100 to Morgan Davis, 100 to Francis Lloyd, and 100 to James Thomas, of Merion, who gave it to the said James Thomas, his son, (subsequently of Whitland tp., Chester Co.), who sold as above to Morris Llewellyn, of Haverford, by deed of 9 Feb. 1708-9.

Francis Howel devised his 100 acres, 15. 1mo. 1695, to his brother, Thomas Howell, who by deed dated 17 June, 1708, for five shillings and natural affection conveyed the land to the aforesaid Morris Llewellyn. The old farm house of the Llewellyns, called "Castle Br'th," is still standing.

The will of "Francis Howell, of Merion, yeoman," signed 15. 1. 1695, proved 25 Sep. 1696, names wife Margaret sole executrix, names brother Thomas Howell, and sisters Elizabeth, Margaret, Mary and Susan Howell. Legacy to James Mortimer. Witnesses, John Bevan, William Howell and John Humphreys.

The will of his wife, and relict, Margaret Howell, of Merion, was marked in the presence of Edward Jones, David Habard (or Havard), and John Humphreys, 12 Sep. 1696, and proved 25 Sep. following. She names brother James Mortimer, nephew James Mortimer, sister Margaret Thomas, cousin Betty Thomas, brothers-in-law David Jones and David (Haubot?), cousin James . . . . . . and legacies to Lewis David, John Hastings, Katherine Pris, her maid servant, "the residue of her time to be free," to Lewis Waker, to my negro, to John Simons, Nathan Thomas,* Owen Thomas, John, William, and Ann Habart (Habard), Elizabeth and Katherine Thomas, Betty and Margaret Lewis, David Pugh, Mary Waker, John Pris, Mary, wife of Benjamin Humphrey, and her son John Humphrey, Mary, wife of David Morris, and to John Humphrey, Sr., and Jr. Legacies also to the "Meeting Houses of Merion and Haverford." Executors, Morris Llewellyn and James Thomas, Jr.

1713, 22. 5mo., the Commissioners confirmed his land to Morris Llewellyn, amounting to three lots, 100, 130, and 400 acres—bought of Lewis David, gent.

---

*The will of "Nathan Thomas, of Merion, yeoman," signed 6. 2mo. 1710, witnesses, Thomas Howell and David Evan, was proved 4 Aug. 1711. He mentions his mother, Margaret Thomas, and "grandmother Thomas," brother Owen Thomas, sisters Katherine Pearson, and Elizabeth Thomas, cousins Thomas and Mary Pearson, and John and Nathan Thomas.

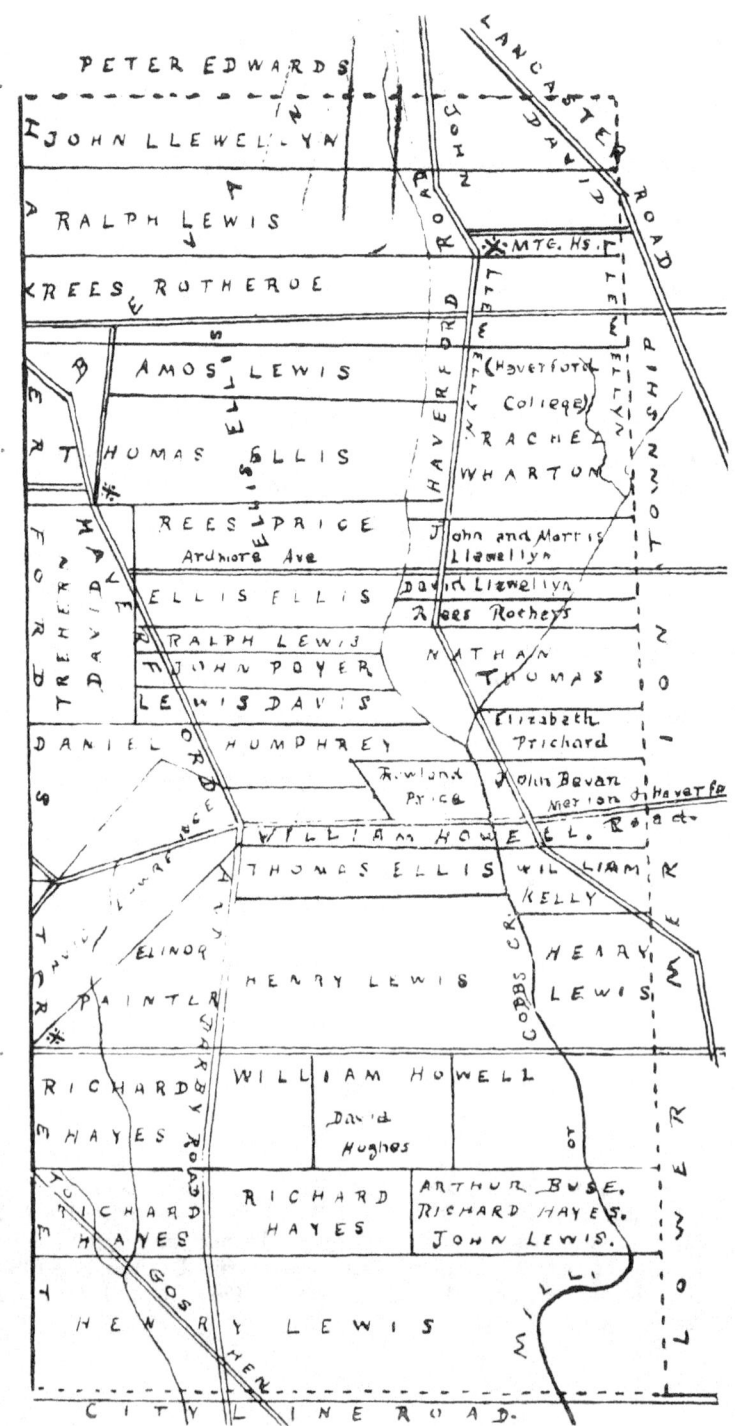

HAVERFORD TP EAST OF THE "STREET," 1690

ADVENTURERS FOR LANDS IN HAVERFORD AND RADNOR

RICHARD THOMAS'S LAND PATENT

Company No. 6—The purchasers of the 5,000 acres of land for which Richard ap Thomas, of Whiteford Garne, subscribed, were not many, and his adventure appears to have been unprofitable. His heir had about the same trouble, as Dr. Wynne's had, in getting his father's land.

From the Commissioners' Minutes 2. 12mo., 1701, we learn that Penn, by deed dated 24th of July, 1681, for £100, conveyed to Richard ap Thomas 5,000 acres, to be laid out "in the Welsh Tract," "of which none has been laid out Saving 600 acres on part of 1.300 Acres laid out to [William] Wood and [William] Sharlow" [or Shardlow, Sharelow, Sherlo, etc.]. This, of course, was "not approv'd of by the Commis'rs". and the "100 Acres of Lib. Land [due, was] taken up by Hugh Roberts." At this Meeting "his Son and Heir, Richard ap Thomas, therefore requets Warr'ts to take up the said Land in the Welsh Tract."

"The said Richard haveing been a Verry great Sufferer by his Father's embarquing for this Province, and deceasing before, or upon his Arrival, by which means he has been reduced to great hardships, 'tis Ordered that a War't be forthwith granted to take up 2,000 A's of Vacant land where to be found in the said Tract, and that War'ts be also Issued for the remainder as fast as he can be accommodated." This was a very fair accommodation all things considered. But on 2. 3mo. 1704, he was assessed the quitrent to run "from the first laying out of the Welsh Tract." Before 7mo. 1702, Philip Howel bought 700 acres from said Richard.

As to the 100 acres in the City Liberties, they were surveyed, 4. 7mo. 1701, "in pursuance of the Proprietor's Warrant, dated 8. 11mo. 1700," to Hugh Roberts, to whom patent for same was issued by the Commissioners 24 Nov. 1701.

WELSH SETTLEMENT OF PENSYLVANIA

This land was located "upon the Indian Creek and the Mill Creek (Cobbs Creek), in Blockley tp., near Adam Rhode's Land," "in Right of Richard Thomas, first Purchaser of 5,000 Acres."

Richard Thomas, Jr., in the Spring of 1703, had considerable trouble about his land, because the surveyor laid it out on a spot that the Commissioners had granted to "R'd Ingels, of Philad'a, Gent." in 2mo. 1686, in the Welsh Tract. On a resurvey, it was found that Ingels had too much land, and with this "overplus" and some unclaimed land adjoining, Richard Thomas was accommodated.

Minute of 8. 9mo. 1703, Richard Thomas, the younger, was granted "a High St. Lott of 132 foot in right of his Fathers Purchase, and 51 foot [lot] in the Front Street."

On 3. 2mo. 1704, Richard Thomas, Jr., made returns of the following sales "of his 5,000 acres Purchased by his Father":—

To Philip Howel, 700 acres.
To Robert Williams, 500 acres.
To Edward Jones, 200 acres.
To Hugh Roberts, 100 acres Liberty Land.
To David Howel, 200 acres.
To Robert David, 861¼ acres.

"In all 1786¼ acres. [He] has taken up and Patented 1,665 acres, which Make 3,451¼, and there remains 1,548¾. To which 320 Being added, allowed to him (for which he is to Pay Rent for the whole 3,200 from the first Location of the Welsh Tract as well P'r agreement), for the 1,665 acres already Patented as for the Rem'd, makes 1,868¾ acres to be Confirmed forthwith, he Paying the said arrears." See also letter of David Powell to James Logan, 5. 12mo. 1701, *super.*

It appears from the Minutes of 1mo. 5th. 1715-16, that the 600 acre part of Richard ap Thomas's original purchase which was sold to Messrs. Wood and Sharlow, was laid out in New Town tp., Chester Co., and that Richard Thomas,

Jr. claimed this tract, but the heirs of Wood and Sharlow protested, whereupon the Commissioners issued a patent to him, dated 8. 1mo. 1716-7, for 243 acres in the "Chester County Welsh Tract," "in part of 600 allowed him instead of the like quantity confirmed to him in New Town."

On 8. 2mo. 1717, "Richard Thomas, Son and Heir of Rich'd ap Thomas, haveing formerly obtained the Grant of a Lott of Ground on the River Schuylkill, to be laid out to him in Right of his ffather's Purchase, besides those Lotts laid out to him on Delaware side of Philad'a, which Lott on Schuylkill not being survey'd to him, he now desires that he might risign his Right to the said Lott, and that he would instead thereof grant him one whole Lott in the Back streets on Delaware side. The Comm'rs considers his disappointm'ts in not haveing his Lotts and Lands laid out to him before he came to age, Grants his Request, and a Warrant is signed and dated ye 25 of 7ber, 1717." This was done "for Richard ap Thomas in full of all his Demand."

RICHARD AP THOMAS, described as gentleman, as he was the owner of a freehold of £300 per annum, resided in Flintshire, at "Whitford Garden," or Crossforth, when he first appears in the history of the "Welsh Tract." Nothing is certain of his ancestry. He was one of the early converts to Fox's teachings.

He made arrangements to remove with his wife, and two children, to Pensylvania, but his wife backed out at the last moment, and remained at home with their daughter. It is tradition among their descendants, that Mrs. Thomas was never converted to Quakerism, and therefore was not "inclined for Pensylvania."

Mr. Thomas, with his only son, Richard Thomas, Jr., aged about ten years, and some servants, joined the Hugh Roberts party, and sailed from Mossom, in the ship Morning Star, of Liverpool, in Sep. 1683, and arrived at Philadelphia on 16 Nov. 1683. Mr. Thomas arrived in ill health, and died shortly, in town, without having had opportunity to attend to the locating of his land, or even the disposal of the goods he brought over to sell. His will, dated 18 Nov. 1683, was probably drawn up just before he died, though it was not proved till 15 Jan. 1695-6, when Richard, Jr., was of age. He devised his lands in Wales and Pensylvania to Richard, his heir, and appointed Dr. Thomas Wynne the executor and guardian of young Richard. To his wife and only daughter, he devised his personal estate in Wales.

Richard Thomas, Jr., lived with his guardian, at Lewes, in Co. Sussex, (Delaware), until Dr. Wynne died, in 1692. In 1693, he had considerable litigation over his Welsh land, attended to by his attorney, Gov. Thomas Lloyd.

The difficulties he experienced, when he became of age, over his Pensylvania grant, are mentioned above. Of his father's 5,000 acres, he sold 1,785 acres to sundry parties. In 1703, he had patents for two tracts, one of 1,065 acres, on a part of which the present city of West Chester stands; the other, 600 acres, laid out in Newton tp., he lost through bad surveys. In 1704, he had a third patent for 1,548 acres, but when it was laid out in Whiteland amounted to 1,869 acres.

In 1699-1700, Richard Thomas, Jr., visited the place of his birth in the old country. His descendant, Col. Richard Thomas, in his memoirs, records that he heard that Richard found his sister "reduced to indigence," and his mother had married again, and was deceased, and that his step-father had dissipated all their joint property.

When Richard returned to Pensylvania, he brought his sister with him, and married her to Llewellyn Parry. They had a family, and descendants may be found in Chester Co., Pa.

After his return, Richard Thomas, Jr., married Grace Atherton, and finally settled in the Chester Valley. In 1704, he is described as of Merion tp., a carpenter, and in 1711, as of Blockley tp.

COMPANY NUMBER SIX

It is of record that Richard Thomas, Jr., was married, by Friends' ceremony, (though there is no evidence that he was a Friend, or member of any Meeting here, so the ceremony may have been performed by a Justice of the Peace), to Grace Atherton, at his own house, in Whiteland tp., on 15. 11mo. 1712-3, and that she was the daughter of Henry and Jennet Atherton, late of Liverpool. Richard Thomas, Jr., died at home, in Whiteland, in 1744, and was survived by his wife, who was buried with him in "Malin's Graveyard," in East Whiteland tp., Chester Co. They had six children, and of these, Hannah, *b.* 14. 11mo. 1716-7, *m.* James Mendenhall; Mary, *b.* 14. 5mo. 1719, *m.* John Harrison; Grace, *b.* 9. 7mo. 1722, *m.* Thomas Stalker; Elizabeth, *m.* 28. 4mo. 1750, Jonathan Howell, and removed to No. Car., and

Richard Thomas, 3d, only son, heir to the Whiteland homestead, *b.* 22. 2mo. 1713, *d.* 22. 9mo. 1754. He *m.*, at the Goshen Meeting, 10. 2mo. 1739, Phebe, daughter of George and Mary (Malin) Ashbridge, of Goshen tp., *b.* 26. 8mo. 1717, *d.* 14. 6mo. 1784, and had five children, namely, Lydia, *m.* John Trimble; Grace, *m.* William Trimble; Hannah, *m.* Joseph Trimble; George, (see below), and

Richard Thomas, 4th., of "Whitford Lodge," in West Whiteland tp., *b.* 30. 10mo. 1744, *d.* 19. 1mo. 1832. Although a birthright Friend, on the outbreak of the war for independence he entered the army, and became colonel of a Pensylvania regiment, and served throughout the war. He was elected to the Pensylvania Assembly, in 1786, and in 1789, and the State Senate in 1790, and member of U. S. Congress, 1794, '96, and '98, in the 4th, 5th and 6th Congresses. He *m.* Thomazine, *b.* 26. 8mo., 1754, *d.* 4. 5mo. 1817, daughter of Richard Downing, 1719-1803, son of Thomas Downing, the founder of Downingtown.* *Issue.*

---

* Thomas Downing, 1691-1772, a farmer, merchant miller, and a Friend, had also a daughter Sarah, who *m.* Thomas Meteer, a farmer and paper maker, member of the Falls, Birmingham, Wilmington,

WELSH SETTLEMENT OF PENSYLVANIA

George Thomas, *b.* 21. 12mo. 1746-7, *d.* 17. 8mo. 1793. He inherited 600 acres of his father's estate, in West Whiteland tp., and when the Uwchlan Friends' Meeting House was used as a hospital, during the Revolutionary War, the Friends held their meetings at his house. He *m.*, at the Merion Meeting, on 26. 5mo. 1774, Sarah, daughter of John Roberts, and his wife, Jane Downing, (daughter of the founder of Downingtown), of Merion, *b.* 11. 1mo. 1750, *d.* 20. 2mo. 1840, and had nine children.

---

and Baltimore Friends' meetings, and had Thomas Meteer, Jr., who *m.* Hannah, a daughter of Captain John Quandrill, of the Chester Co. militia, and had Ann Meteer, 1798-1872, who *m.* Eli Sinex, 1797-1830, of Staunton, Del., and had Thomas Sinex, 1820-1899, of Philadelphia, father of John H. Sinex, of Philadelphia, and Edge Water Park, N. J.

RICHARD DAVIES'S LAND PATENT

Company No. 7. The purchasers of the 5,000 acres for which "Richard Davies, of Welshpool, gent.," subscribed and had deed, date 14. 7mo. 1681, were as follows, with the parishes in which they resided, their deeds, bearing dates, 19 June, and 30 July, 1682, give their occupations and station in life.

Merionethshire.

	Acres.
Rowland Ellis, gent, Bryn Mawr	1100
Richard Humphrey, gent, Llan Glynin	150
Ellis Maurice, gent, Dolgun vcha	78
Lewis Owen, gent, Gwanas	183
Rowland Owen, gent, Gwanas	182
Evan John William, gent, Llangylynin	156¼
Evan ap William, gent, Llanvachreth	156¼
David ap Evan, gent, Llanvachreth	156¼
Edward Owen, gent, "Late of Dalserey"	

Carmarthenshire.

James Price, gent, Mothvey.................... 300

Caernarvonshire.

John Roberts, gent, Llangian................... 150

Unknown.

Ellis ap Hugh, [Pugh], (possibly of Merioneth)....160
Petter Edwards 100

WELSH SETTLEMENT OF PENSYLVANIA

Radnorshire.

David Kinsey, carpenter, Nantmele	100
John Evans, gent, Nantmele	350
Ellis Jones, weaver, Nantmele	100
Margaret James, spinster, Newchurch	200
Richard Miles, weaver, Llanvihangel Velgyen	100
Roger Hughes, gent, Llanvihangel Rhydyithan	250
David Meredith, weaver, Llanbister	100
Richard Corn, glover, Langunllo	50
Richard Cooke, glover, Langunllo	100
Thomas Jones, gent, Glascombe	100
Evan Oliver, gent, Glascombe	200
John Lloyd, glover, Dissart	100
Edward Jones, gent, St. Harmon	250
David James, mariner, Glascram	100

Their purchases were laid out in Merion, Radnor, Goshen and New Town townships, in the Welsh Tract, and the following is his own account of the purchases from Richard Davies.

"Rich'd Davies Purchase & Alienation of 5,000 acres pr Rowl'd Ellis." is the endorsement on the document, owned by the Historical Society of Pensylvania, and is, as its subhead states: "Richard Davies purchases 5,000 acres as by the original Deed doth appeer, sold & subdivided to ye severall purchasers hereafter named."

"Names—first purchasers in England:—

"To Rowland Ellis 1,100 acres as per deed apears, whereof 600 is taken up & setled att Merion; 483 acres att Goshen in ye Welsh tract laid out & both entered in ye Survey'r Generalls Office [&] 17 acres of Lyberty land.

"To John Roberts 150 acres taken up in the Township of Merion, & in's own possession.

"To Richard Humphrey 156¼ acres taken up in ye Township of Radnor—he died, John Humphrey's Executor, did assign right thereto William Tho.

COMPANY NUMBER SEVEN

"To Evan Jno Williams 156¼ acres laid out Goshen in ye Welsh Tract—he died, by's will bequeathed the same to Evan ab William, by's will bequeathed ye same to's son Philip Evan, it being laid out as by patent doth appear in ye Welsh tract—ye s'd Philip died without issue—brother David Evan possess ye same.*

"To Lewis Owen, Rowland Owen, Ellis Maurice, Ellis Pugh, 625 acres, sold to Thomas Ellis their title & interest therein—ye sd quantity was taken up together in Merion—he dec'd, Executor's sold ye same to Joh: William.

"To James Price 300 acres, he sold same to David Price, ye sd David to Henry Rees † the present possessor thereof —in ye Township of Radnor.

"To John Evans 350 acres—out of s'd tract he sold 100 acres to John German now deceased—his widow in possession. Another pt thereof he sold vizt: 100 to John Roberts,

---

*The will of David Evan, of Radnor, signed 16. 12, 1709, witnesses Hugh William, Humphrey Ellis (marked), William Davies, and John Morgan, was proved 17 May, 1710. by wife Mary. Names children Caleb, Joshua, Evan, David, Philip, John, Mary, Gwen, (and her children, John and Gainor), and Sarah. Overseers, Rowland Ellis, Sr. and Jr., Rees Thomas, Rowland Powell, Richard Ormes, and John Morgan.

† The will of Henry Rees, signed 1 Feb. 1704-5, witnesses, Richard Moore and David Evan, was proved 30 June 1705, by wife Elizabeth, names children David, Gwen, and Margaret.

The will of David Rees, (or Reece), of New Town, Chester Co., yeoman, signed 14. 11mo. 1705-6, witnesses, Evan Davis (marked), and John Reece, was proved by wife Eleanor, 30 March 1706. Son Thomas Reece, to be executor. Names son Lewis Reece. Overseers, David Morice, of Marple tp., Henry Lewis, of Haverford tp., and Richard Hayes.

The will of Thomas Reece, of Haverford, yeoman, marked 7. 7mo. 1713; present Rowland Ellis, Henry Lewis, Rowland Powell, and David Morris (marked). was proved 10 Oct. 1713, by son Samuel Reece, executor. Other children, Sarah, Daniel, Mary, David, Isaac, Philip, Miriam, Thomas, and John. Names sister Margaret Reece, of Pembrokeshire. The witnesses, with Rees Thomas, to be guardians and trustees.

the sd John sold the same to John Morgan who has it in possession—the remaining pt ye sd John Evans hath in's possession, all in Radnor.†

"To Richard Corn 50 acres, deceased, his son William Corn convey'd right therein to John Evans as by deeds doth appear & being posses'd thereof, lying in Radnor.

"To Edward Jones 250 acres, one James Morgan purchased's right to ye sd quantity. Late deceased's son & heir John Morgan now possessor.

"To Ellis Jones 100 acres, he assigning's right & title therein to William David, the said William to John Morgan the possessor thereof.

"To Roger Hughes 250 acres, he selling one moety thereof, vizt: 125 acres to Tho Parry, the sd Parry assigning over's right to Richard Moore, ye other half ye sd Roger sold to David Meredith—now in his possession.

---

†The two following wills were probated at Philadelphia. John Evans, of Radnor, marked in the presence of William ap Edward (marked) and Hugh William, 19. 11. 1707-8, was proved 19 Jan. 1708, by his wife, Mary. Names brother Edward Evan. Appointed John Roberts, William ap Edward, Edward Rees, and Hugh William guardians to his children, named Evan, Edward, Mary, and Sarah Johnes.

John Evans, of Radnor, [from Nantmele, Radnor], signed in the presence of Abel Roberts, John Jarman, Evan Rees, David Lloyd, and Philip Howell. 17. 6mo. 1703, was proved by wife, Deliah, 22 Nov. 1707, Names daughters, Mary, wife of David Evan, Sarah, wife of John Morgan, Margaret, wife of Hugh Samuel, Phebe, wife of Edward Jones David, (and "her three children"), and Jane Jones' sons, Rees Jones and Thomas Jones. Brother Edward Evans, and his daughter Elizabeth. Overseers, David Evan and John Morgan.

John Morgan, mentioned in this will, was a brother of Cadwalader Morgan, one of the Thomas & Jones Company. He came over with his father, James Morgan, from Vaenor, Radnorshire, and took up land in Radnor, some of which is still held by descendants. John's daughter, Hannah Morgan, *m.* James Hunter, of Radnor, and their daughter, Mary, 1757-1820, *m.* Hugh Jones, 1748-1796, of Radnor, (and had Mary, *m.* 1804, Nathan Brooke, of Gulph Mills, 1778-1815), son of Hugh Jones, 1705-1790, who, with his father, owned at one time 700 acres, part of it is the farm land called "Brookfield," North of Bryn Mawr, owned by Mr. Wayne MacVeagh.

"To Richard Cook 100 acres, taken up for him in Radnor.

"To John Lloyd 100 acres, laid out for hime likewise [in Radnor].

"To David James 100 acres, deceased—his daughter Mary James Executrix of ye sd father sold ye title & interest therin to Stephen ab Evan present possessor.

"To Margaret James 200 acres, Samuel James in right of's wife the sd Margaret possesseth ye same.

"To Richard Miles 100 acres, settles thereon.

"To Thomas Jones [100] by his heirs the title thereof was made to William Davies the possessor.

"To Evan Oliver 200 acres, deceased, his heirs sold ye sd quantity to ye sd William Davies the possessor.

"To David Kinsey 100 acres, the Execut's of the deceased Kinsey sold the said tract to James James,* & ye sd James to Lewis Walker, who possesseth ye same.

"To Petter Edwards 100 acres, he sold's title and interest to Thomas Parry, and the sd Parry to Tho Rees, ye present possessor.

"The whole subdivided among ye above named first purchasers in England comes 5,000.

"Whereof 2,656 accers & ¼ is laid out in ye Township Rodnor, the remainder of ye property hath been laid pt in Merion the rest where the [mutilated] lives in ye Welch tract.

"Here followeth some acc more of lands taken up in ye said Township, part whereof by purchase & part rent land:

"David Meredith 250 acres, purchased as by patent doth appear.

"Samuel Miles 100 acres, formerly took up att Rent, sometime after paid for as doth appear.

---

*Will of "James James, of Haverford, yeoman," signed 18. 6mo. 1708, witnesses, Richard Hayes, Rowland Powell, and Adam Roades, was proved 28 Aug. 1708. Wife probably dead. Names children, George, David, Sarah, and Thomas James (executor). Son-in-law David Lewis, and his children, not named.

WELSH SETTLEMENT OF PENSYLVANIA

"John Evans 100 acres, took up att rent, in his possession.

"William Davies 150 acres, formerly took up att Rent.

"Stephen ab Evan 100 acres, hath taken up likewise att Rent.

"all by orders in Radnor Welch tract."

In pursuance of the order made by the Commissioners, 23. 10. 1701, on 16. 12mo. 1701-2, the lands of these grantees of Richard Davis were resurveyed. John Roberts, malter, 150 acres in Merion tp., and William Thomas 153¼ acres in Merion tp., Radnor Tp., John Roberts, malter 150 acres in Radnor tp. The will of "William Thomas, of Radnor, planter," was marked in the presence of Philip Evan, and John Humphrey, 18. 7mo. 1687, and proved 4. 9mo. 1689, by wife Ann, to whom he left his estate, with remainder to William Thomas, if he will come to this country, otherwise his property was to be sold, "and the proceeds equally divided between the children of my brother, and of my sister," unnamed. Legacies to cousin Rees Petter, Ellis Ellis, Humphrey Ellis, David Lawrence, Katherine Morgan, Ellis Pugh, Evan Harry, Hugh Haney, and Daniel Haney. To Owen Morgan* one sow, and his son (Owen's) "to be released after my departure, and if my wife depart before the time of his daughter be over, she also may be released." To brother-in-law David Davies, sister-in-law Katherine Davies. To be overseers, David Lawrence, Rees Petter, David Evan, and John Humphrey.

Richard Davies' "alienation of his 5,000 acres" was long the cause of misunderstanding by purchasers under him, especially as to city lots, and "Liberty lands" which went

---

*Will of Owen Morgan, of Merion, signed 23. 9mo. 1703, in presence of Daniel Thomas (marked), John More, and John Bevan, was proved 26 Feb. 1703-4, by wife Blanche. Names son Humphrey Morgan, and daughters, Katherine Morgan, and Mary Carply. Friends Edward Morgan, and John Lloyd. To be overseers, William Lewis, Ralph Lewis, Ellis Ellis, and John Bevan.

with such a purchase. Frequently the Land Commissioners had to explain that Richard Davies had no right to such extras on account of the whole purchase, because he had made it only in trust, and had conveyed the tract to parties interested, himself only being one of them, who had taken up lots in several parts of the city according to their shares purchased out of the 5,000 acres grant. And that Davies, himself, was only entitled to a twenty-five foot lot, which he had in High Street and Front Street, Philadelphia, Pa., on account of his share, namely, 1,250 acres of the grant. His Pensylvania land was managed and sold by many mentioned as his attorneys, as Thomas Lloyd, William Powel, Hugh Roberts, David and John Humphrey, Griffith Owen, Rowland Ellis, and David Lloyd.

The Land Commissioners's "Welsh Minutes" give a few further details concerning the distribution of Richard Davies's land. He sold 2,656 acres in Radnor tp., and balance was located in Merion and Goshen.

Rowland Ellis sold, by deed 31 July, 1682, his 17 acres of the Liberty lands, to John Goodson. Of his 600 acres tract in Merion he gave 100 acres "to Edw'd Jones, of London, gent., for settling it," by deed of 6. 12mo. 1687. By deed, dated 11. 2mo. 1702, he bought back this land. Besides this Merion land, he had 483 acres in Goshen tp.

"John Roberts's, gent.," deed for his 150 acres in Merion, dated 30. July, 1682, recorded 24. 4. 1684, was witnessed by Rowland Owen, Ellis Morris, David Evan, Owen Lewis, Sr., and Jr., Evan Harry, and Rowland Ellis. He also held 60 acres adjoining where he resided, which he had from Andrew Wheeler, a Swede, 3 June 1699.

(Will dated 25. 7mo. 1688, of "Jance John Morgan, alias Jane Roberts, of Haverford," left all her estate to "friend John Roberts, of Merion," who was to be sole executor. Signed in presence of William Howell and Blanche Sharples).

WELSH SETTLEMENT OF PENSYLVANIA

Richard Humphrey died without issue, and his 150 or 156¼ acres, located in Radnor tp., were sold by his cousin, heir and executor, John Humphrey, 23. 10mo. 1693, to William Thomas.

Richard Humphrey, "of Radnor, in the Welsh Tract," was the cousin and brother-in-law of John Humphrey, of Haverford. He had resided in the parish of Llangelynin, or Llan Glynin, Merioneth, and had the usual Friends' certificate, dated 27. 5mo. 1683. His will, marked, and witnessed by Theodore Robert (marked), Benjamin Humphrey, and Rowland Ellis, 12. 12mo. 1691, was proved at Philadelphia, 18. 12mo. 1692-3. He bequeathed all his land "to my brother-in-law, John Humphrey," who sold it. He gave legacies to brothers John Humphrey and Owen Humphrey, sister Katherine, or her children, unnamed, cousin John Owen, Lyddie Ellis, Rebecca, Ann, Daniel, Benjamin and Joseph Humphrey, also to the "Friends' Monthly Meeting for the service of Truth."

Rebecca Humphrey and Elizabeth Owen, spinster, also came from this parish, bringing certificates which they filed with the Haverford Monthly Meeting. Elizabeth's certificate was signed by Hugh Rees, Owen and William Humphrey, Robert, Evan, and Humphrey Owen, Humphrey Reinald, John William, Richard, Sr., Elizabeth, and Richard Stafford, Jr. Rebecca's was signed by the same, and Griffith Robert, Edward Ellis, Hugh David, Lewis Robert, Owen Lewis, Lewis Owen, David Edward, Ellis Moris, Robert Richard, Katharine Price, Janne Robert, Ellin Ellis, Anne Hugh, Margaret Robert, and Ann Humphrey.

Evan John William, gent., divided his right to 156¼ acres, laid out in Goshen tp., giving part to his nephew, Richard Rees, and the other to "John Roberts, cordwainer, of Philadelphia, who is Rees Peter's wife's son." "Rees Petter, of Machanlleth, Montgomeryshire" brought certificate, dated 27. 5mo. 1683, from the Quarterly Meeting at Dolyseerey, which he filed with the Haverford Monthly

Meeting. It was signed by Robert, Humphrey, and Richard Owen, Griffith and Owen Lewis, John Evans, Hugh Reece, Amos Davies, William Thomas, and Evan, William, and Rowland Ellis.

Evan ap William died at sea coming over. A letter of attorney, dated 27 July, 1683, recorded 8. 5. 1684, at Philadelphia, was given by Evan ap William, gent., and David Evan, both of Llanfachreth, to John Roberts, of Langian, Caernarvonshire, in a matter concerning their 312½ acres purchased of Richard Davies. It was witnessed by Tho Ellis, John Humphrey, Evan Ellis, and Rowland Ellis. By his will, his son Philip ap Evan, inherited his purchase, which was laid out near the New Town Friends' Meeting House, patent being confirmed to him, 27. 11. 1687. Philip died without issue, when his brother, David ap Evan, succeeded to the farm. The will of David Evan, of Haverford, was marked in the presence of John Bevan, Evan Bevan, and Elinor Bevan, 16. 1. 1698, proved 20 April, 1706, names his children, Harry, Sarah, and Elizabeth David.

David ap Evan (David Evan) was himself a purchaser of 156¼ acres from Davies, which tract was laid out, 22. 11mo. 1687, along with his brother's tract, at New Town, in the Welsh Tract. In 1701, David Evan had 308 acres in two parcels, in Radnor.

Edward Jones's 250 acres were in Radnor. He, by deed, dated 4 Feb. 1690-1, sold same to James Morgan, who, in 1701, had altogether 450 in Radnor, whose son and heir, John, inherited the place, but John Worrall had most of it in 1703.

Ellis Jones assigned, on 12. 10. 1687, his 100 acres to William David, who sold the same to John Morgan, by deed of 15. 10. 1702, so the said John had 450 acres in Radnor tp. He sold 80 acres to Henry Lewis, of Haverford, who sold the same to John Worrall, or Worrell.

Roger Hughes had deed, dated 20 June. 1682, for 250 acres laid out in Radnor tp. By deed, 11. 7. 1691, he sold

WELSH SETTLEMENT OF PENSYLVANIA

125 acres to David Meredith, who sold to Richard Moore. Roger sold his balance, in 1699, to Thomas Parry, after whose death, Richard Moore had it.

Thomas Parry,* or Thomas ap Harry, a weaver, who bought this land, was the son of Harry ap Rees, of Henllan parish, Cardiganshire, and came to Pensylvania from Llanelwith, in Radnor, bringing a certificate of membership from the Radnor Quarterly Meeting, dated 5. 5mo. 1699. He *m.* Elinor, daughter of John Edward, of Lanelwi parish, Radnor, and had two sons, Edward Parry, who *m.* 6. 8mo. 1710, Jane, daughter of Robert Evans, and *d.* 28. 2mo. 1726, and Thomas Parry, Jr., who *m.* 27. 8mo. 1715, Jane Phillips, daughter of Philip Philip, of Radnor, (who *d.* 25. 12mo. 1697), and had ten children.

Roger Hughes subsequently bought 250 acres from the Commissioners, the money being paid to James Harrison. Of this, he sold, 20. 5. 1691, 150 acres to Stephen Evans, who had also 100 acres from David James.

Richard Cooke located his 100 acres in Radnor tp., but did not come over from Wales, and probably lost his rights. Witnesses to his deed, 19 June, 1682, were Ed Jones, Tho Davies, Ric Jones, David Jones, Daniel Morris, Samuel Miles, Evan Evans, and others.

"John Lloyd" remained in Wales, but had his 100 acre right laid out in Radnor tp. This probably should be Francis Lloyd, who died, and his widow, Mary Lloyd, and son, Joseph Lloyd, cordwainer, both of Haverford West, gave power of attorney to Samuel Carpenter, a Philadelphia merchant, and William Howell, of Haverford, to sell the 100 acres, which they did to Mary, widow of David Haverd.

---

*Will of Hugh Parry, of Merion, signed 26 April, 1731; witnesses Hugh Evans, Thomas Lloyd (marked), and Robert Jones; proved 5 June same year, mentions brothers Henry and Robert, and sisters Ellin, Jane, Elizabeth, and Katherine Pugh.

COMPANY NUMBER SEVEN

Cook and Lloyd tried to sell through David Meredith, and Stephen Evans, but they only disposed of their city lots in Walnut Street, near Fifth Street, in 1702, to Enoch Story.

David Jones died, and his only child, Mary, sold his right to 100 acres, to Stephen Evans, in Radnor.

Margaret James, spinster, after receiving deed, dated 20 June, 1682, for her 200 acres, married by Friends' ceremony, and in Welsh, at the house of Ann Thomas, in New Church parish, Radnorshire, 24. 4mo. 1682, Samuel Miles, of Hamhanghobyeholgen parish, Radnor, and they located the land in Radnor tp., removed to it, and bought 150 acres more from Thomas Lehnman. They sold 50 acres to brother Richard Miles, and, in Sep. 1705, had remaining 258 acres in Radnor, which, on resurvey, amounted to 352 acres, the excess they bought, paying 6s. 8d. per acre, and eighteen months' interest on the price of the surplus from the date of the original grant.

Samuel Miles's will, signed in the presence of Edward Rees, Richard Miles, David Thomas, William Davies, and John Reece, 24. 4mo. 1707, was proved by his wife, [Margaret James], not named, 28 Apr. 1708. Names his children, Tamar, Phoebe, and Ruth, [*m.* Owen Evans]. To be overseers brother Richard Miles, Stephen Bevan, and Edward Reece. Their first child, Tamar, was *b.* 21 Feb. 1687, and was the first Welsh child born in Radnor tp. She *m.* Thomas Thomas, of Radnor, and, after 62 years of married life, *d.* 28. 7mo. 1770, a member of the Radnor Meeting.

Richard Miles also located his right to 100 acres in Radnor, which re-surveyed amounted to 233 acres. He also bought from his brother, Samuel Miles, 50 acres, which was found to be 92 acres on a re-survey, and 20 acres from Ellis Jones, "the Govern's miller." By the first surveys in 12mo. 1701, he supposed he had only 170 acres in Radnor, but the later survey showed he had 325 acres, so he bought the excess from Penn, 155 acres, and paid interest on the cost of the "overs" from dates of the grants.

WELSH SETTLEMENT OF PENSYLVANIA

Thomas Jones, of "Laulanread in Elvel," or Glascombe, Radnorshire, gave his 100 acre right to his nephew, John Jones, who by deed, dated 30 8ber, 1685, conveyed the same to William Davies, who sold it to David Evan, of Radnor tp.

Evan Oliver's 200 acres were sold by his heir to William Davies, who, by deed, dated 18 Jan. 1702, conveyed 50 acres of the same to David Evan, of Radnor, and on 19 July, 1697, 100 acres to Edward David.

David Meredith, besides the 100 acres from Davies, bought 100 from Corn (and on re-survey it was found 37 acres over, which amount he bought, paying a noble an acre), and 125 acres from Roger Hughes, which he sold to Richard Moore. David Meredith, his wife Katherine, and children Richard, Mary, John, Meredith, and Sarah, came from Llanbister parish, Radnorshire, bringing the usual certificate of membership in good standing in the Society of Friends, dated 20. 5mo. 1683.

To Lewis Owen, 183 acres, Rowland Owen, 182 acres, Ellis Morris, 78 acres, and Ellis ap Hugh, 182 acres, were conveyed 625 acres, in proportions named, in four deeds, dated 31 July, 1682. Witnesses to the deeds of the first three, as grantees, were the men of Merioneth, Owen Lewis, Sr., and Jr., Rowland Ellis, Evan Harry, and David Evan, and as grantors, were same, and Morris Ellis, and John Humphrey.

The first three grantees, by deed dated 30 June, 1683, sold their rights to 443 acres for £19. 17. 2, English, to Thomas Ellis, as also did Ellis Pugh,* by deed dated 16 July, 1686. This land, Thomas Ellis had laid out in Merion. By his will, signed 1. 11mo. 1688, he ordered it sold to pay his debts, which was done 5. 7mo. 1698.

---

*Evan ap Hugh (Evan Pugh) made his will 21 May, 1703, and signed with his mark in the presence of Thomas Edward, Humphrey Bate, and John Robert. Proved 7 June, 1704, by wife Ann. Names only son David Pugh, (but had other children) and nephew Hugh Edward. Overseers, John Humphrey, Edward Foulke, and Robert John.

COMPANY NUMBER SEVEN

James Price, who had right to 300 acres in Radnor tp., by deed, 19 June, 1682, rented his land for three year from 16 July, 1684, to David Price, and in case James did not come over to use the land, he could have it forever. "James never came," so David sold the place, by deed 6. 1. 1696-7, to Humphrey Rees. David Price was also granted a city lot, "among the rest of his countrymen in Chestnut Street," between Fourth and Fifth Streets, and this by deed, 7 July, 1693, without even locating the lot, he conveyed to William Thomas, of Radnor, who sold it to Gov. Lloyd, whose executor, David Lloyd, requested confirmation of sale, as said Thomas lost his life by accident before he executed the deed of sale. His widow gave the deed, 27. 2. 1702.

John ap Evan, or John Evans, Sr., received his right to 350 acres by deed of 19 July, 1682, witnessed by Edward Jones, Thomas Davies, David Jones, Richard Jones and David Morris. He located his land in Radnor tp. On resur-

---

Roger Robert, of Radnor, marked his will, 5 July, 1720, in the presence of Robert Jones, Rees Thomas, William Thomas, and Robert Evans, and mentions his children, Robert, John, Owen, and Jane, and grandsons Roger Robert and Roger Pugh.

Will of Thomas Pugh, a mason, signed 3. 3. 1723: witnesses John Roger, Thomas Ellis, Ellis Robert, and Meredith David. proved 1 Oct. 1723, by wife Ann. Mentions brother Job Pugh, and own sons Jesse and Roger Pugh. To be trustees, Robert Jones, of Merion, Meredith Davis, Robert Roger, Job Pugh, and Ellis Robert.

Will of Henry Pugh, of Merion, yeoman, signed 11 June, 1730, proved by wife Katherine, 1 May, 1731. Witnesses, Ellen Thomas (marked) Ellin Jones, Ann Jones (marked), Lowry Evans, Hugh Evans, and Robert Jones. Names children, Hugh, Robert, Jane, Katherine, Elizabeth, Ellen, Henry, and Moses Pugh. Trustees, Thomas Thomas, Thomas Lawrence, Hugh Evans and Robert Jones.

Will of William Pugh, of Radnor, yeoman, marked 19 June, 1705, witnesses Daniel Harry (marked), Susanna Williams, and William Davies. Proved 19 June, 1798. Wife probably deceased. Names son, "Hugh Williams," and his children William, Catherine, Susanna, and Elizabeth Williams. Grandsons, Hugh Jones and Joseph Jones. Mentions "friends Richard and Ann [Roberts,] brother and sister of John Roberts, of Merion, and Jane, daughter of Robert Ellis."

vey it amounted to only 300 acres, and was surveyed again, and came out only 250 acres, and even then he had to buy an "over plus" of 25 acres. By deed, 4. 4. 1688, Evans conveyed 100 acres to John German, or Jarman, whose relict, "Margaret Jermain," held it. On survey, it was made out to be 42 acres over, which her son, John, paid for at a noble an acre. "John Jarman, of the parish of Llangerig," in Montgomeryshire, and his wife Margaret, and children Elizabeth and Sarah, brought certificate, dated 20. 5mo. 1683, from the Radnorshire Men's Meeting, which they filed with the Haverford Monthly Meeting. It was signed by Owen Humphrey, Daniel Lewis, Nathan Woodliffe, David Griffith, Jon Lloyd, Edward Moore, Richard Watkins, Thomas Parry, Edward Jones, Richard Cooke, John Watson, Roger Hughes, John Robert, and Rees ap Rees. At same date (4. 4. 1688), John Evans sold 100 acres to "Jno. Robert, of Haverford, smith," adjoining German or Jarman, on the north. The will of "John Robert, blacksmith," dated 26. 7. 1702, was proved 5 Jan. 1702-3. To daughter Margaret, wife of Thomas Kenderdine, and her children. Mentions his son John, and daughter, Elinor Jenkins, living in Wales. Executors, John Bevan and John Rees. Among the witnesses was William Howell. John Robert, by deed of 9. 1mo. 1699-00, sold same land to John Morgan, who also had 100 acres more of John Evans's land. Edward David, on 19 July, 1697, bought "the remaining 150 acres," and this lot, with 50 acres, he bought of William Corn (the son of one of Davies's grantees), was in Radnor tp., and he sold it to John Evans, "together with 500 acres of 'rent land,' of which he sold 50 to Edward David." In 12mo. 1701, the Land Commissioners supposed John Evans had 2,200 acres in Radnor.

Richard Corn, or Conn, got his 50 acres in Radnor, by deed, 20 June, 1682, his son and heir, William, sold it to John Evans, 6 Jan. 1690.

COMPANY NUMBER SEVEN

By a triparty deed, dated 19. 6mo. 1686, between—
Richard Davies, Thomas Ellis, William Howell.
Francis Howel, Ellis Ellis.
Morgan David.
Francis Lloyd.
James Thomas.
there was conveyed 410 acres of land, for £30, being part of 500 acres out of Richard Davies's 1250 acres, to William Howell and Ellis Ellis (son of Thomas Ellis), that is to say: —for Thomas Ellis, 10 acres, Francis Howel 100, James Thomas 100, Morgan David 100, and Francis Lloyd 100.

The will of David Morgan, "of Merion, yeoman," marked 15. 12mo. 1694, in presence of Robert Owen, Robert Powell, and of John Humphreys, proved 18. 7. 1695, by wife Catherine, sole executor. William Howell, Morris Llewellyn, Francis Howel and David Lawrence, overseers. His estate to go to his two eldest sons, John and Evan, mentions son David. Legacies to daughters Katherine and Elizabeth, and to the Meeting House in Haverford. By deed of 8. 3mo. 1695, the relict and the overseers conveyed David Morgan's 100 acres to James Thomas, who willed the same to his second son, Nathan Thomas. In 12mo. 1701, James Thomas had 100 acres of the Richard Davies patent located in Merion, and altogether, at this time, he held 300 acres in the Welsh Tract.

"David James, from Llandigley and Glaseram [or Glascum] parish, in Radnorshire," and his wife, Margaret, and daughter Mary, wrote to the Radnorshire Men's Meeting, from Pensylvania, in 8mo. 1682, asking for a certificate of membership, &c., which was given, dated 20. 5mo. 1683, and filed with the Haverford (Radnor) Monthly Meeting.

David James had his purchase of 100 acres laid out in Radnor. His sole heir, Mary James, by deed, dated 23. 10mo. 1702, conveyed the same property to Stephen Evans, of Radnor, yeoman, who came from Llanbister parish, Radnorshire, bringing to the Haverford (or Radnor) Monthly

WELSH SETTLEMENT OF PENSYLVANIA

Meeting, his certificate from the Radnorshire Men's Meeting, dated 20. 5mo. 1683.

Stephen Evans bought by deed of 20. 5mo. 1691, 150 acres of David Meredith (who held 350 acres in Radnor, but in 1701, had only 200). Mary James also sold her father's head right, or servant land, to Stephen Evans, whose son John Stephens had the whole surveyed. He declined to pay quit-rent to the land officer, alleging that Penn was under some obligation to him for personal services. He probably satisfied the Commissioners, as there is no further mention of this matter.

Roger Hughes, David Meredith, Richard Cook, David (or James) Price, and John Lloyd, had city lots, in Chestnut Street, between 4th and 5th Streets, reserved for the Welsh settlers, granted to them on account of purchases of land from Richard Davies, which lots were resurveyed to them 28. 2mo. 1702. Hughes sold his lot to Meredith. Cook and Lloyd sold their lots to said Meredith and Stephen Evans. By deed of 20. 9mo. 1702, they conveyed the four lots to David Lloyd, who then owned five city lots altogether, in Chestnut Street, between 4th and 5th Streets, which he sold, by deed of 23. 10mo. 1702, to Enoch Story, of Philadelphia.

Stephen ap Evan, or Stephen Evans aforesaid, bought 100 acres from Richard Davies, and, with the two lots purchased as above, he had 350 acres in Radnor, and on resurvey, in 6mo. 1703, it was discovered he had 47 acres "overplus," which he bought, paying Penn a noble an acre. The Land Commissioners found that he owed Mary James £11, and rent-money for her land from in 1684, and ordered this all paid.

Other land transactions in the account of Richard Davies.

David Lloyd bought from attorneys of Richard Davies, 15. 6mo. 1687, 90 acres, which he sold, 7. 7mo. 1687, to David Powel, who sold it, by deed 10. 10mo. 1687, to Evan Harry, and said Evan Harry also bought 74 acres from Powel, so that in 12mo. 1701, he had 164 acres in one tract, in Radnor. Evan Harry, who had land in Merion—164 acres he bought, which on the survey, amounted to 214 acres, in 4mo. 1704.

Griffith Owen, John Humphrey, Rowland Ellis, and David Lloyd, acting as Davies's attorneys, and Edward Evans, conveyed by deeds of 6. 1mo. 1698-9, and 6. 1mo. 1696, 90 acres to Joseph Growdon.

"Richard Davies *alias* Prees," in 12mo. 1701, held 76½ acres in Goshen tp., part of Richard Davies's 5,000 acres.

Thomas Howell, in 12mo. 1701, held 100 acres in Haverford, being part of Richard Davies's 1250 acres there.

Daniel Humphrey bought 5. 3mo. 1694, 50 acres of "overplus land," due several purchasers of Richard Davies, in Haverford. He also held in Haverford, in 12mo. 1701, 200 acres in rights of "T. Ellis, L. David and J. Poyer."

Richard Moore, in 12mo. 1701, held 245 acres in Radnor, and Henry Price,* 300 acres in same township, bought out of the Richard Davies tract there.

Griffith Owen bought some of this land in Goshen tp., which by first survey amounted to 401½ acres. But on resurvey, in 9mo. 1703, amounted to 775 acres. He was allowed 40 acres "for measure," and promised to pay for the difference.

---

*Price families were numerous in the Welsh Tract.

Will of Isaac Price, signed 4 Sep. 1706, witnesses, David William, Thomas Rees, and Rowland Ellis, proved by his wife, not named, 1 Mar. 1706-7. Names children, Isaac, Mary, and Gwen Price. Overseers same as the witnesses.

Will of Philip Price, of Merion, yeoman, marked 11 Dec. 1719, in the presence of Rees Thomas, Owen Roberts, and Richard Thomas. proved 22 Nov. 1720, by wife Margaret. Names daughter Sarah Lewis, grandchildren Isaac Price, and Samuel, Daniel, Sarah, Mary, David, Isaac, Philip, Miriam, and John, the children of Thomas Rees, "late of Haverford," also grandchildren, ("children of John Lewis, of New Castle, Delaware county"), Elizabeth Stout, Philip, Stephen, Josiah, Sarah, Mary and Ann Lewis. Mentions Joan, wife of Hugh David, Lettice, wife of Samuel Rees, and Rebecca, wife of Thomas Rees. Overseers, Rees Thomas, Norris Llewellyn, and Robert Jones.

WELSH SETTLEMENT OF PENSYLVANIA

Henry Harry, only son of Daniel Harry, grantee of 100 acres in Radnor, in 168—, asked confirmation by the Land Commissioners of this land to him, 25. 9mo. 1724.

"From Macchinleth, in Montgomeryshire, Hugh Harris and Daniel Harris," is recorded on the passenger list of the ship "Vine of Liverpool," which arrived at Philadelphia 17. 7mo. 1684, and from the minutes of the Haverford, or Radnor Monthly Meeting, 8. 2mo. 1686, "William Howell and George Painter are ordered to speak to Hugh and Daniel Harry concerning their Parents money," and, in same, 10, 4mo. 1686, "George Painter & William Howell according to former order did speak with Hugh and Daniel Harry, who have promised yt if any friends would lay out money in England upon their parents account they would out of the Product or growth of this Countrey make them satisfaction." Their surnames, as assumed, were variously Harry and Harris in different families. Hugh Harris, a weaver, and Elizabeth, daughter of William and Ann Brinton, of Birmingham tp., declared their intentions of marriage, at the Chichester Meeting 1. 1mo. 1686. By deed 11. 4mo. 1695, Mr. Brinton conveyed 250 acres of land in Birmingham, to them, where they went to reside, and 19 Nov. 1707, Hugh bought 430 acres in East Marlborough tp., Chester Co. Hugh Harris died in 1708, having nine children. His four sons, Evan, William, Hugh, and John, and their descendants, had "Harry" as their surname.

The will of Lewis Harry, of Radnor, marked 12. 7mo. 1699, witnesses David Davies, Benjamin Humphrey, David Lewis, and Benjamin Lewis, was proved 1 April, 1700, by wife Abigail. Children named Harry, Mary, and Eleanore. The will of his son, Harry Lewis, of Radnor, signed 20 March, 1701-2, in the presence of Peter Worrell, Edward Thomas, and David Evan, was proved 13 April, 1702, by brother-in-law John Worrell, names sisters Mary Worrell, and Eleanor Lewis. His father's servant, Richard Faddery, mentioned in both wills.

COMPANY NUMBER SEVEN

John Evan Edwards, held at one time 625 and 194 acres, in Radnor. He bougth 200 acres of this land from John Williams, by deed of 10. 5mo. 1700, which was a portion of the estate of Thomas Ellis, whose administrator, Daniel Humphreys, had conveyed it to Williams. David Powel conveyed, by deed of 22. 5mo. 1687, to John Evan Edwards 100 acres, which was a part of the 500 acres he received from the Land Commissioners, by patent, dated 4. 4mo. 1686. On resurvey, it was found to be 123 acres, and Edwards bought the difference.

The will of Thomas John Evan, of Radnor, who may have been a son of this landowner, signed 31, 1 mo. 1707, in the presence of friends Rowland Ellis, Sr., Joshua Owen, and Rowland Ellis, Jr., was proved by his wife "Lowry John Evan." Children named, John, Joseph, and Elizabeth.

All of these "Radnor town" original deeds had about the same witnesses, namely, Edward Jones, Thomas Davies, David James, Richard Jones, Daniel Morris, Samuel Miles, John Evans, and Daniel Meredith.

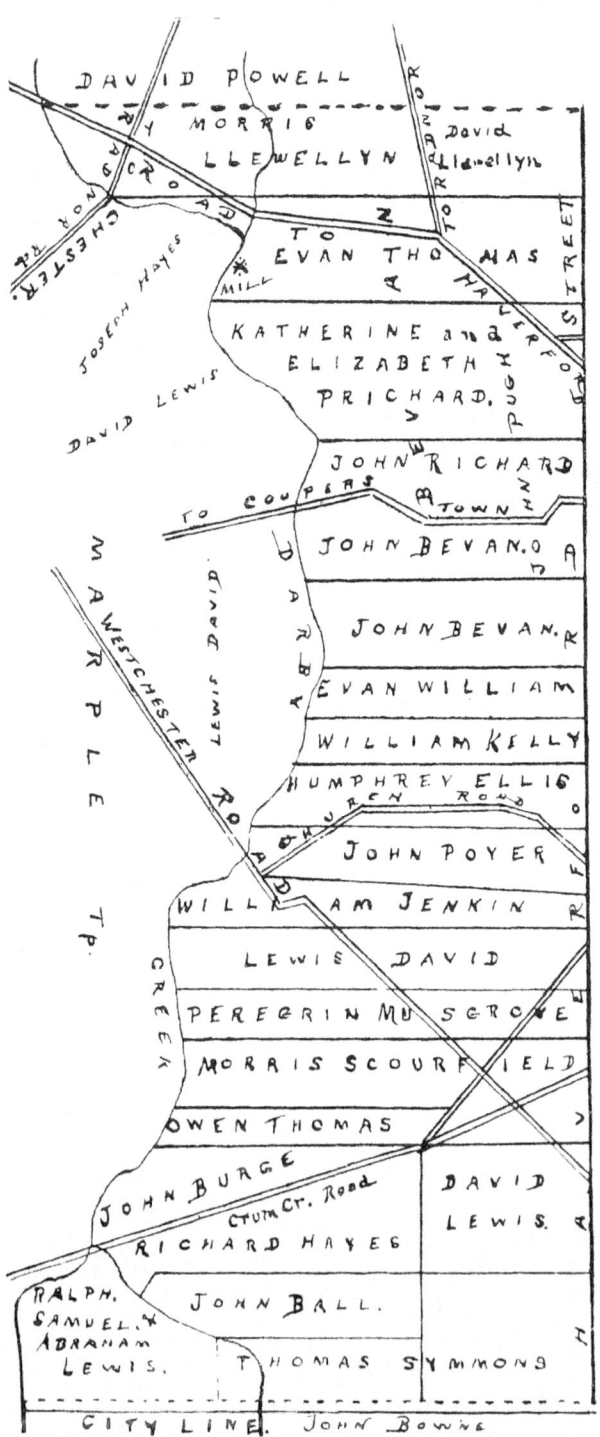

HAVERFORD TP., WEST OF THE "STREET," 1690.

RICHARD DAVIES'S LAND PATENT, II.

RICHARD DAVIES was a recognized minister among the Friends in Wales, and, as it appears, was an active friend of Penn, since he sold so much of his land. But, strange to say, he sold none of it in his home county. "The Journal of that ancient Servant of the Lord, Richard Davies," giving his autobiography, has frequently been printed. He was born at Welshpool, Montgomeryshire, in 1635. His parents were "Church of England people," but being apprenticed to an "Independant," a felt-maker, he became acquainted with Morgan Evan, of South Wales, a minister among Friends, who made the young man a convert to Quakerism. In 1659, he married in London, Tace ...., by whom, who died in 1705, he had a daughter Tace, who married ———— Endon, and had a son, David Endon. Mr. Davies died at his home, Cloddan Cochion, near Welshpool, on 22. 1mo. 1707-8.

See the "Friends' Library," vol. XIII., for "An Account of Richard Davies," written in 1708, and a copy of the "Testimonies concerning him," given at the Quarterly Meeting held at Dolobran, 25. 11mo. 1708.

"Rowland Ellis, gent," a minister among Friends, with a good estate, the largest purchaser of land from Richard Davies, and subsequently one of the prominent men of the Welsh Tract, was born about 1650-2, on his father's farm, called "Bryn Mawr," near Dogelly, Dyffrydan tp., in Merionethshire, where he resided till his removal to Pensylvania, having sold the old homestead, a modest stone house, which is still standing in a state of good preservation.

Like other Welshmen who came over to settle here, he wrote out and brought his family genealogy, in Welsh style, still extant in the Evans family, so as to be in touch with

WELSH SETTLEMENT OF PENSYLVANIA

"home." From it, we learn that he was the only son of Ellis ap Rees, or Ellis Price, whose father, Lewis ap Sion Griffith, of Nannau, built "Bryn Mawr House" in 1617. And that Rowland's mother, Ann Humphrey, was a daughter of Humphrey ap Hugh, of Llwyngrill, (the marriage settlement dated 1 Jan. 1649), and sister to John and Samuel Humphrey, purchasers of Welsh Tract land from the Lloyds. He is of record, 8. 10mo. 1704, as filing an account of his kindred and life with the Merion Meeting.

Rowland Ellis became a Quaker about 1673, and like other Friends of his neighborhood, suffered imprisonment in 1676, in Dolgelly goal, but, although he bought the largest block of land in the Welsh Tract purchased of Richard Davies, and helped get up his company, he did not remove to his purchase permanently till after sixteen years, when "beyond the Schuylkill" was no longer a wilderness.

In 1683, Rowland Ellis sent in Hugh Roberts' party his farmer, Thomas Owen, who was said to be a relative, and Thomas's family, to have his land properly laid out, some in Merion, and some in Goshen, and to make a settlement on his Merion land, build a house, clear some fields, and begin a farm, and make the usual preparations for the coming of himself and family when convenient. Four years later, Rowland Ellis, then a widower, bringing his son and namesake, came over to look over the situation, with a view of permanently removing with all his family.

On this trip to Pensylvania, he sailed in a Bristol ship from Milford Haven, on 16. 8mo. 1686. Many of his neighbors, about 100, all from about Dolgelly, accompanied him, and they had a long and tedious passage of 24 weeks, as they were obliged to come by the way of the Barbadoes, where the ship was detained six weeks, much to the discomfort of some of the passengers, but the saving of others, for coming, the immigrants generally experienced great suffering from being crowded in a small boat, and from the lack of proper accommodations for so large a party, and as it is recorded, "many died through want of necessary provisions, others from the remaining effects of their 'sufferings' [in Wales] and some that survived never recovered their former strength." If these passengers had not had the opportunity for recuperation at the Barbadoes, it was thought all would have perished before reaching the Delaware, so great was their suffering through bad food and sickness.

Mr. Ellis remained here only about nine months, and then returned to "old Bryn Mawr," leaving young Rowland behind with uncle John Humphreys. So pleased was Mr. Ellis with the outlook in the Province, that he bought a great deal of wild land in various localities at this time, and shortly after, and these land speculations eventually caused his financial ruin.

Mr. Ellis seems to have made his second visit after 1687, and before his second marriage, as he brought a certificate of good standing from some Meeting (not named, and undated), probably the one held at Tyddier y Gareg, near Dolgelley, Merioneth, which he filed with the Haverford (Radnor) Mo. Mtg. It mentions him as "returning to his own country namely Pensilvania." It says that "he was free and clear from any promise or Ingagement up on the account of Marriage, as far as we know when he parted from us." Signed by Robert Ellis, Owen Lewis, Rowland Edward Humphrey, Robert and Harry Owen, Ellis Powell, Owen Humphrey, John Harry, and William Bevan. How long he stayed here is not known.

In 1696, Mr. Ellis resolved to remove altogether, with his family, excepting his daughter Ann, who was left in possession of "Bryn Mawr," and who was then married to the Episcopal clergyman, to his American possessions. He sailed from Liverpool again, with a hundred passengers from his neighborhood, who having the experience of their former neighbors, provided against the discomforts of a long voyage. They arrived at Philadelphia in 4mo. 1697. He brought his certificate from the Garthgynfawr Meet-

WELSH SETTLEMENT OF PENSYLVANIA

ing, dated 7. 11mo. 1696-7, signed by Lewis Owen, Rowland Owen, David Jones, and others.

He resided for several years in the little house erected by Mr. Owen, on his improved land, which he named after his paternal home, "Bryn Mawr," a name perpetuated by a beautiful town and a college, as his farm adjoined the Bryn Mawr College on the North. About 1704, (or was it 1714?), he erected a more pretentious two-story stone mansion on his "Bryn Mawr" farm, which is still standing, but renamed "Harriton" by a subsequent owner.

An interesting and long letter from Mr. Ellis, written in 1698, to his son-in-law, Rev. Mr. Johnson, is preserved, (see Pa. Mag. 1894), and tells considerable about his new home. He wrote:—"Our house lies under ye Cold N. W. wind, and just to the South Sun, in a very warm bottom near a stream of very good water. We have cleared about this run about 10 or 12 acres for meadow land, very good soil, black mould moist over.... We have as much more such ground for meadow, when we may have to enclose it. Few, or none of our countrymen have the like conveniency of meadow land. We have above six acres of wheat sown in good order, and an accer and half of ye last summer fallow for barley. We now begin to clear in order for to sow Oats....We are about to enclose with rail fence about 40 accre."

He said his farm property here was about forty perch in length, and four perch in breadth. From his statement, it may be imagined Mr. Ellis had but little of his land under cultivation, and hardly crops enough to sustain his family, and this all seems a very miniature farm, in his great holdings, for from the minutes of the Land Commissioners, 12. 2. 1703, we learn that Rowland Ellis, having purchased of Richard Davies 1100 acres, by deed dated 30 July, 1682, recorded 30. 5. 1684, witnesses being Ellis Morris, Row Owen, Owen Lewis, Sr., and Jr., David Evan and Evan Harry, he had 500 laid out in Merion, and 483 in Goshen tp., having sold 117 acres. And that on resurvey, he had

COMPANY NUMBER SEVEN

in Merion 881 acres, and in Goshen 341 acres, and altogether 1222 acres of land. It was found that he had only 39 acres of "over plus" land, and this he promised to pay for, so patent was issued to him for 1222 acres.

By deed of 24 Feb. 1708, Mr. Ellis, for £180, conveyed to Rees Thomas, of Merion, and William Lewis, of New Town, 300 acres, "wherein the said Rowland Ellis now dwells, with the tract of land thereunto belonging." But Mr. Ellis's residence, still standing, was on the following property.

In 1717-9, Rees Thomas and William Lewis sold 700 acres, (the above 300 acres included), and apparently "Bryn Mawr," which lay on what is known as the Gulf Road, (that is, this road passed diagonally through the South part of the tract, and bounded it on the South-West), to Richard Harrison of Herring Creek, in Maryland, whose second wife Hannah, a Friends' minister, was a daughter of Judge Isaac Norris, and a granddaughter of Gov. Thomas Lloyd. 1719, Oct. 23, Mr. Ellis confirmed by one deed of this date, his whole tract of 718 acres to the said Richard Harrison, and for which he paid £600. The land of John Williams, Hugh Pugh, Thomas Lloyd, Hugh Evans, Owen Roberts, Thomas Nicholas, Philip Price, and Peter Jones, were bounds to Mr. Ellis's land in 1719. On this land is the "Harrison Family Cemetery," where Richard Harrison was buried in 1747-8.

Mr. Harrison's son-in-law, Charles Thomson, the well known secretary of the Continental Congress, lived in Mr. Ellis's stone house, on the Gulph Road, some three miles from Gulph Mill, and changed its name to "Harriton." He was buried in the Harriton Cemetery, in 1824, with his wife. It was while Mr. Thomson lived here, "12 miles from the State House," that Gen. James Potter, of the American army, wrote the following report to President Wharton, of Pensylvania dated 15 Dec. 1777.

WELSH SETTLEMENT OF PENSYLVANIA

"Last Thursday the enemy march out of the City with a desine to Furridge, but it was Nessecerey to drive me out of the way; my advanced picquet fired on them at the Bridge; another party of one Hundred attacted them at Black Hors. I was encamped on Charles Thomson's place, where I staeconed two Regiments who attacted the enemy with viger. On the next Hill, I staeconed three Regments, letting the first line know, that when they were over powered, they must Retreat and form behind the second line, and in that manner we formed and Retreated for four miles; and on every Hill we disputed the matter with them. My people Behaved well, espealy three Regements, Commanded by the Cols Chambers, Murrey, and Leacey. His Excellencey Returned us thanks in public orders.* But the cumplement would have been much more substantiale had the Valant Generil Solovan Covered my Retreat with two Devissions of the Army, he had in my Reare, the front of them was about one half mile in my Reare, but he gave orders for them to Retreat and join the army who were on the other side of the Schuylkill about one mile and a Half from me, thus the enemy Got leave to plunder the Countrey, which they have dun without parsiality or favour to any, leaving none of the Nessecereys of Life Behind them that they conveniantly could Carry or destroy."

In those days, fifty years after he left the neighborhood, there were strenuous times about the old home of the mild Quaker minister.

In 1700, Rowland Ellis represented the Welsh Tract, or at least Merion, in the Assembly, and generally he was an active man in Welsh affairs, and because of his sound judgment in all cases, civil and religious, he was highly respected,

---

*"The Commander-in-Chief, with great pleasure, expresses his approbation of the behavior of the Pensylvania Militia yesterday, under General Potter, on the vigorous opposition they made to a body of the enemy on the other side of the Schuylkill." From "Orderly Book," 12 Dec. 1777.

COMPANY NUMBER SEVEN

not only by the Welsh Quakers, but in the Province generally. His last attendance at Quarterly Meeting was in Philadelphia on 31. 6mo. 1731.

Mr. Ellis was taken suddenly ill, after attending meeting at Gwynedd, and died in 7mo. 1731, in his 80th year, at the home of his son-in-law, John Evans, in "North Wales," or Plymouth, Philadelphia Co. (where he lived in 1717), and was buried there in the ground of the Gwynedd Monthly Meeting, which Meeting prepared a Memorial respecting him, stating he had "a gift in the ministry which was acceptable and to edification."

About 1672, Rowland Ellis* was married first to his cousin, Margaret Ellis, daughter of Ellis Morris, of Dolgun, and by her had a son and a daughter:

Ann Ellis, "married out," in 1696, to the Rev. Richard Johnson, of the "Established," or P. E. Church, who was the curate of Dolgelly, and had issue. Mr. Ellis was much attached to his wayward daughter, but as she was disowned, he did not know, in 1699, if she was living, and wrote to inquire "whether she is quite dead."

Rowland Ellis, Jr., who came over with his father in 1686-1687, seems to have died without issue. On 19. 3mo. 1725, he requested warrant of the Commissioners for the survey on 3,000 acres which he had purchased, paying £130, by deed, dated 3 April, 1724, of Daniel Warley, Jr., the son and heir of a London wool merchant, who had bought the land in 1695.

Mr. Ellis married secondly, after his second trip to Pensylvania, his cousin Margaret Roberts, daughter of Robert ap Owen Lewis, of Dyffryddan, and had by her, who died at

---

*In her will, marked in the presence of Edward Rees and Rowland Ellis, on 9. 8mo. 1716, proved 19 Aug. 1717, Rachel Ellis, of Haverford, mentions cousin Rowland Ellis and Elizabeth Ellis, and her brother Evan Ellis, and William Ellis, and sisters Elizabeth, Bridget, and Rebecca Ellis.

WELSH SETTLEMENT OF PENSYLVANIA

Plymouth, about 1730, four children, of whom *Elizabeth, Robert,* and *Catherine, b.* 1697, died unmarried, and

Ellin Ellis, (or Eleanor) who *d.* 29. 4mo. 1765, aged 76 years. She married at the Merion Meeting, on 8. 4mo. 1715, John Evans, of Gwynedd, Philadelphia Co., a Friends' minister, (a son of Cadwalader Evans, 1664-1745, of Gwynedd), and had by him, who *d.* 23. 9mo. 1756, (his will dated 16. 9mo. 1756, proved 22 June, 1757), eight children. Of these the only known grandchildren of Rowland Ellis, of "Bryn Mawr,"—

Cadwalader Evans, 1716-1773, *m.* Jane Owen.
Rowland Evans, 1718-1789, *m.* Susanna Foulke.
Margaret, wife of Anthony Williams.
Jane, wife of John Hubbs.
Ellen, second wife of Ellis Lewis.
Elizabeth Evans, spinster, 1726-1805.
John Evans, 1730-1807, *m.* Margaret Foulke.

Thomas Ellis, of Dolserre, in Merionethshire, having bought a great deal of the Robert Davies land, is included in this section though he was not one of his subscribers, but was originally an independent purchaser from Penn. He was one of the party of Welsh Quakers who interviewed Penn, in London, in May, 1681, about land in his Province, and, being a personal friend of John ap Thomas, accompanied him. Becoming convinced of Penn's representations, he bought from him 1,000 acres, on his own account, and not as a trustee, or "Adventuring Company," which land was subsequently laid out to him in the upper part of Merion.

It is supposed that Thomas Ellis was born in Montgomeryshire, though there is nothing definite known of his people. When he first came into notice, he is a minister among Friends, and travelled much throughout Wales, often in the company of the missionary, John Burnyeat, and was arrested at Machynlleth, and at Aberystwith, for being at meetings and preaching, and was imprisoned, and "suffered"

COMPANY NUMBER SEVEN

in other ways, and by 1683, he had had enough of Wales, joined the party of Hugh Roberts, and came over to Pensylvania.

He filed with the Philadelphia Mo. Mtg. his certificate from the Dolserre Quarterly Meeting, dated 27. 5 mo. 1683. He also filed with the Haverford Mo. Mtg. his certificate issued to himself, his wife, and family, from the Mo. Mtg. at Redstone, in Pembrokeshire, dated 2. 7mo. 1683, signed by Edward Lloyd, John Poyer, John Bourge, James Thomas, William Jenkins, Evan Rowen, Lewis James, James Lewis, Richard White, David John, David Rees, and Peregrin Musgrave.

Where Mr. Ellis, with his wife and family, resided after settling here, is not known, but from the following letter, of 1685, it was not far from the Haverford Meeting house, and, afterwards, in the city, on account of his public life, and because of his travels. In the Province, he became a man of considerable prominence, even among the English, and, at the time of his decease, he was the register-general of the Province. His speculations in land were extensive and intricate, and on this account his estate was involved in litigation which caused his executor considerable trouble.

There is a rather interesting letter, printed in full in the Journal of the Friends' Historical Society, London, (issue of Nov. 1909), written by Thomas Ellis, while at Dublin, dated 13. 4mo. 1685, addressed "To Phillipp ffoord att Hood an Scarff in Bow Lane, London, for G. ff, these deliv'r with Care." This was the Mr. Ford with whom and his shrewd wife Mr. Penn had certainly peculiar relations, of which elsewhere, and which are fully set out by Mr. Shepherd in his "History of Proprietary Government in Pensylvania."

Mr. Ellis's letter was written on his return from Pensylvania, where he writes he had "left a tender wife and a considerable family of children and Servants well settled and ordered, considering the time, in a good neighborhood."

WELSH SETTLEMENT OF PENSYLVANIA

"Abt 15 families of us have taken our Land together and are to be abt 8 more that have not yet com, we took (to begin) 30 accres a piece, we built upon and doe improve [this land], and the other Land we have for Range to our cattell."

"We have our buriyng place where we intend our [Haverford] meeting house [shall be], as neer as we can to the Center, [of the settlement]. Our first day and week dayes meetings [are] well observed, besides our mens and womens meetings, and another Monthly Meeting [besides the great Philadelphia Mo. Mtg.], both in week dayes, unto wch four townships, [Merion, Haverford, Radnor and Schuylkill] at least belongs."

Mr. Ellis advises Friends to remove from Wales to Pensylvania, because there is no hope, so far as he can see, of their ever doing so well, or of ever being better off than now, in the old country.

"I cam from home since the 12mo. intending to be at the yearly meeting but could not have any shipping for 6 weeks being there was so much winter wether the like was hardly known, and so no seasoning wether for their tobacco, and a sore visitation in Mariland, in so much that hundreds dyed there in this last falls and winter of all sorts of people, 3 or 4 doctors [died] on the easter shore while I was there. dear Thomas Taylor and his wife [of Maryland], and Bryan Mele and Thomas ffurby, and many others, servicable friends, by a violent feaver, but it seems to be well over before I cam thence."

"I suppose you have had an account of Pensilvania affairs by newyork as was intended at the monthly meeting at Philadelphia," he asks Mr. Fox, whom he addressed as "My dear and fatherly friend," and informs him, "the president [Thomas Lloyd] was not then at home, but was expected from newyork."

"Several young people continue to com over without certificates which is a trouble to friends.   I am like to con-

COMPANY NUMBER SEVEN

tinue in Wales a while when I would be glad to meet with William Bingley or such.

[Signed] "Thou knowest Tho Ellis."* He requests his mail lying in London be forwarded to him in care of "Peregrine Musgraves, clothier, in Haverford west, in Penbrokeshire, South Wales."

In the "P. S.", Mr. Ellis continues, "I have sent a few lines for W. P."...."dated here abt 4 dayes agoe." "If W. P. [has] not received it let him have part of this" [letter].

Thomas Ellis's first grant, by general description, was 1,000 acres, located in Merion. On survey it came out 819 acres, and on a resurvey only 735 acres, which gives us a fair idea of the ability of Penn's official surveyors at that time.

"Of the Richard Davies purchase Thomas Ellis, gent., of Jsoregenan, in Merioneth, bought of the mesme purchasers," namely, Lewis Owen and Rowland Owen, of Gwanas, Ellis Maurice (or Morris), of Dolgunucha, and Ellis Pugh, 625 acres in Merion, for himself, and 1,000 acres as agent for cthers. These purchases were conveyed by deeds dated in 1684 and 1686, and witnessed by Owen Lewis, Evan Harry, and John Humphrey, of Llanwddyn. Mr. Ellis took up these lands by warrants, dated 3. 11mo. 1687., and kept for his trouble all of the lands in the city Liberties, due on account of the purchases, besides all of the "overs." From the land records, he seems to have had over 3400 acres at one time, made up of Penn's grant, Davis' land, sundry rights, and "over-plus," but he had only between 800 and 900 acres in various places when he died.

Mr. Ellis was buried in the ground of the Haverford Mtg. By his will, dated 1. 11mo. 1688, he desired that all of his land should be sold by his executors to pay his debts, but those he named as executors declined to act, because

---

*For other particulars as to Thomas Ellis, see George Smith's "History of Delaware County," Pa., and "The Philadelphia Friend," magazine, XXVII.

of the tangled state of his lands. Nor would his relict administer, and settle up his estate, for the same reason, and by her will, threw all this trouble to her executor Daniel Humphrey, and he generously undertook the task with the assistance of the meeting.

As executor, Mr. Humphrey, by deed dated 5. 7mo. 1698, conveyed what was remaining of the Penn grant, about 625 acres, and 194 acres, in Merion to John Williams, and settled Ellis's account with William Penn, as he owed Penn £12.7.9, (being the balance due on the "1,000 acres," or 763 and 84 acres, at 5s. per acre)—with a credit of £30 Penn owed him. Some of Mr. Ellis's land lay in Duffryn Mawr, and Bertha Rowles bought 250 acres out of it, and in 1701, his daughter, Rachel Ellis, held 250 acres there, in his right.

A further account shows that Mr. Ellis had also about 790 acres in Haverford, as there were the following distributions and sales:—To his widow, Ellin, 30; son Ellis Ellis, 200; (and 30 from John Bevan); daughter "Brigid" 100; son Humphrey Ellis, 90; (60, 20 and 10 acres), sold to Daniel Humphrey, 100 (90 only in Haverford); to George Painter, 90; (sold to John Lewis, Sr.); to Daniel Lawrence, 90, (who also bought Humphrey Ellis's 90); to same, 60; to Daniel Humphrey, 20; to William Howell, 10, (sold to Rowland Powel). Or, there was sold 690 acres, and daughter Rachel Ellis had besides 101 acres in Haverford.

In 1700, Daniel Humphrey, of Haverford, held some 200 acres, made up of 90 acres bought (23. 12. 1684) from Thomas Ellis; 30 acres from Mr. Ellis and wife Ellin; 20¾ acres from Humphrey Ellis, son of said Thomas, by deed, 8. 9mo. 1694, and 60 acres from William Rowe, by deed of 30 May 1700.

Thomas Ellis was survived by his wife, Ellen, (surname unknown). Her will to which she put her mark, witnessed by David Llewellyn, Benjamn Humphreys, Theodore Robert, and John Humphrey, 27. 1. 1692, was proved 18. 12mo.

1692-3. She left her estate to daughter Rachel Ellis, and if she died before receiving it, then to the six children, unnamed, of her sisters, Lowry and Gwen. Appoints as executor, nephew Daniel Humphrey. To be trustees, Griffith Owen, William Howell, Edward Jones, John Roberts, Robert Owen, and John Humphreys.

Of their children:—

Ellis Ellis. He received some of his father's land, and held a warrant for re-survey, 18. 12mo. 1701, two parcels; found to be 330 acres, including 63 acres "over plus," which he promised to buy at 7s, 6d. per acre. He *m.* Lydia, daughter of Samuel and Elizabeth Humphrey, of Haverford.

The land deeds of the old Haverford School, and Haverford College, show the college land was originally part of the 410 acres which Richard Davies conveyed, on 19. 6mo. 1686, to Thomas Ellis, gentleman, Francis Howell, yeoman, James Thomas, yeoman, Morgan David, husbandman, and Francis Lloyd, shoemaker. And also that land which Ellis Ellis, of Haverford, yeoman, conveyed, by deed dated 25. 12mo. 1703, to "Robert Wharton, cordwainer," and his wife, Rachel, (a daughter of Thomas Ellis), namely 255 acres of his father's land, for fifty shillings, Pensylvania money, is part of the college land.

Humphrey Ellis, living in 1699.

Rachel Ellis, *m.* Robert Wharton.

"Brigid Ellis," who *d.* in England.

Eleanor Ellis, who *m.* David Lawrence, of Haverford. He came over from Wales about 1683. His will, signed 12. 2mo. 1699, in the presence of John Roberts, Rowland Powell, and John Bevan, was proved 1 July 1699. He left his estate to his wife and eldest son, Daniel. Names sons, Henry and Thomas, and daughters, Margaret, Eleanor and Rachel Lawrence, overseers, "brothers Ellis Ellis and Humphrey

WELSH SETTLEMENT OF PENSYLVANIA

Ellis," and William Howell. Thomas Lawrence* *m.* Sarah, *b.* 1685, daughter of William ap Edward, of Blockley, and his second wife, her sister, Ellen, *b.* 1691, *m.* Henry Lawrence, and their brother "Edward Williams," of Blockley, *m.* Eleanor Lawrence.

John Williams who bought in 1698, the balance of Thomas Ellis's Merion land, as above, sold 10. 5. 1700, some of it to Hugh Jones and John Evans (John Evans held 200 acres of this land, in 12mo. 1701).

Mr. Humphrey, the executor to both Thomas Ellis and his wife, as above, by deed dated 20. 1mo. 1701, conveyed 409½ acres of Ellis's land to Robert Lloyd, and Hugh Jones, aforesaid, and let Robert have 150 acres, which he conveyed to his brother, Thomas Lloyd.

The brothers, Robert Lloyd and Thomas Lloyd, came over in Hugh Roberts's and John Bevan's party, in 1683, from Merioneth, and were young and unmarried. They next appear as subscribing witnesses at the marriage of Robert Roberts and Katherine Jones, at the Haverford Meeting, 5. 3mo. 1696. Robert was one of the overseers to the will of Robert Owen, of Merion.

Robert Lloyd's first purchase of land, as above, was located North of "Bryn Mawr" (Rowland Ellis's tract), and was a portion of the Richard Davies grant from Penn. Robert had 259½ acres of this surveyed and laid out, in 12mo. 1701.

1703, 8mo. 4. Before the Land Commissioners, Robert Lloyd produced return of 432 acres, in Merion, on re-survey, on warrant dated 20. 2mo. 1703, to survey to him 409 acres, "being part of 819 acres out of Thomas Ellis's land." He requested a patent. Granted. And on 6. 12mo. 1707-8, he had title to his land confirmed to him, and this for good reasons, as explained elsewhere.

*From him are descended Abraham Lewis Smith, of Media, and Benj. Hayes Smith, of Philadelphia, who are also descended from Dr. Thomas Wynne, Dr. Edward Jones, Robert Owen, of Merion, Ralph Lewis, etc.

COMPANY NUMBER SEVEN

Robert Lloyd* died 29. 3mo. 1714, and was buried at the Merion Meeting House. His will, signed 30 April, 1714, witnessed by Edward Foulke, William Roberts (marked), and Thomas Albin, was proved 16 Nov. same year, by his wife, Lowry. He names his children, David, Robert, Rees, Richard, Hannah, Gwen, Sarah, and Gainor. Mentions Edward Thomas and Owen Roberts, and his brother Thomas Lloyd, and named as trustees, Robert and Richard Jones, Thomas Lloyd, Jr., and friends Robert Evan, Rowland Ellis, and Robert Jones, of Merion.

He married at the Merion Meeting, on 11. 8mo. 1698, Lowry Jones, who died 25. 11mo. 1762, aged 80 years, and was buried with her husband. She was a child of Rees John William, of Merion. Of their children:—

Hannah *m.* first, John Roberts, Jr., (grandson of Owen Humphrey) and had John Roberts, 3d. *b.* 1721, and *m.* secondly, William Paschall, *issue,* and *m.* thirdly, Peter Osborne, *issue.*

Richard Lloyd, 1714-1755, of Darby, *m.* at Darby Mtg. 24. 9. 1736, Hannah daughter of Samuel and Sarah Sellers, and had Hugh Lloyd, 1742-1832, of Chester Co., colonel of 3d Battalion, presidential elector and associate judge.

Robert Lloyd, *m.* Catherine Humphrey. *Issue.*

Thomas Lloyd, the younger of the brothers, held in 12mo. 1701, the 150 (or 154½) acres in Merion, which had been a part of the Thomas Ellis estate, and lay North of "Bryn Mawr," and by deed, dated 10 Feb. 1709, his brother Robert further conveyed to him 154 acres of his land North of "Bryn Mawr," on payment of £40. He was a farmer, and his will, marked 26. 5mo. 1741, was proved 6 Feb. 1748;

---

*From Robert Lloyd are descended Howard Williams Lloyd, Wm. Supplee Lloyd, and the brothers Samuel Bunting Lewis, Davis Levis Lewis, George Harrison Lewis, and Osborn G. L. Lewis, of Philadelphia, descendants also of William Lewis, who came over in 1686-7. Samuel Marshall, of West Chester, Pa. is also descended from Robert Lloyd, and from Rees John William, of Merion.

witnesses, David Davids and Richard Lloyd, trustees to be "neighbors Richard Lloyd and Griffith Llewellyn."

Thomas Lloyd was married about 1698, by a justice of the peace, to Elizabeth, *b.* 1672, who survived him, daughter of William ap Edward, or Edwards, of Blockley, by his first wife. They appeared before the Merion Meeting, on 8. 6mo. 1700, and humbled themselves for "marrying out." Her will, signed 2 Dec. 1748, was proved 6 Feb. 1748-9. They had seven children: Thomas, 1699-176-, resided in Bucks Co., Pa.; Sarah, *m.* at Merion Mtg. 8. 9mo. 1721, John Morgan (son of Edward, of Gwynedd); Jane, *m.* first at Merion Mtg. 8. 8. 1725, Lewis Williams, of Gwynedd; John 1704-1770, *m.* at Merion Mtg. 31. 10. 1731, Eleanor, daughter of Henry and Catherine Pugh; Elizabeth, *m.* at Merion Mtg. 9. 8mo. 1728, Joseph Morgan (brother to above John); Evan and William.

Having now brought nearly all of the Welsh "first purchasers," and the early settlers to their new homes in the great Welsh tract, a review of the peculiar claims they made on Penn, or set up for themselves, and how they tried to substantiate them, and, failing in this, see how it was that "the Welsh tract," as a district and indentity was wiped-off the map of Pensylvania should be interesting.

WELSH TRACT PLANTERS

The following is the summary of the foregoing transactions, and others in the Welsh tract, set forth in "D. Powels Acct of ye Welch Purchasers in Genl," in which he gives his personal "Account of the purchasers Concurned in the Welch Tract Granted by the Generall war't by wich the said Tract was Laid out and such Lands as hath bin Laid out by war'ts Dulie Executed within the same and ist of ye ould England Parishes":—

	Acres.		Acres.
Charles Lloyd, and Margaret Davis	5,000	Henry Right	500
		Daniell Med———	200
Richard Davis, [Davies]	5,000	Thomas Ellis	1,000
William Jenkins	1,000	Tho Ellis for B. Roules	250
John Poy, [Poyer]	750	Th. Ellis on ac't Humph. Tho.	100
John Burge	750		
William Mordant	500	David Powell	1,000
William Powell	1,250	Burke and Simson	1,000
Lewis David	3,000	John Kinsy	200
Morris Llewlin	500	John Kinsy	100
Thomas Simons	500	David Meredith	250
John Bevan	2,000	John Day	300
Edward Prichard	2,500	David Davis	200
John ap John, and Thomas Wyn	5,000	Henry Joanes	400
		Thomas John Evan	250
Edward Joanes, and John Thomas	5,000	John Evans	100
		John Jormon	50
Richard Davis	1,250	David Kinsy	200
Richard ap Thomas	5,000	Evan Oliver	100
Daniell Hurry, [Harry]	300	Samuel Mills	100
Mordicia Moore in Right of	500	Thomas Joanes	50
		David Joanes	100
John Millington	500	John Ffish	300

"The whole Compl'nt 50,000 acres."

As there are only forty-one grants in this list, and Holme's map indicated more than twice this number of land owners

WELSH SETTLEMENT OF PENSYLVANIA

in the Welsh Tract, it may be presumed that Holme did not compile his map as early as he claimed, when testifying before the Council as to the positions of the townships of Haverford and Radnor, as will appear.

In this summary by Surveyor David Powel, without date, we find the names of the first large purchasers of land in Merion township, John Thomas and Dr. Jones, and those of the other six "Companies," or adventurers for Welsh Tract plantations, and also those of the other large independent "first purchasers," some of whose land was laid out in Merion, besides in Haverford, Radnor, and Goshen townships, and it may be noticed that there were very few not strictly Welsh had been granted land in the tract.

Although the acreage given by Powel exceeded the original total of the grants to the Welsh, namely 40,000 acres, and took in much of the supplementary 10,000 acres reserved for them, it did not come up to "the whole Compl'nt 50,000 acres." Mr. Powel, however, may have inadvertently overlooked some grantees, but it appears that he remembered to record a tract of 1,000 acres in his own name, and its future location he had probably selected, for which he had deed from Penn. It seems to have been for services as a surveyor, but the grant was not confirmed to him till in 1705, as mentioned below.

For the above reason, the date of Powel's list cannot be approximated by the mention of his own land, 1,000 acres. For his surveying work for the Land Commissioners, he probably received from them little cash; but he was granted small parcels of land, and realized what he could by the sale of them. He had a patent from the Commissioners, dated 14. 3mo. 1686, for 611 acres, which he laid out in Radnor tp., in two tracts, 500 and 111 acres, and this is his first land-ownership of record. This represented £100 to him. On 22. 5mo. 1687, he sold 100 acres of this patent to John Evans, adjoining the land of Hugh Samuel. On 17. 11mo. 1690, he sold 100 acres more to said Hugh Samuel, (servant to Thomas Ellis), adjoining the land of David

PLANTERS AND SERVANTS

Hugh. On 17. 3mo. 1690, he sold another 100 acres to James Pugh (servant to Steven Bevan), adjoining land of David Pugh, and by another deed of this date, he sold 200¾ acres and closed out his 500 acres, to William Davis and Griffith Miles, the land adjoining Hugh Samuel. Of this land, William and Griffith sold 150 acres to Philip Philips, whose widow, Phoebe, sold the same to David Pugh, and, by deed 22. 6mo. 1690, William and Griffith sold their balance of 50 acres to James Pugh, aforesaid, and here was the "Pugh District" in Radnor.

John Evans, aforesaid, by deed of 10. 5mo. 1700, bought 200 acres in Merion, adjoining Rowland Ellis, from John Williams, who had it from the Richard Davies tract, (Company No. 7), through Thomas Ellis and Daniel Humphrey.

Evan Harry, by deed of 10. 10mo. 1687, bought 90 acres from Surveyor Powel, who received it, 7. 7mo. 1687, from David Lloyd, the lawyer, as a fee, who bought it from the attorneys of Richard Davies, 15. 6mo. 1687. Evan Harry also bought 74 acres more from Powel, and Abel Roberts, son of Ellis Roberts, of Radnor, also bought 100 acres from Powel, by deed of 1. 6mo. 1693, confirmed 9. 6mo. 1703, and these sales exceeded his patents.

In 1704-5, Powel was still the Proprietor's surveyor in the Welsh Tract on the Schuylkill, and receiving no cash for his work, as he states in his petition, he asked the Commissioners, 28. 11mo. 1705, to grant him 1,000 acres he had selected in the Welsh Tract. He asked this, because he had been compensated with only the above mentioned 500 acres. Petition granted, providing he could find any vacant land, which, as an old surveyor in that section, he easily could, and apparently had. His lands were quickly disposed of, as he may have been a good judge of land, and guaranteed his bounds.

The following transportation agreement between Mr. Powell and a skipper, suggests that he brought over the passengers to buy land from him about this time.

WELSH SETTLEMENT OF PENSYLVANIA

"Articles of ffreightment, covenanted, indented and made the seventh day of March, 1697-8, between Owen Thomas, of the county burrough of Carmathen, mercer, owner of the good shipp called the William Galley, now residing in the river of Towny, of the one part, and

"David Powell, of the parish of Nantmell, in the county of Radnor, and John Morris, of the parish of Karbardamfyneth, in the said county of Radnor, yeomen, of the other part,

"Contract to take to Pensilvania after 10th of May, starting with first good wind and weather, from said river Towny, and town of Rhaygsder, to Philadelphia in Pensilvania, with them and passengers and goods." The charge for transportation to be £5 for each adult over 12 years old, persons under 12 years, fifty shillings, sucking children and freight up to twenty tons, free. The head of each family was also charged "ffive shillings encouragement to the doctor belonging to said shipp, and all single persons except servants, to pay one shilling each."

The following is the list of principals in this venture, and how many each paid for in his party:

David Powell paid for 11 passengers.
John Morris paid for 6.
Margaret Jones paid for 3.
Edward Moore paid for 4.
Thomas Powell paid for 3½.
Thomas Griffith paid for 2.
Rees Rees paid for 4½.
Edward Nicholas paid for 4.
Thomas Watts, 1.
Winnifred Oliver paid for 5 passengers.
Evan Powell paid for 5.
Thomas Jerman paid for 3.
John Powell paid for 2.
James Price paid for 2.
John Vaikaw (?) 1.
Lumley Williams, 1.

PLANTERS AND SERVANTS

Ann Lewis, 1.
Walter Ingram, 1.
Benjamin Davis, 1.

"John Burge, of Haverford-West, Pembrokeshire, clothier," mentioned in Powel's list, was another of Penn's personal customers for Welsh Tract land. He bought by deed, dated 24. 8mo. 1681, 750 acres which were to be laid out in Haverford in several tracts. One of these, 250 acres, it was discovered, was laid out on land owned by Humphrey Ellis, and after a litigation, Burge had to look elsewhere to locate this parcel, so he sold the 250 acre right to William Kelly, of Haverford-West, a weaver, who had 141 acres of it laid out in Haverford, and 30 acres in city liberties and lots. On 2. 10mo. 1694, said Kelly sold the 141 acres to Humphrey Ellis, who had also bought 79 acres from John Burge, or from Kelly, which he sold, for £8.9. Pensylvania money, 15 Feb. 1703, to Henry Lewis.

Edward ap Richard, or Prichard, on Powel's list, was another of Penn's personal customers. He took 2,500 acres, deed dated 14 April, 1682, which was confirmed by patent dated 18. 3mo. 1685; 1,250 acres were to be laid out in Merion, and balance in Radnor. Many of his deeds are of record in the office of the Recorder.

John Poyer, on Powel's list, also purchased of Penn, by deed dated 24. 8mo. 1681, 750 acres, and by deed of 3 June, 1686, he sold the rights to 250 acres to Henry Sanders, who had the same resurveyed to himself, on Commissioner's warrant, dated 16. 12mo. 1701, when Owen Thomas requested a warrant to take up this land.

"William Jenkins, of Tenby, in Pembrokeshire, emasculator," (subsequently of Abington tp.), on Powel's list, bought of Penn 1,000 acres by deed dated 24. 8mo. 1681. Of this grant, 245 acres were laid out to him in Duffrin Mawr tp., 12. 11mo. 1689. By deed of 30. 7mo. 1686, he conveyed 250 acres to James Thomas, late of Landboyden, Carmarthenshire, a husbandman, which, on resurvey, amounted to 300 acres, and Penn issued a warrant for that amount, 2. 7mo. 1701. Afterwards, James was astonished to learn that his purchase was not within the Welsh Tract, and, on 16. 12mo. 1701, requested a new warrant for Welsh Tract land to this amount, which the Commissioners granted, provided he could find such an amount of unclaimed land in the tract. But it seems he could not, as by his will he devised to his son, Nathan Thomas, lands in Duffrin Mawr.

William Jenkins, by deed of 3. 7mo. 1686, sold 500 acres to Francis Howel, of Lancilio, in Carmarthanshire, who devised 300 acres of the purchase to Thomas Howel, which he sold, by deed 1. 7. 1700, to above James Thomas,

From the number of these sales of land, it might be supposed that Penn had no difficulty in getting rid of his land; but he had, even before Ford's persecution cast a shadow on the titles. For some reason the bottom dropped out of his real estate business after the first boom, and when he supposed 100 "barons" in the "House of Lords"—each to buy 5,000 acres, was too small a number to stop at, he suddenly discovered that he might not be able to have even half that number of "Lords." And his order that "no 1,000 acre lot could be increased contiguously, unless within three years there was a family settled on each 1,000 acres," shows how sparsely the country must have been settled at that period.

In the early land records of Chester Co., for the townships of Radnor and Haverford, there are records of the following early grantees.

These had deeds for land:

1681.			Acres.
March	3.	Lewis David	3,000
"	"	Thomas Rowland	1,000
"	"	David Powell	1,000
March	17.	John Bevan	2,000
"	22.	Thomas Ellis	1,000
"	"	Thomas Holme	5,000
"	"	Joseph Powell	250
"	"	Thomas Powell	500
June	16.	Richard Davies	1,250

1681			Acres.
July	13.	Thomas Rudyard	5,000
Sept.	14.	John & Wynne	5,000
"	"	Richard Davies	5,000
Oct.	24.	John Poyer	750
Jan.	19.	Morris Llewelyn	500
"	"	William Sharlow*	5,000

These had patents for land.

Haverford tp.

1684. 11. 29.	Thomas Ellis	791
1688. 5. 23.	Charles & John Bevan	230
1703. 8. 25.	Ellis Ellis	425
1703. 8. 25.	Daniel Humphrey	241
1704. 2. 4.	John Bevan	508
1706. 5. 20.	Henry Lewis	488

Marple tp.

1688. 5. 23.	Charles & John Bevan	750
1694. 2. 21.	Thomas Ellis	330

Radnor tp.

1684. 5. 29.	Thomas Wynne	250
1685. 5. 30.	David Davis	200
1686. 3, 14.	David Powell	611
1687. 7. 9.	David Powell	300
1688. 8. 1.	Reese Prece	200
1689. 3. 26.	David Meredith	350
1701. 7. 30.	Evan Rodderch	122
1703. 8. 25.	John Evan Edward	123
1703. 8. 25.	Margaret Jarmon	152
1703. 8. 25.	David Pugh	174
1703. 8. 25.	James Pugh	162
1703. 9. 1.	Thomas John Evan	340
1703. 9. 1.	Edward David	155
1704. 1. 14.	John Evans	300
1704. 3. 1.	David Meredith	253

* William Sharlow was a London merchant. He purchased from Mr. Penn, by deed dated 2. 5mo. 1683, besides the above, 500 acres, which was laid out and surveyed to him, 30. 7mo. 1684, and named "Mount Ararat." It lay on the Schuylkill, above the Thomas & Jones tract, but not adjoining it, as in Holme's map. Mr. Sharlow's Pensylvania attorney, by deed of 5. 10mo. 1692, conveyed 150 acres of "Mt. Ararat" to Thomas Potts, who by deed of 2. 2mo. 1695, conveyed his purchase to David Hugh, who sold the same to "Robert Jones, of Meirion, Labourer," or "Robert Jones, Yeoman, of Meirion," who was a son of John ap Thomas.

WELSH SETTLEMENT OF PENSYLVANIA

Some of the properties of early settlers were located about as follows:

Along the East boundary, (a line and the Haverford road, about $3\frac{3}{4}$ miles), of Radnor, in Merion, on the upper side, where are the settlements of Villa Nova and Rosemont, were the great estates of Rowland Ellis and John Eckley. And in Radnor, along and between this line, and where "Radnor Street," (or the present Radnor road, crossing Eagle road, if continued straight to the opposite line), was to have been, passing through the center of the township, North and South, beginning at the upper end, were the properties of Evan Lloyd, Abel Roberts, John and William Thomas, Matthew Jones, David David, Richard Humphrey, John Morgan, Henry Lewis, John Jarman, John Evans, Roger Hugh, David Prees, David Meredith, David James, Thomas Rees and Stephen Evan.

In the same position in Haverford, that is between the line of the proposed "Haverford Street," through the center of the township from North to South, and the Eastern boundary line, about $3\frac{1}{2}$ miles long, were the properties of Hugh David, William Lewis, Thomas Rees, David and Ralph Lewis, Rees Rotherow, William Ellis, Ellis Ellis, Robert Wharton, Thomas Ellis, Lewis David, Daniel Humphrey, William Howell, all lying above the road passing the Haverford Meeting House towards the road to Darby. And below this road, John Lewis, John Havard, Henry Ellis, David Hugh, Henry Lewis, Daniel Lawrence, Richard Hayes, Samuel Lewis. In both townships, West of the imaginary streets, were the properties of some others. And in Merion, along the Haverford township line, at Haverford College station on the railroad, and below Wynnewood station, were the great estates of John Humphrey and John Bevan.

In 1734, the following Welshmen each paid assessments on 100 acres of land in Philadelphia county: Hugh Thomas, Daniel Jones, David George, John Thomas, James Jones, William Roberts, Evan Rees, John Humphrey, George

PLANTERS AND SERVANTS

George, Lewis Jones and Edward Williams; "Robert Roberts, of Mirian," 50; David Morgan, 19, and "Thomas Winne," 50 acres in Blockley.

In an undated paper (1693?) at the Historical Society of Pensylvania, giving "The Valuation of the Estates of the Inhabitants of the Township of Merion," and the amount of tax each was to pay ("one penny on the pound"), we have a list of Merion people, many of whose names are familiar, as follows:—

Merion.	Valuation.	Merion.	Valuation.
John Roberts	£120	Robert Owen	100
Hugh Jones	40	John Roberts "of the Wain"	100
Cadwalader Morgan	90	Robert Jones	72
Rowland Richard	30	David Hugh	60
Robert David [collector]	100	Katherine David	30
Hugh Roberts	150	John Williams	30
Katherine Thomas	100	Benjamin Humphreys	60
Griffith John	110	Reece Thomas	100
Richard Walter	70	Philip and Isaac Price	60
Abel Thomas	30	Peter Jones	30
Reece Jones	60	John Robert Ellis	30
Edward Jones	90	Edward Jones	72
Edward Reece	120	Edward Griffith	72
Richard Cuarton	80	William Cuarton	30
David Pugh	30	Thomas Rees	30
David Price	30	Owen Morgan	30
Daniel Thomas	50	John Moore	30
Evan Bevan	80	Thomas Howell	40
David Havard,		James Thomas, Sen'r	70
"with 200 acres of Land"	82	James Thomas, Jun'r	40

The following men of Merion were each assessed six shillings, without valuations, (which was the tax paid on all estate valuations of £72), and probably were freemen:—

Evan Harry.
Thomas Jones.
David Ryederch.
Meredith Davids.
Joshua Owen.
Edward Edwards.
Robert Lloyd.
Thomas Jones.

William Roberts.
Robert William.
Philip Wallis.
Owen Thomas.
Robert David.
Robert Hugh.
John Owen.
Evan Harry, weaver.

WELSH SETTLEMENT OF PENSYLVANIA

Robert David, who lived in Merion fifty years, was the collector of this tax, and he endorsed on the list, "Paid to James Fox, Recorder." If Mr. Fox was a recorder of Philadelphia County, none of the accepted-as-correct printed lists of them include his name. Mr. Fox was commissioned, 12 Feb. 1697-8, a justice of the Philadelphia county court, and was a member of the Assembly 1688-1699; will proved at Philadelphia, 10 April, 1701.

It is presumed that the aforesaid assessment was made in 1693, because it is known that in this year there was one made in Chester Co., as below, for the same amount of tax, namely, "one penny per pound on Estates," and "six shillings per head on freemen." This was probably the levy noticed in the minutes of the Welsh monthly meeting, 8mo. 1693, "tax levied of one shilling per hundred towards the taking of wolves."

The following names are on the Chester Co. lists for the townships of Haverford and Radnor. The total amounts received were: Haverford, £3.14.5, and Radnor, £2.19.3. The estates in these townships were appraised lower than those of Merion, as may be seen.

Haverford.	Valuation.
John Bevan	£50
William Howell	40
Morris Llewellyn	40
Thomas Reese	30
William Lewis	48
John Richard	30
Humphrey Ellis	30
Ellis Ellis	33
Ralph Lewis	30
William Jenken	45
Daniel Humphrey	40
David Lawrence	36
Radnor.	
John Evans	£45
David Meredith	70
John Evans	30
John Jarman	44
John Morgan	32

Haverford.	Valuation.
Lewis David	30
John Lewis	40
Henry Lewis	50
John Lewis, Jr.	30
Richard Hayes	43
Benjamin Humphrey	32
William Howell, for Thomas Owen	72
Richard Hayes, for David Lewis	72
John Bevan, for Evan William	72
Philip Evan	43
David Evan	41
William Davis	31
Samuel Miles	33
Richard Miles	34

PLANTERS AND SERVANTS

William David	31	Evan Prothero	43
Richard Armes	52	John Richard	33
Matthew Joanes	30	Stephen Bevan	45
Howell James	44	Thomas Johns	32

Following the custom long established in Virginia, Penn granted fifty acres for each indentured servant brought into his Providence. In Virginia, this head-right, as it was called there, belonged to the person importing the servant. In fact, the importer, or master, received in Virginia lands, fifty acres not only for each of his servants, but the same amount for each member of his family, or particular party, whose passage he paid. While Penn not only granted (or intended to do so), fifty acres to the servant himself, and gave him a deed, and warrant of survey for the same, at the expiration of his term of servitude, or when his master freed him, but fifty acres to the master for each servant brought. This was a better arrangement, because in Virginia it was notorious that the same servants and other head-rights, were used over and over, often with the same names, to procure lands, hence some of the great tracts of tide-water land in Virginia, held by Colonial worthies.

In neither Virginia or Pensylvania were all of the "servants" of the lowest social class; nor were these, men and women, all servants as we now understand the term. In either colony, many of these servants were relatives of their "masters," even were their children, and frequently were at "home," and here, of equal social standing to their masters. Many reasons can be assigned to account for their servitude, or indenture, and many whose earliest record in America is that of "servant," in a short time became prominent for good in social, religious, or civil life.

According to the Minutes of the Board of Property, 26. 9mo. 1701, it was the intention of William Penn to set aside a township of 6,000 acres, to be used only as "head-land" for servants brought into his Province, in the years 1682-3, where they could settle when their "time" expired; but this idea was probably abandoned, because it was found the servants nearly always conveyed away for a small consideration their rights to land.

For instance, Philip Howel purchased their head-lands from the following servants, they uniting in a deed for the same to him, dated 18. 2mo. 1702:—

"Humphrey Edwards, servant to John ap Edwards.
"Inemry (?) Osborn, servant to Griffith Jones.*
"Elizabeth Osborn, his wife (born Day), servant to same.
"Jacob Willis, servant to William Cloud.
"Evan Williams, servant to Thomas Ellis.†
"Margaret Williams, his wife (born Richard), servant to John Bevan.
"Edmund MacVeagh, servant to Thomas Holme.
"Alice MacVeagh, his wife, (born Dickinson), servant to James Harrison."

Robert Turner's servants, like himself, were from Dublin, and all named Furness:— John, Henry, Joseph, Daniel, Mary, Sarah, and Rachel. John Furness was Mr. Turner's barber, and in 8mo. 1683, was granted by the Commissioners 350 acres, on account of himself, and the other servants of his surname.

Reuben Ford, servant to John Gibbons, received headland on his own account, by warrant of 8. 9. 1703.

---

* Griffith Jones was one of the prominent Welsh Quakers of the Province. In 1703, he was chosen as Mayor of Philadelphia, but for some reason he declined to serve, and, as was the custom then, he was fined £20, but did not pay. On 3 Oct. 1704, he was again chosen for the mayoralty, and would have again declined, but being threatened with a like fine, or a total of £40, he accepted the office, and it was such an honour to have him as the Mayor, the first fine was remitted. David Lloyd, another Welsh Quaker, was the Recorder of the city at this time.

† Thomas Ellis came from a hamlet, near Dolgules, in Merionethshire, the name of which was variously written Dolserre, Dolserey, Dolyseerey, Dolyserry, Doleyseere, Dolyserre, Doleyserre, etc.

PLANTERS AND SERVANTS

The following were servants to the prominent families of Merion, the first settlers:—

Edmund Griffith, and Katherine Griffith, "formerly wife to Edmund Griffith," were servants of Hugh Roberts.

John Hugh was servant to Rees John William.

Hugh Samuel was servant to Thomas Ellis.

Mary Hughes was servant to John ap Edward.

John Roberts and William Roberts were servants to Robert David.

William David was servant to John Bevan.

James Pugh was servant to Steven Bevan.

Thomas Rees was servant to Evan Thomas.

Susanna Griffith was servant to John Richards.

Thomas Armes, John Ball (had four years to serve), Robert Lort (had eight years to serve), Jean, Bridget and Elizabeth Watts, and Alexander Edwards (who each had three years to serve), were servants to Griffith Owen, in 1684.

These were servants to Katharine, relict of John ap Thomas, in Merion, Elizabeth Owen, Thomas David, and Ann David.

Frequently servants were given certificates of good character by the Friends' Meetings they belonged to in the old country. There are a number of these preserved on the books of the Haverford, now Radnor, Monthly Meeting, as John ap Evan and family, and Ralph Lewis, from Treverig Meeting, dated 10. 7mo. 1683, and John Richard, and William Sharpless, from the same Meeting, of whom the Certificate describe them "of small abilitie," and "harmless men"; but "ready to hear and Receive the Truth." And that they were "low in the Outward, yett lived Comfortable enough." John Lloyd, a servant to Mr. Bevan, was also thus described.

Servants who claimed to have served their "time," require a strong certificate of the fact before being released. For instance, in the case of Humphrey Edwards, mentioned above; on 9. 4mo. 1702, Edward Jones, William Jenkins, and Philip Howel, declared before the Commissioners, that

WELSH SETTLEMENT OF PENSYLVANIA

Humphrey, "now of Gwynedd, came into this Province about the year 1683, as a servant to John ap Edward, and served his time to him faithfully, and according to Indenture." This occurred on his request for fifty acres of headland.

Thomas Jones also had a servant named Ellis Roberts, who according to the minutes of the Merion Preparative Meeting, 6mo. 6. 1703, was made free, having according to his certificate, which was read to the meeting, as was usual, served Mr. Jones's mother, brother, and himself twelve years.

The certificate of Robert Goodwin, who had been a servant for four years to Evan Harry, was also read in Merion meeting, on 2. 1mo. 1704-5, and, on 4. 6mo. 1704, that of Hugh Humphreys from his master, Benjamin Humphreys, and that of John Roberts from his master, Robert Jones.

A letter from Thomas Jones, of Merion tp., to his cousin, Robert Vaughan, in Wales, tells of Owen Roberts' (son of the Friends' minister, Hugh Roberts), adventures at sea, coming to Pensylvania, and that his company was captured by the French near the mouth of the Delaware, and carried as prisoners to the West Indies. Nine of the servants he was bringing were "pressed on board a ship"; "Morris Richard, the Tailor, died at sea"; but the others finally reached Philadelphia. Among the latter were Humphrey Williams, Thomas Owen, Cadder John, Robert Arthur, Hugh Griffith, Edward Thomas and James Griffith. Thomas Owen died after reaching here. Owen Roberts returned to Antigua, to try and recover his impressed men, but could not find them.

These were some of the servants who came over in the ship Vine, in Sept. 1684, besides Griffith Owen's servants:— Edward Edwards, a boy, Lowry Edwards, Margaret Edwards, Ann Owen, Hannah Watts and Charles Hughes. It appears from the monthly meeting minutes, 11. 2mo. 1695, that Charles Hughs "married out," and that because David Potts, Owen Thomas, and Evan Harry were at the wedding, "which marriage friends had no unity with," "they were

PLANTERS AND SERVANTS

dealt with by Robert Owen and Edward Jones, and thereupon gave forth the following paper of condemnation, viz. For as much as we whose names are hereunto written, for want of due consideration have unadvisedly been at the dishonorable marriage of Charles Hughes, and by so doing have transgressed against this good order as established among friends of Truth," &c., hereby acknowledging publicly before the meeting the mistake they made. But in 1722, 5mo. the Radnor Mo. Mtg. was not so certain of its stand as to "dishonorable marriages," as it instructed its representatives to the quarterly meeting "to report that the monthly meeting was concerned whether it was necessary to disown such persons as go to the priest to marry, or only advise them."

The Gwynedd meeting was formed by sanction of the Radnor Mo. Mtg. at the desire of Friends there, and they were "to meet second weekly Third day of every month" beginning in 2mo. 1699. But they were not authorized till in 6mo. 1702, "to keep a preparative meeting among themselves."

Recorded at the Radnor Monthly Meeting is the undated, unsigned, certificate, from some Meeting in Wales, unnamed, of "Treharn David, who hath gone now 13 or 14 months since for Pensylvania with Janne his wife, being noe more in family but they both." "Treharne lived with our friend John Bevan for many years," in Wales.

William Morgan, and his wife Elizabeth, who came over in the "Morning Star," 20. 9mo. 1683, had been "servants," but in the passenger list they were described "both free," having served their "time."

From the burial records of the Merion Meeting come the following particulars about other servants, white and black, of early times, who should not be passed by, for they, like their masters, had a part in the opening and settling of this new country.

1714. 8. 9. "David Lewis, servant of Morris Llwellyn."
1714. 10. 8. "Morgan Thomas, servant to Robert Evans"

WELSH SETTLEMENT OF PENSYLVANIA

1714-5. 11. 16. "Robert Vincent, servant to Jon Jones."
1714-5. 12. 27. "Bumbo, a young negro."
1716. 4. 5. "Catharine Griffith, servant to Evan Harry."
1717. 10. 30. "George Eves, burnt at Edward Jones'."
1718. 10. 14. "Rowland Ellis' tenant," (? Thomas Owen).
1719. 7. 14. Thos. Evans, "living at David Mirick's place."
1719. 10. 27. "Ship, Henry Pugh's Negro."
1720. 1. 5. "William Worm, servant to Hugh Evans"

This Hugh Evans had considerable trouble when he proposed to marry the lady of his choice, according to a minute of the Radnor Mo. Mtg. He desired to marry Lowrey Lloyd, the daughter of Rees John William, of Merion, and widow of Robert Lloyd, of Merion, who died in 1714, but the union was objected to by friends on the ground "of too near affinity," "she being Hugh's deceased wife's mother's sister's daughter." Hugh held that Lowrey was of no kin at all to him, but the monthly meeting thought otherwise, so the matter was referred to the quarterly meeting, which allowed the marriage to take place, and the wedding was at the Merion meeting house, on 13, 12mo. 1716-7.

1720-1. 11. 26. "A young Negro of Edward Reese."
1720-1. 12. 17. "old Bassel, negro to Edward Reese."
1726-7. 1. 13. "Black Hannah."
1745. 6. 2. "A child of Edward Williams' maid."
1746. 9. 2. "Will, a Negro of Edward Price."
1748. 8. 29. "Black Peter."
1749. 10mo. "Old Caesar, Reese Reese's negro."
1749. 6. 28. "A Dutch........from Evan Jones place."
1752. 10. 10. "A Dutch woman from Evan Jones' place."
1754. 11. 20. "A dutchman from Anthony Tunis's."
1754. 10. 22. "Dutch girl from Philip Creakbeam's."
1756. 4. 13. "A Dutch Woman from William Stadleman's. Supposed to be Poisoned by a Dutchman, from Lancaster, who was Tryed & Convicted, but Repreived"

The Welsh monthly meeting several times issued instructions to the preparative meetings, that as the matter of discharging servants, whose time had expired, was an important one, masters were commanded to give the new freemen certificates as to conduct, &c., as a protection to the community (hence, possibly, our servant's "references"). It also ordered, none should encourage servants to buy their time, by lending them money to do so, or going bond for them without master's consent.

In an advertisement in the *American Weekly Mercury*, Philadelphia, 26 May, 1720, "Samuel Lewis, of Harford in the county of Chester," offers thirty shillings reward for the return to him of his runaway servant, Thomas Roberts, aged about thirty years. The description of the clothes of this servant may give some idea of how his "betters" dressed. "He wore a duroy coat lined with silk, a leathern jacket and breeches."

It is singular but never in all the wills of the ancient Welsh Friends, which frequently mentioned purchased Negroes, and bequeathed them as chattel, have I found an instance of a devisor liberating his slaves. It was the custom of the day to own "blacks," and Penn himself then was only interested in "regulating Negroes in their Morals and Marriages," and in "the regulations of their trials and punishments." His whole interest in the negro was, that "he should receive proper treatment while in bondage." In 1688, the German Friends were the first to protest to the Yearly Meeting against slavery of Negroes, but for fifty years, the Yearly Meeting went no further in the matter than to advise against buying newly imported Negroes, although Ralph Sandiford, a Philadelphia Friend, worked hard in 1730-40, with pamphlets and addresses to suppress slavery altogether in Pensylvania.

Of the second and much smaller "Welsh Tract" much has been printed, but there never seemed to be the same interest in it for the Land Commissioners, which they had in the first and greater, and, in fact, they had no particular reason to watch it, for its settlers made no singular claims, nor were many of its men remarkable in provincial affairs.

WELSH SETTLEMENT OF PENSYLVANIA

Of these "Gwynedd Welsh," it is said they "in general did not at first profess with the Quakers, [being "Baptists"], but afterwards they, with "many others" as the neighborhood increased, joined the religious society with them, and were an industrious, worthy people." One of the longest to be remembered was Ann Roberts, who died 4 June, 1750, aged 73 years, having been a minister among Friends for fifty years.

The nucleus of this second Welsh Tract was a large tract of land in the upper part of old Philadelphia county, owned by Robert Turner, and purchased by people from North Wales, and afterwards was generally known as "North Wales," and the "Gwynedd Settlement." This emigration Mr. Jenkins* places in 1698, and ascribes it to the influence of Hugh Roberts, the minister, who was in Wales the previous year; but why Hugh did not secure these settlers for the greater Welsh Tract, in which he was certainly more interested, rather than for Gwynedd tp., where he owned no land, is not apparent.

On 22 March, 1681, Penn granted by patent of this date, 5,000 acres of Pensylvania land to Robert Turner,† who,

---

*"Gwynedd" by Howard M. Jenkins (1884). P. 22.

† Mr. Turner, who became an important official in Philadelphia, had been frequently roughly handled for being a Quaker. In 1657, "being at Meeting in Londonderry, he was haled out and dragged along the streets by his Armes and Leggs, the Mayor of the City helping with his owne hands, and so turned him out of the City. And about two or three Dais after haled him again in like manner as before, and tied him upon a bare Horse Back with a Hair Rope, and so far their Sport, and Mocking led him at their Pleasure." But Mr. Turner's experience was not singular in Ireland, for there are hundreds of similar "sufferings" of Friends mentioned in the works of Fuller and Holme, (1671); "Sufferings of the People Call'd Quakers," (Dublin, 1731); Stockdale's "The Great Cry of Oppression," (1683); Wight, (1700), in his "History of the People Called Quakers," Dublin, 1751, and Myers's "Immigration of Irish Quakers into Pensylvania."

A score of Mr. Turner's deeds for lands to the Welsh at Gwynedd may be seen in Exemplification Book, No. 7, pp. 381, &c. Recorder's office, Philadelphia.

PLANTERS AND SERVANTS

with Robert Zane, and other Dublin Friends, six years before this, had been a grantee for tracts of West Jersey land, purchased from Friend Byllings, and had started the settlement of English speaking people in that country, which furnished William Penn with the idea for another such scheme for himself. Mr. Turner increased his holdings as follows:—

By deed, 8 Sep. 1685, he bought 2,500 acres which Penn had sold to John Gee, of King's Co., Ireland, and, 29. 7. 1685, 1,250 acres from Joseph Fuller, of King's Co., and 8 March, 1695, 1,250 acres from Jacob Fuller, of King's Co., making Turner's holding in Pensylvania 10,000 acres. Of this Penn confirmed to him 7,800 acres, laid out in Philadelphia County. By deed, 10. 1mo. 1698-9, Turner sold this tract to two Welshmen, William ap John and Thomas ap Evan, of Philadelphia, and they, by several deeds in 1699, sold this land to the following parties, who, on 25. 11mo. 1702, having had their parcels of land resurveyed, according to the order, to find "overplusage" for Penn, rendered the following statement, showing their correct acreage:—

	Acres.	Over.		Acres.	Over.
Ellis, or Da'd Pugh.	220	231	Edward Pugh.*	100	
Evan Hugh	100	110	Cadwall'dr ap Evan.	500	609
John Hugh	500	648	Owen ap Evan	400	538
John Humphrey	450	561	Rob't ap Hugh	200	232
Rob't ap Evan	5,005	1,034	William John	1,900	2,866
Edward Faulk	400	712	Thomas Evan	700	1,049
Robert Jones	500	720	William John	150	322
Robert Evan	200	250	Evan Robert	100	110
Evan ap Hugh.*	400	1,068	Hugh Griffith	200	376
David Pugh.*	200				

*"(Brothers, Evan holds all, other two dead.)"

It may be seen that the overplus on these 7,800 acres was 11,436 acres. No wonder that Penn had new surveys made of old grants. However, he allowed these unfortunates to purchase in all 2,846 acres of the "overs," and, in 11mo. 1702, these Welsh grantees, and their heirs, and those who had bought of them, obligated themselves to pay Penn

WELSH SETTLEMENT OF PENSYLVANIA

the amounts as below. This table also shows the amounts owing, or "continued," after a cash payment:—

	Obligation.	Continued.
Rob't John, Wm. John, Edw'd Faulk.	£535.10. 8	£269. 5. 4
Tho. Evan, Cadw. ap Evan, Rob't ap Hugh	140.18.11	80. 7. 5
Owen ap Evan, Robert Evan	216. 5. 3	104. 2. 7
Robert Evan, Evan ap Hugh	134.12. 6	67. 8. 3
Jno. Humphrey, Jno. Hugh	75.00. 3	37.10. 2
Hugh Griffith & Son	22.17. 9	11. 8.10
Robert John		3.00. 0
Owen ap Evan		5.
William John, (Pd by Ja. Logan)		15.
Thomas Evan, (Pd by Ja. Logan)		10.
Robert Evan		10.
John Hugh		15.
Edward Faulk		10.
Evan Pugh		5.

In the latter end of the year 1698, the purchasers of these lands began removing to "North Wales." Among the early arrivals were Thomas, Robert, and Owen Evans, William Jones, Cadwalader Evans, 1664-1745, (an ancestor of Mr. Lewis Jones Levick, of Bala, as elsewhere), Hugh Griffith, John Hugh, &c., as in these lists. Some of these gentlemen subsequently purchased considerable land in the first, or great Welsh Tract, and removed there, having become Quakers, and intermarried with the Welsh pioneer families there, as may be seen in the following chart.

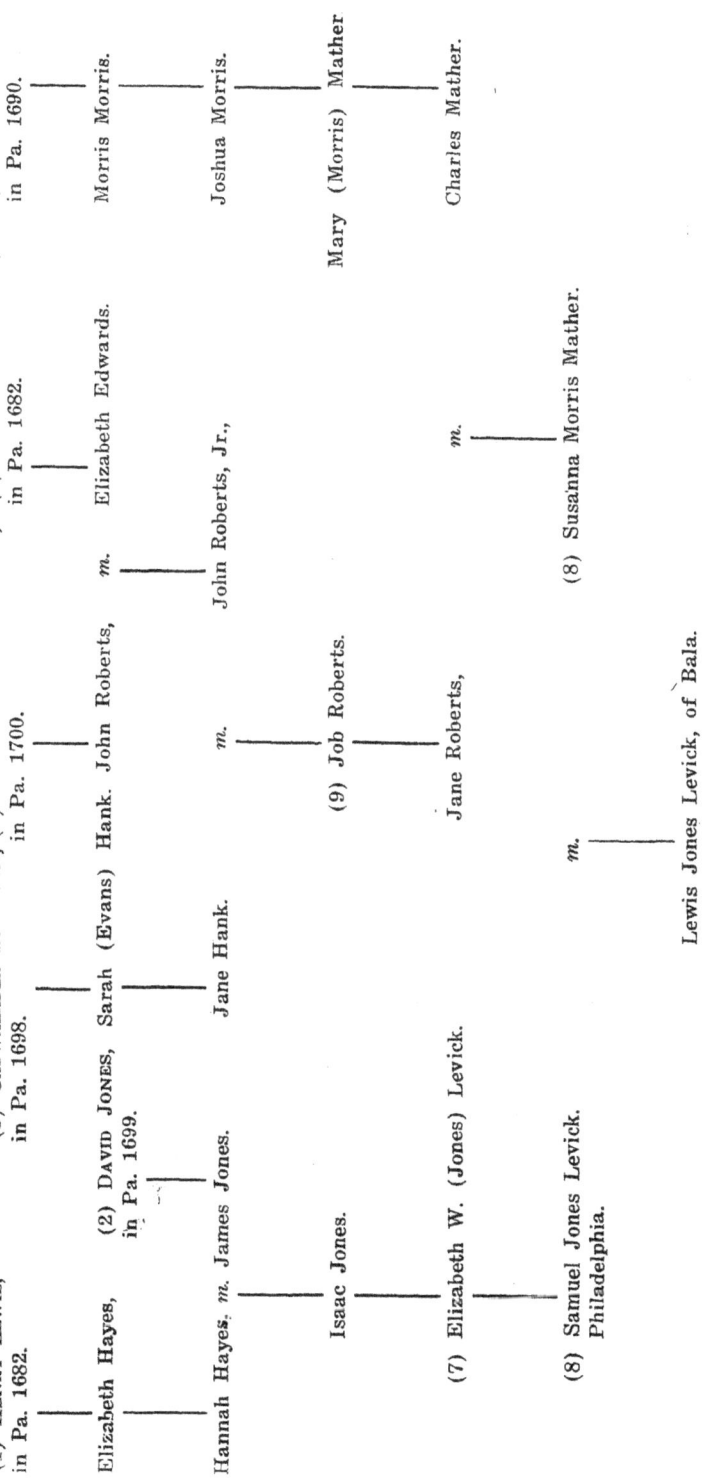

WELSH SETTLEMENT OF PENSYLVANIA

Notes to the aforesaid chart.

(1)—Some account of HENRY LEWIS, and his Welsh Tract land, has been given. He came with his wife Margaret, from Narbeth, Pembrokeshire, in 1682. In 1684, when still a member of the Philadelphia Monthly Meeting, he was of a committee appointed "to visit the poor and the sick, and administer what they should judge convenient, at the expense of the meeting." Besides being the foreman of the first Grand Jury of Philadelphia County, he was one of the three "peace makers," he being the representative from the Welsh Tract, appointed by the county court, an office created by act of assembly, at the second session. Their duty was to determine matters in litigation, and subject to appeal to Court; they were to prevent law suits if possible, and discourage litigation, and "to hear and end differences betwixt man and man." It has been said he was the beloved and trusted friend of William Penn. His daughter, Elizabeth, *b*. at Narbeth, 14. 12mo. 1677, married in 1697 Richard Hayes, Jr., who removed from Ilminston, Pembrokeshire, to Haverford, in 1687, with his parents. His mother, Isatt Hayes, is frequently mentioned in Haverford Monthly Meeting minutes as active in work among the Haverford Friends. Richard Hayes, Jr., was a justice of the court in Chester Co., and member of the Pensylvania Assembly for many years. His wife *d*. 25. 3mo. 1742, and the Philadelphia Quarterly Meeting has recorded the testimony respecting her:— "She was a faithful Elder among us for several years, a good example to the flock."

(2)—DAVID JONES removed from Wales with his wife Katherine and two children, about 1700, and bought 350 acres of land, located in Blockley tp., at Haverford road and 63d street. His sister, Ellen Jones, *m*. Robert Jones, of Merion, a son of John ap Thomas, the associate of Dr. Jones. He was a prominent Friend in both countries. The Friends' minister, William Edmundson, in his Journal (printed), mentions him. He brought his certificate from

PLANTERS AND SERVANTS

the Monthly Meeting at Hendri Mawr, dated 24. 12mo. 1699-00, signed by Robert Vaughan, Cadwalader Ellis, Evan Rees, Edward Ellis, Thomas Richards, Edward David, Owen Lewis, Ellis Lewis, Rowland Owen, Thomas Cadwalader, and John Robert. He also had a certificate from the men's meeting in Haverford West, dated 4. 1mo. 1699-00, and among the signers were Andrew Llewellyn, James Lewis, Peregrine Musgrave, Evan Bowen and John Roger. The records of the Haverford Monthly Meeting say of him, "he was one of the first appointed an Elder in the Haverford Meeting." He d. 27. 6mo. 1725, and was buried at the Merion Meeting House. His wife was also an active member of this meeting, being "an inspector of conversation," and a "visitor," and represented Haverford in the Quarterly Meeting. After her husband's death, she had a certificate from the Radnor Monthly Meeting to the Philadelphia Monthly Meeting, and d. 23. 5mo. 1764. Their Bible, "printed yn Llundian," 1678, records the births of James Lewis, on 8th mo. 10th, 1638, and "Katerin Lewis, ye 25th of 12th month 1640," who may have been the parents of David's wife, Katherine, who had a brother James Lewis, of Llanddewy, whose letters to her are extant. Their son James Jones, b. 31. 5mo. 1699, d. in Blockley tp. 27. 3mo. 1791, aged 92 years. He m. Hannah Hayes, at Haverford Meeting, 10. 8mo. 1727, and had Isaac Jones, who m. at Burlington (N. J.) Meeting 26. 11mo. 1778.

(3)—CADWALADER AP EVAN, mentioned elsewhere, came from Fron Gôch, Merionethshire, and died in the Gwynedd settlement, in 1745, age 81 years. He married in Wales, Ellen, daughter of John Morris, of Bryn Gwyn, and their daughter, Sarah Evans, married John Hank, of White Marsh, and had issue as mentioned before.

(4, 5, 9)—The ancestry of ROBERT ap CADWALADER is unknown. He was one of the early settlers of Gwynedd, and his son, John Roberts, who married Elizabeth, daughter of the Merion settler, (5) JOHN ap EDWARD, of whom

WELSH SETTLEMENT OF PENSYLVANIA

elsewhere, was the founder of the Roberts family of "Woodlawn" plantation, Whitpain tp., Montgomery Co., Pa., where seven successive generations of Roberts blood have resided. On this property is another stone mansion, erected in 1715, acccording to the date-stone, called "Woodlawn Farm," which was the home of (9) Job Roberts, who was known as "the Pensylvania farmer," and was the pioneer of scientific farming, on which subject he published a book in 1804. He was a magistrate for twenty-nine years. This family was also remarkable for longevity, as Job Roberts died aged 96 years, his father, John Jr., died at 90 years, and his grandfather, John Roberts, at 96 years.

(6)—EVAN MORRIS was an early settler in the Gwynedd district, and a prominent Friend. He and his wife, Gainor, brought certificates, dated 8. 5mo. 1690, from the Quarterly Meeting at Tyddyn y Garreg, Merioneth, filed with the Philadelphia Monthly Meeting. His son, Morris Morris, gave the land on which the Richland meeting house was built, and also endowed the Friends' school there, which many of his descendants attended. His wife, Susanna Heth, or Heath, was "an eminent minister in the Society of Friends."

(7)—ELIZABETH WETHERILL JONES, (wife of Ebenezer Levick, and mother of the Friends' minister, Samuel J. Levick), whose interesting "Recollections of Her Early Days," in Philadelphia, were printed in book-form, in 1881, was born at No. 17 Pine Street, Philadelphia, her parents' home, on 5. 6mo. 1789. She was the youngest child of Isaac Jones, and his wife, Mary Wetherill, (who is buried at the Merion Meeting House), married at the Burlington Meeting, 26. 11mo. 1778, and died at the home of her son, Dr. James Jones Levick, at 12th and Arch streets, Philadelphia, 21. 11mo. 1886, aged over 97 years and six months, and was buried in Friends' Southwestern Ground, Philadelphia. Dr.

Levick mentioned, was noted for his interest in the Welsh settlement of Pensylvania, and published many valuable articles about the settlers of "Merion in the Welsh Tract." He *d.* 25. 6mo. 1893, aged 69 years. She also had a son, William Manlove Levick, of Philadelphia, a lawyer.

(8)—SAMUEL JONES LEVICK, of Philadelphia, whose Life was written and published, in 1895, by Hugh Foulke, of Philadelphia, was the son of Ebenezer Levick, a Philadelphia merchant, and Elizabeth Wetherill Jones, married at the Pine Street Friends' Meeting, Philadelphia, 1. 5mo. 1816, and was born 30. 8mo. 1819. He was educated at the Friends' Westtown Boarding School, in Chester Co., and according to the memorial of him, prepared for the Philadelphia Monthly Meeting, and approved by the Quarterly Meeting, 2. 5mo. 1889, "he became a public ambassador for Christ in his twenty-first year, continuing in the work of the ministry for over forty-five years. His gift therein was acknowledged by the Richland Monthly Meeting in Fourth month, 1842, and confirmed by Abington Quarterly Meeting of ministers and elders, in Fifth month of the same year."

The memorial tells that Mr. Levick travelled much in the work of the Friends' ministry in all parts of the Union, and that "he was a man of strong and earnest convictions, and very plain and outspoken in the expressison of his views." "He was deeply interested in public affairs, both national and local, active in the work of organized charities in our city." At the time of his decease, he was the secretary of the Society for the Prevention of Cruelty to Animals. In early life, Mr. Levick became an active worker for the abolition of slavery, and was a member of the Junior Anti-Slavery Society. He was also a member of the "Peace Society" of Philadelphia, which, in January, 1839, took up the matter of forming a "Congress of Nations," in which such matters that led to war between nations could be peacefully adjusted,

WELSH SETTLEMENT OF PENSYLVANIA

which is a prominent proposition of the present day. Mr. Levick died at his home in West Philadelphia on 19. 4mo. 1885, and was buried at the Merion meeting house, as he desired, when "testimonies were borne by several Friends in the ministry from different meetings," of both branches of the Society of Friends. He was twice married, first to Ellen, daughter of Caleb Foulke, at the Richland Friends' Meeting, on 3. 4mo. 1841; she died in 1842, and he married secondly, on 17. 10mo. 1844, Susanna Morris Mather, who died 9. 4mo. 1904, and was buried at the Merion meeting house. Mr. Levick had by his first wife an only child

Jane Foulke Levick, who m. first, Edwin A. Jackson, issue died young. She m. secondly, in Philadelphia, 17 Oct. 1910, William W. J. Cooke.

Mr. Levick by his second wife, Susanna Mather, who was the granddaughter of Isaac Mather (and Mary Morris), son of Richard (and Sarah Penrose), son of Joseph Mather and his wife, Elizabeth, only child of John Russell, who purchased several hundred acres of land from Penn, in 1683, in Cheltenham tp., much of which still remains with Mather descendants, had,—

1—Lewis Jones Levick, of Bala, and Philadelphia, m. Mary d'Invilliers, of Philadelphia, and had,—

    I. Henry Lewis Levick, of Bala.

    II. Mary Sabina Levick, m. Winthrop C. Neilson, of Philadelphia, and had Lewis Winthrop.

    III. Louise Jamart, wife of George B. Atlee.

    IV. Suzanne Levick, of Bala.

2—Charles Mather Levick, deceased. He m. Henrietta Wilson, his brother's widow. No issue.

3—Samuel Jones Levick, Jr., deceased. He m. Anna E. Bullock, and had,—

    I. Anna Lucile Levick, m. Dr. Deemer.

    II. Florence Levick, m. Joseph Sullivant.

    III. Elizabeth Wetherill Levick, m. William Hicks.

PLANTERS AND SERVANTS

4—William Ebenezer Levick, deceased. He *m.* Henrietta Wilson. No issue.

5—James Jones Levick, Jr., unmarried.

On an abandoned road, near Norristown, which was a short cut between the two Welsh settlements, was the little smithy of Ellis Robert, patronized by people we have heard of, as may be learned from his extant "Day Book," in which it is written that he bought it of Thomas Pugh, a Welshman, and a Philadelphia bookseller, on 21. 6mo. 1703. The blacksmith's first entry in it was on "ye 13th of ye 3rd month, 1703," when he records, "Cadwalader Morgan, dr. 1 day's harvest work, 3s. 6d." And "26th day of ye 4th month, 1703, Ellis David of Goshen, 1 day's work, 1 shilling." In 5th month, next, "For soying with Griffith Jones 12 hundred of Oak & Poplar, £1. 15s. 6d." "ye 18th day of ye 3 month, 1703, Cadwalader Jones dr. for 2 days' work, 3s. 4d." His account book runs into the year 1705, and he had customers of many kinds, and from various places, but principally North Wales inhabitants, and for these he repaired plows, sharpened hoes, mended implements, and harness, besides did some horse shoeing. Among his customers in these years were, Richard Pugh, Edward Jarman, John Williamson, Thomas Craffot, Samuel Brockes, Jacob Cofing, Hernell Cassel, John Good, Morris Roberts, the widow Clancy, John Michinar, Richard Blackham, Matthew Jones, David Hughes, John Meredith, Evan Griffith, William Thomas, John Welles, William Robert Ellis, Thomas Griffith, Rowland Richard, John Morgan, Thomas David, of Valley, John Evans, John Roberts, David Howel, Thomas Louis, John David Thomas, David Harvey Rees, William Thomas Hugh, Robert Williamson, of Goshen, Edward Watgin, John Davis, of ye Gulfe, and John Cadwalader, who "paid for the bell, 4s. 3d. Three pounds remain unpaid." John Cadwalader, who died in Oct. 1742, in the island of Tortola, W. I., where Thomas Chalkley died 4 Nov. 1741, was in debt to another man, in the following item. The long will, all in Welsh, of Cadwalader David ap Hugh, of Gwynedd, dated 23 Nov. 1700, gives to Hugh ap Edward £18, and appoints brother Evan ap Hugh, and Edward Foulke to be guardians, and overseers. He had considerable money loaned out at interest, although he was a "workingman." Among his borrowers were John Cadwalader, Hugh William, David Evan, of Radnor, Hugh ap William, Edward Griffith, Robert Hugh, and Robert John, for whom he was working when the will was made.

APPENDIX

Page 26. "No where was persecution [of Quakers] more severe" [than in Wales]. The Welsh Quakers "stood it all heroically, and when William Penn offered them a haven of rest, they found an honourable way of escaping the trials which seemed practically endless. But they loved their old country; its language and customs, and a committee of them obtained from William Penn the offer of a Barony, where they could have a new Wales, and, as they hoped, a government of their own, unmixed with alien influences". (See pp. 442-3, "The Quakers in the American Colonies", by Rufus M. Jones, Isaac Sharpless, and Amelia M. Gummere, 1911).

Page 27. An exception can be given to this statement, for Lady Anne Conway was prominent as a Quakeress in time of Mr. Fox. She was the daughter of Sir Heneage Finch, speaker of the House of Commons, died in 1631. She married (his first wife), in 1651, the Hon. Edward Conway (son and heir of Edward, Viscount Conway, of Ragley), who succeeded his father in 1655, and in 1679, was created Earl of Conway. Lady Conway's brother, Heneage Finch, 1621-1682, was created Earl of Nottingham, and was Lord Chancellor.

Page 80. The location of the Merion meeting house was rather on the northeastern line, than corner of Rees's first land.

Page 80. The deeds of 1695 and 1714, have cleared up all doubt as to on which lot the Merion Meeting House was built.

Page 96. "Elizabeth William Owen" (not "Katherine Robert") was the wife of Robert Pugh, Gent., and mother of Hugh Roberts. See pp. 125-6.

Page 98. The six lines at the foot of this page were badly pied by pressman, and should read:

In Radnorshire, he visited Roger Hughes; at Lanole, Edward Jones, David Powel, Thomas Goodin, near Llwyn-du. From North Wales he travelled to many places in South Wales, then back to Merionethshire, in the North, where he visited Lewis Owen, near Dollegelley, then to Bala, and "Penllyn where I was born and bred," and visited there his old friend, Robert Vaughan, and then made another pilgrimage through Wales.

WELSH SETTLEMENT OF PENSYLVANIA

Page 110. At the top of this page, between the third and fourth lines, should be the lost line:
   Goch of Byrammer, in the parish of Cerrig y druidion.

Page 110. Thomas Ellis and Hugh Roberts filed Memorials as to John Thomas with the Haverford Mo. Mtg.

Page 117. The difficulty that the heirs of John Thomas had in getting a bonus lot in the city, as in the following petition, is an example of what other Welshmen experienced.

"The Case of Robert Jones in Relation to a high Street Lot appurtenant to his father's purchase Stated.

May it please the Proprietor.

My father John Thomas and Edward Jones for themselves and Company in 7ber in the Year 1681 purchased 5000 acres of Land in this Province of which Quantity my father's part was 1250 acres.

In the year 1682 Edward Jones arrived here with several others of that Company by whom my father sent some Effects and agreed with them to make some provision for him against his intended coming and on the 18th of the 2d Month 1683 The proprietor issued his Warr^t to the Surveyor Genl to lay out to my father a front lot on Delaware proportional to his purchase of 1250 ac as afores^d.

In the beginning of the year 1683 my fathers intended Voyage hither was prevented be Death But his Widow and family about 20 in number arrived here in November 1683 and found one half of the purchase taken up in the place since called Merion and some small Improvement made on the same where we then settled And as we were soon after informed a lot was laid out in the City on Delaware front by one Richard Noble a Deputy Surv^r in pursuance of the Warr^t afores^d soon after wch s^d Noble left these parts and on Enquiry no Return found of the s^d Lot the Warr^t also was mislaid and not found for several Years during wch interval one Herriot (If I mistake not) possess^d himself of the lot laid out to us as afores^d.

On the 16th of 7ber 1684 the Comm^{rs} granted a Warr^t to my mother for the high Street lot appurtent to the purchase afores^d.

About the Year 1692 the Warr^t for the front lot being found we thereupon applied to the Comm^{rs} for relief but upon enquiry the Surv^r alleged there was no vacant front lot on Delaware the s^d Comm^{rs} therefore issued their Warr^t dated the 24th. 10th M^o 1692 to the Surveyor to lay out to my Mother a Lot of 50 foot front on Delaware second Street adjoining John Griffiths wch lot was laid out accordingly.

But the High Street lot we were told fell at Skulkil and we refused to accept of it there it being as we conceived without any one president that our front lot should lie on Delaware and our High Street lot on Skulkil.

APPENDIX

About the year 1700 the Second Street lot laid out to us as afore^{sd} was again taken from us, but on the 6th: 2^d M^o. 1702 the Comm^{rs} granted us another Warr^t for a Second Street lot in lieu of the former, but of 34 foot broad, no more (as we supposed) being then vacant and to compensate its deficiency in breadth, a small lot of 20 ft broad on third Street was joined to it, and afterwards confirmed to us by patent But no high Street lot has yet been laid out to us

I therefore desire the proprietor would be pleased to grant a Warr^t for the high Street lot in such manner as has been usual to other purchasers."

Robert Jones's mother, whom he mentions above, (and of whom in page 117), was known in her widowhood by her maiden name, after Welsh custom, as well as by her husband's name, "Katharine Robert" and "Katharine Thomas." Her certificate of removal which she brought over, and is preserved with Merion Meeting MSS, it may be seen was more than the usual, formal indorsement from one meeting to another.

"To all whom it may concern:

Whereas, Katerin Robert, of llaithgwm, in ye County of Merioneth, widdow, hath declared before us her intention in order to her and her families removal to Pensilvania in America, wee thought it convenient to certify in her and their behalfe yt she is one yt received the truth for these ten years past, and that hath walked since answerable to the truth according to her measure. She is a woman yt never gave occasion to ye enemies of truth to open their mouths against ye truth which she owned; her children taught and educated in the fear of the Lord from their infancy Answerable to ye duty of parents, both professing and possessing ye truth.

from our mens & womens

meetings ye 18 of 5mo. 1683.

Robert Owen, Cadd Lewis, Richard Price, Edward Griffith,

Elizabeth William Bowen, Elizabeth John, Margaret Cadwalader."

As stated in page 121, this Robert Jones married (11 May, 1693), Ellen Jones, sister-in-law to Mrs. Katharine Jones, (p. 270), whose certificate of removal is also among the Merion Meeting archives. In a few years, these two remarkable pioneer women, related to each other by consanguinity in their native country, became more closely connected by subsequent intermarriages between their descendants. In this connection, it is interesting to know that Mr. Lewis Jones Levick, of Bala, Philadelphia, has a handsome cabinet made by combining, without changing, the two sea-chests, handsomely carved, which were brought to the New World by these two ladies, "the two Katharins". The chest of Katharine Robert, or Thomas, carries her initials: K R 1664.

WELSH SETTLEMENT OF PENSYLVANIA

Page 121. "1756, Aug. 30. Robert Jones, Dr.
On acc't his purchase.
The Estate of Jo Williams.
To the Gulph Mill & plant'n
sold him this day at Vendue,—1005
Pd for Deeds & recording   1. 7.6.

£1006. 7.6.
Pd Cash £290, (& by 5 Jan. 1757, had pd all but 14.18.9, bal due), it is paid".

Above item from the "Jones Papers", (in the Levick collection), where may be seen the marriage certificate of the above Robert Jones and Ellen Jones, with seventy-five signatures. Their wedding took place at the house of Katharine Thomas, 3. 11. 1693. Also marriage certificates of James Jones, of Blockley, and Hannah Hayes, dau. of Richard, 10. 8mo. 1727, (and the birth dates of their children); and of Jonathan Jones, (son of Jonathan and Gainor Jones), and Sarah Jones, (dau. Thomas and Ann Jones), dated 8. 11mo. 1741; and of Evan Jones, (son of John Pugh), and Hannah (Davis) Jones, dau. of Hugh David and Mary Elizabeth, in 1712, and also of Lewis Jones and Katharine Jones, dau. of Thomas Jones. dated 29. 10. 1732 (and births of their children).

Page 129. Sidney Rees's father was "Evan Rees", of Penmaen.

Page 160. In the Book of Memorials of the Haverford Mo. Mtg. may be read the memorial prepared by John Humphreys as to Robert Owen, and his wife, Jane. He said, "They were the man and woman to my knowledge that first opened the door for a reformation of religion in the country (Merionethshire) where they lived, after the Civil War between King and Parliament began." Rowland Ellis also testified as to their worth:—"After the time of Oliver and Richard Cromwell, Robert was commissioned captain of the militia, and governor of Bewmares, a seaport town upon the Irish coast." But when Robert Owen was required to take the Oath of Allegiance and Supremacy, he refused, and was imprisoned for —— years. His wife then was the mother of nine sons, and her relatives, "yt then bore ye chieffest sway in ye whole county," urged her to prevail on her husband to yeild, and save his estate for his children, but she declined to interfere. Robert and Jane died within five days of each other, in 5mo. 1685.

Page 167. Line 18 from bottom should be, "and married his second wife" (?). See pp. 168-9.

Page 168. Line 7 from bottom, omit comma between "sensible" and "she".

Page 178. Line 2 from bottom, should be "Ruabon."

APPENDIX

Page 179. Will of "Daniel Medlicott, of Haverford," signed in the presence of Stephen Evans, John Roberts, and Daniel Meredith, 16. 7. 1688, was proved at Philadelphia, 20 March, 1697-8. He left his estate to his wife, Martha, and mentioned his daughter, Mary Medlicott, and overseers Edward Jones and Francis Howell. He had property "near Schoolkill beyond the Gulff". His widow, Martha, married James Keite (his second wife), who died in 1713.

Page 181. I do not know who was the compiler of the pedigree, so cannot speculate on its authenticity, or reliability, and this, too, since no authorities are given for important statements made, nor are the sources of the information cited, but there is a "long distance" pedigree of Dr. Thomas Wynne printed in page 618, of Jordan's "Colonial Families of Philadelphia." It says that the Doctor was the son of Thomas ap John Wynne, and that "he was born in parish of Yskeiviog, near Caerways, Flintshire." The Doctor's immediate pedigree as given, runs,

"John ap Rees ap John Wynne" married at Bodfari church, 29 Oct. 1588, Grace Morgan. (It is not known when either died). "Their only son,"

"Thomas ap John Wynne," lived on Brovedog farm in Yskeiviog parish. He was *bapt.* at Yskeiviog par. church 20 Dec. 1589. (His wife's name not given). (According to the Doctor's statement, his father died about 1638). "He had five sons. His third and fourth were,"

3. John Wynne, *bapt.* at above church, 13 April, 1625. He came to Pensylvania with his brother, and lived in Sussex county.

4. Dr. Thomas Wynne, *bapt.* at above church, 20 July, 1627.

Page 182. Line 5 from top, should be "Gwydir."

Page 191. Line 13 from top, should be "Mary Southworth."

Page 236. The certificate of removal of Rowland Ellis and his wife was read in the Haverford Mo. Mtg., 12. 6mo. 1697. It appears that meetings for worship were held at his house during the cold weather of 1713-4, and for weddings also.

INDEX

ABEL Thomas 154
ABRAHAM Joseph 130
ALLEN Sarah Catherin 160
ANDREWS Roger 191
ARMES Richard 259
  Thomas 261
ARTHUR Robert 262
ASCUE John 97
ASHBRIDGE family 135
ASBRIDGE George 136, 211
  Phebe 211
ASHCOMBE/ASHCOM Charles 51, 52, 67, 71, 88,
ATHERTON Grace 210, 211
  Henry 211
  Jennet 211
ATKINSON James 122
ATLEE George B. 274
AUBREY/AWBREY Barbara 163
  Elizabeth 172
  Martha 172
  Thomas 172
  William 167, 168, 171, 172

BACON Charles L. 73
  Charles W. 73
BALL John 196, 232, 261
BARNES Alice 189
  John 189
BARTLETT Walter 98
BATE Humphrey 224
BEALER Jacob 130
BEARDSLEY Alexander 146
BEDWARD William 85
BESSE Joseph 185
BETTALY/BETTLY Humphrey 178, 191
BEVAN family 166, 167
BEVAN's house 162
BEVAN's land 163
BEVAN Ann 103, 170
  Awbrey 169
  Barbara 167, 170
  Catherine 170
  Charles 163, 168, 169, 170, 255
  Elinor 221
  Elizabeth 170
  Evan 103, 168, 169, 170, 221, 257
  Henry C. 170
  Jane 169
  John 25, 33, 95, 98, 103, 117, 124, 138, 163-170, 171, 191, 199, 203, 204, 218, 221, 226, 232, 244, 245, 249, 254, 255, 256, 258, 260, 261, 263
  John, Jr. 163, 168, 169
  John L. 170
  Richard 168
  Stephen 223, 251, 259, 261
  Thomas 168
  William 235
BIDDLE family 159
BIDDLE Clement 159
  John 159
BINGLEY William 242
BLACKHAM Richard 275
BLACKSTONE 97
BLACKWELL Gov. John 143
BOND Elizabeth 103
  Joseph 87
BOULTON Job 65
BOURGE John 241
BOWEN Evan 271
  John 173, 180
  Mary 197
  Owen 98
  Thomas 107
BOWLE John 174
BOWNE John 232
  Samuel 101
BRADFORD Andrew 152
BRINTON Ann 230
  Elizabeth 230
  William 230
BROADBER Will 163
BROCK John 189
BROCKES Samuel 275
BROOKE Hugh Jones 133
  Hunter 133
  Nathan 216
  William T. 133
BROWN Martha M. 190
  William 174
BROWNING Charles H. 159
  Edward 73, 130
BUFFSTIN Levin 98
BULLOCK Anna E. 274
BURGE John 25, 196, 197, 232, 249, 253
BURNYEAT John 29, 240
BURR John 159
BUSE Arthur 204

BUTTALL Martha 189
  Jonathan 189
  Nathaniel 185
  Samuel 188, 189

CADWALADER family 107, 109
CADWALADER David ap Hugh 276
  ap Evan 267, 269, 271
  Thomas Hugh 111
  Dr. Ch. E. 74
  Edward 107
  Gen. George 74
  Hannah 73
  John 73, 74, 77, 84, 109, 138, 190, 192, 193, 275, 276
  Gen. John 74
  Judge John 74
  John L. 74
  Col. Lambert 74
  Margaret 96
  Mary 73
  Morgan 107
  Rebecca 73
  Richard M. 74
  Sarah 107
  Thomas 73, 84, 122, 198, 271
  Dr. Thomas 74
  Gen. Thomas 74
CARPENTER family 146
CARPENTER Samuel 97, 146, 222
CARPLEY Mkary 218
CASSEL Hernell 275
CHALKLEY Thomas 72, 275
CHAMBERS Benj. 146, 164, 196, 199
  Colonel 238
CHARLES ab Evan 163
CHEW Samuel 74, 193
  William 193
CHILDS George Wm. 165
CHORLEY John 189
CLAPP B. Frank 130
CLANCY Widow 275
CLARK John 171
CLOUD William 260
COATES Edward H. 133
  George M. 133
  Henry T. 133
  Joseph H. 133
  William M. 133

INDEX

COCHRAN George 74
  Travis 74
  William 74
  William Greene 74
COCK Peter 68
COFING Jacob 275
COLKET George H. 133
COLLET George 201
COLLINS family 146
COMFORT Howard 73, 190
COMPTON Capt. John 64
COOK Francis 100
  William 98
COOKE Richard 214, 217, 222, 223, 226, 228
  William W. J. 274
COOPLAND John 98
COPPOCK Jacob Jonathan 104
CORSON Charles F. 73
  Joseph K. 73
  Robert R. 73, 190
CORN Richard 214, 216, 224, 226
  William 216, 226
COWPLAND Caleb 135
COX Martha 103
CRAFFOT Thomas 275
CREAKBEAM Philip 264
CRESSON William 73
CROSBY Richard 178, 191
CROSS Mrs. Arthur D. 170
CROSSMAN Capt. 68
CROTHEFRS Mrs. Stevenson 190
CUARTON Richard 149, 257
  William 146, 149, 257
CULLY Hugh 130

DAVID ap Evan 213, 221
  Harvey Rees 275
  ap Rees 200
  Anne 22, 261
  Caleb 164
  David 164, 256
  Ebenezer 163
  Elizabeth 221
  Edward 198, 224, 226, 255, 271
  Ellis 54, 55, 57, 59, 80, 84, 97, 105, 133, 275
  Evan 173
  Harry 221
  Hugh 154, 164, 220, 229, 256
  Janne 263
  Jenkin 86, 173
  Joan 229
  Jonathan 164
  John 111, 166
  Katherine 257
  Lewis 153, 164, 165, 166, 195, 197, 203, 229, 232, 249, 254, 256, 258
  Llewellyn 173
  Margaret 96, 108, 154
  Martha 164
  Meredith 225
  Morgan 227, 245
  Owen 21, 22, 114
  Richard 56
  Robert 21, 54, 55, 57, 58, 83, 84, 104, 116, 120, 127, 208, 257, 258, 261
  Samuel 164
  Sarah 221
  Thomas 147, 179, 261, 275
  Treharn 204, 263
  William 216, 221, 259, 261
DAVIE John 114
DAVIES Amos 149, 151, 152, 221
  David 89, 117, 149, 151, 175, 218, 230
  Ellis 115, 152
  Evan 149, 150
  Katherine 218
  Margaret 33, 55, 141, 145, 147
  Maurice 84
  Richard 24, 25, 29, 33, 104, 112, 127, 149, 150, 151, 153, 174, 177, 183, 185, 213, 227, 249, 251, 255
  Thomas 146, 222, 225, 226, 231
  William 178, 215, 217, 218, 223, 224, 225
DAVIDS David 248
  Meredith 257
  Thomas 78

DAVIS Benjamin 253
  David 84, 135, 161, 249, 255
  Ellis 84
  Elizabeth 84
  Evan 215
  Jane 84
  John 275
  Katherine 161
  Lewis 204
  Margaret 142, 149, 249
  Meredith 225
  Morgan 202
  Richard 124, 177, 179, 249
  Robert 47, 48, 79, 82, 84
  Thomas 84
  William 158, 251, 258
DAY --- 260
  John 249
  Richard 73
DEEMER Dr. 274
d'INVILLIERS Mary 274
DICKINSON family 146
DICKINSON --- 260
  James 98
  Jonathan 101
  John 193
  Philemon 74
  Samuel 193
  Sarah 107
DILLARD Henry K. 133, 190
DOWNING Jane 212
  Sarah 211
  Richard 211
  Thomas 211
  Thomasine 211
DREEL John R. 133
DUCKETT Thomas 174

INDEX

DUER Mary Ann 160
  Capt. William 160
DUNBABIN Alice 189
  Margaret 189
  Samuel 189

ECKLEY John 124, 171, 256
  Sarah 171
EDGE Jacob 135
EDMUNDSON William 270
EDWARD David 220
  Evan 85
  Hugh 224
  Jane 135
  John 47, 48, 91, 222
  ap John 64, 85
  Jones David 216
  ap Rees 63, 64, 79
  ap Richard 253
  Thomas 85
  William 47, 48, 54, 55, 89, 91, 138
  Edward Jones & Co. 63

EDWARDS Alexander 161, 261
  Edward 257, 262
  Elizabeth 269, 271
  Ellen 246
  Evan 21
  Humphrey 260, 261
  Lowry 262
  Margaret 107, 108, 161, 262
  Martha 161
  Peter 204, 213, 217
  Sarah 245
  Thomas 161, 173, 224
  William 54, 71, 79, 100, 174, 178, 179, 248
EHRET Alvin 192
ELIZABETH William Owen 126
ELLET family 146
ELLIS family 146
ELLIS Ann 235, 239
  Bridget 239
  Cadwalader 96, 97, 100, 101, 133, 198, 271
  David 80
  Edward 220, 271
  Eleanor 245
  Elizabeth 82, 239, 240

Ellis 82, 152, 154, 202, 204, 218, 227, 244, 245, 255, 256, 258
  Ellin 115, 154, 220, 240
  Evan 152, 221, 239
  Gemima 132
  Henry 256
  ap Hugh 224
  Humphrey 196, 201, 215, 218, 232, 244, 245, 253, 258
  Jane 225
  Lyddie 220
  ap Rees 234
  Rees Lewis 180
  Margaret 239
  Mary 132
  Morris 224
  Rachel 239, 244, 245
  Rebecca 239
  Robert 106, 225, 235, 240
  Rowland 49, 82, 95, 97, 106, 115, 124, 134, 135, 149, 150, 151, 152, 153, 154, 156, 157, 180-192, 200, 213, 214, 215, 219, 220, 221, 224, 225, 231, 233, 247, 251, 256, 264
  Rowland, Jr. 215, 231, 234, 235, 239
  Thomas 25, 82, 87, 90, 97, 120, 124, 153, 154, 196, 197, 199, 202, 204, 215, 221, 224, 225, 227, 231, 240, 249, 250, 251, 254, 255, 256, 260, 261
  William 152, 221, 239, 256
  William Robert 275
EMLEN family 146
ENDON David 233
EVAN David 177, 191, 203, 219, 221, 224, 230, 236, 258, 276
  Edward 216
  ap Edward 89
  Griffith 72, 79, 105, 106, 136, 137

  ap Hugh 267, 268, 276
  John 89, 154
  John Evan 166
  John William 132,
  Morgan 233
  Philip 215, 218, 258
  Rees 49, 72, 79, 83, 97, 99, 105, 106, 115, 122, 129, 136, 137, 154
  ap Rees 136
  ap Rees Goch 109
  Robert 107, 112, 126, 247, 267, 268
  Robert Lewis 155
  Stephen 256
  Thomas 267, 268
  ap William 213, 215, 221
  ap William Powell 152
EVANS family 161, 233
EVANS Alice 161
  Caleb 215
  Cadwalader 107, 159, 240, 268-276
  Charles 163
  Daniel 199
  David 152, 158, 215, 216
  Deliah 216
  Edward 229
  Eleanor 105
  Elizabeth 84, 161, 240
  Evan 158, 215, 216, 222
  Evans 240
  Gwen 215
  Hugh 76, 78, 107, 134, 135, 158, 173, 180, 222, 225, 237, 264
  Jane 134, 161, 222, 240
  John 152, 214, 215, 216, 218, 221, 225, 226, 231, 239, 240, 246, 249, 250, 251, 255, 256, 258, 275
  Joshua 215
  Lowry 76, 225
  Margaret 240
  Mary 161, 199, 215, 216
  Owen 223, 268
  Rees 120
  Rowland 240
  Robert 21, 84, 106, 107, 129, 130, 222, 225, 263, 268
  Sarah 161, 271

INDEX

Sidney 158
Stephen 222, 223, 227, 228
Susanna 76, 158
Thomas 122, 133, 264, 268
EVES George 264

FADDERY Richard 230
FISH John 249
FISHBOURNE William 103
FISHER family 189
FISHER Mary 115
  Thomas 189, 190
FLEMING Charles 98
FFLOID Robert 96, 134
FORD Philip 241
  Robert 260
FORSTER B. 174
FOULKE Amos 76, 158
  Caleb 76, 274
  Edward 224, 247, 267, 268, 276
  Ellen 274
  Frank 73, 133, 190
  Hugh 273
  Margaret 240
  Mary 175
  Owen 176
  Susanna 240
  Dr. Richard 73
FOX George 23, 28, 110, 189, 241, 242
  James 258
FULLER & HOLME 266
FULLER Jacob 267
  Joseph 267
FURBY Thomas 242
FURNESS family 260

GALLOWAY Samuel 97
GALLOWELL Elizabeth 98
GARRETT John 130
  Thomas 134
  William 197
GARRIGUES Samuel M. 201
GEE John 267
  Thomas 174
GEORGE Amos 87
  David 107, 130, 174, 256
  Edward 87, 100, 129
  George 257
  Jane 100
  Jesse 100, 158

John 86
Rebecca 100
Richard 78, 100, 121
Richard, Jr. 129
GERMAN John 215, 226
GIBBONS John 260
GLENN Edward A. 77, 160
  Lewis A. 160
  Lewis W. 160
  Col. Thomas A. 160
GOOD John 275
GOODIN Thomas 98
GOODWIN Robert 262
GOODSON John 104, 219
GRAEME Dr. 104
GRAHAM John 74
GRIFFITH David 226
  Edward 22, 54, 55, 83, 96, 97, 105, 118, 179, 257, 276
  Edmund 261
  Evan 121, 275
  Hugh 83, 96, 97, 105, 115, 262, 267, 268
  James 262
  John 121, 130
  ap John 121
  John Evan 96, 136, 137
  Katherine 261, 264
  Lewis 201
  Mary 115
  Susan 161, 261
  Thomas 54, 55, 252, 275
GRISCOM Clement A. 141
GROWDEN Joseph 229
GUEST John 82
"GYNN" Dr. Thomas 178, 179

HABARD David 203
HABART Ann 203
  John 203
  William 203
HALLINS Dr. 182
HANEY Daniel 218
  Hugh 218
HANK Jane 269
  John 271
  Sarah 269
HANKINSON Samuel E. D. 74
HARDIMAN Abraham 165
  Hannah 199

HARPER Henry S. 133
HARRIS Daniel 161, 230
  Hugh 161, 230
  Joseph 145
HARRISON family 146
HARRISON James 222, 260
  John 211
  Joseph 119
  Richard 237
Harriton farm 236
HARRY family 230
HARRY ap Rees 222
  Abigail 230
  Daniel 225, 230, 249
  Evan 152, 218, 219, 224, 228, 229, 230, 236, 243, 251, 257, 262, 264
  Henry 230
  Hugh 230
  John 230, 235
  Lewis 230
  Rees 81
  William 230
HASTINGS John 203
  Jonah 86
HAVARD David 203, 222, 257
  John 122, 173, 256
  Mary 222
HAVID John 122
HAXETT Michael 186
HAYES Benjamin 76, 158, 199
  Elizabeth 199, 269
  Hannah 198, 269, 271
  Isaat (Iseult) 198, 270
  John 163, 198
  John Russell 15
  Jonathan 82, 196
  Joseph 198, 232
  Mary 198
  Richard 158, 165, 166, 195, 198, 204, 215, 217, 232, 256, 258
  Richard, Jr. 197, 198, 270
  Richard, 3d, 198
  Capt. Thomas 95
HEATH Susanna 272
HEIGHT Jonathan 178
HENTON REES 196
HERBERT Morgan 153
HETH Susanna 272
HIBBARD Josiah 159

INDEX

HICKS William 274
HIGGINSON Rev. John 186
HILL Richard 146
HILLING Jone 197
  Henry 197
HINTON James 86
HOFFMAN Edward F. 74
HOGG Ann 81
HOLCROFT Elias 186
HOLLAND John 124, 201
  Joshua 201
HOLLOWELL Elizabeth 98
HOLME Thomas 35, 41, 50, 52, 67, 254, 260
HONE John 74
HOOD Jonathan 77
HOSKINS Martha 103
  Mary 158
  Dr. Richard 158
HOWEL David 208, 275
  Francis 202, 227, 254
  Mary 164
  William 164, 199, 201, 203
HOWELL Daniel 244
  Edward 166
  Elizabeth 203
  Francis 200, 245
  Jenkin 166
  John 49
  Jonathan 211
  Joseph 158
  Margaret 202, 203
  Mary 164, 203
  Mireck 166
  Philip 147, 148, 207, 208, 216, 260, 261
  Rowland 200
  Samuel 135
  Susan 203
  Thomas 166, 202, 203, 229, 254, 257
  William 164, 169, 195, 196, 198, 204, 219, 222, 226, 227, 230, 245, 256, 258
HUBBS John 240
HUDSON Susanna 159
  William 159
HUGH Agnes 115
  Ann 220
  David 121, 196, 250, 255, 256, 257
  ap Edward 276
  Ellis 171
  Evan 267, 268
  John 261, 267, 268
  John Thomas 21, 70, 89, 106, 108, 127
  Robert 257, 276
  ap Robert 96, 111
  Roger 256
  ap William 276
HUGHS John 153
  Mary 90
  Sarah 153
HUGHES Charles 161, 262, 263
  David 204, 275
  Humphrey 21, 113
  Joseph 111
  Mary 261
  Roger 98, 214, 216, 221, 222, 224, 226, 228
HULSE Mrs. Charles F. 190
HUMPHRIES Benjamin 142
HUMPHREY Ann 153, 154, 180, 220, 234
  Benjamin 81, 82, 122, 150, 151, 153, 180, 181, 203, 220, 230, 258
  Charles 152, 153
  Daniel 152, 153, 174, 181, 204, 220, 229, 244, 251, 255, 256, 258
  David 154, 219
  Edward 153
  Elizabeth 152, 153, 154
  Gabbatha 152
  ap Hugh 150, 234
  Jane 151
  Joan 152
  John 49, 70, 95, 124, 141, 150, 151, 152, 153, 155, 180, 199, 214, 218, 219, 220, 221, 224, 234, 235, 243, 256, 267, 268
  John, Jr. 203
  Jonathan 153
  Joseph 151, 180, 220
  Joshua 153
  Katherine 220, 247
  Lydia 152, 153, 154
  Mary 203
  Morris 83, 97
  Owen 49, 97, 115, 134, 151, 153, 220, 226, 235, 247
  Rebecca 81, 154, 220
  Reginald 154
  Richard 49, 95, 150, 151, 152, 213, 214, 220, 256
  Robert 152
  Samuel 81, 82, 95, 150, 152, 153, 155, 181, 234, 245
  Solomon 153
  Tabitha 151
  Thomas 153, 180
  William 23, 220
HUMPHREYS family 95, 150
HUMPHREYS/HUMPHRIES Ann 122
  Benjamin 173, 245, 257, 262
  Daniel 81, 192, 193, 196, 200, 231
  Elizabeth 193
  Hugh 262
  John 156, 203, 227, 229
  Joshua 37
  Lydia 81, 245
  Owen 152, 157
  Samuel 193
  William Penn 190
HUNT Benjamin 82
HUNTER John 216
  Mary 216
HURRY Daniel 249

INGELS Richard 208
INGRAM Walter 253

JACKSON Edwin A. 274
JAMES David 214, 217, 222, 223, 227, 231, 256
  George 217
  Howel 176, 177, 191, 259
  James 217
  John 22
  Lewis 241
  Margaret 214, 217, 223, 227
  Mary 217, 227, 228
  Mordicai 135
  Philip 176
  Samuel 217

INDEX

Sarah 198, 217
Thomas 164, 217
William 191
JANCE John Morgan 219
JARMAN (JARMAIN, JARMON, JERMIN, JERMON, JORMON)
  Edward 275
  Elizabeth 226
  Margaret 226, 255
  John 216, 226, 249, 256, 258
  Sarah 226
  Thomas 252
JENKINS Elinor 226
  Howard M. 266
  Margaret 201
  Stephen 201
  William 25, 86, 198, 200, 232, 241, 249, 253, 254, 258, 261
JENNINGS Samuel 101
JOHN & WYNNE 100, 175, 255
JOHN Cadwalader 262
  Catherine 133
  David 83, 96, 105, 241
  ap David 112
  David John 21
  David Thomas 196, 199, 275
  ap Edward 21, 48, 55, 70, 71, 78, 83, 84, 86, 88, 261, 262, 269, 271
  Elizabeth 96, 115, 116
  Evan 49, 96, 163
  ab Evan 121, 163, 166, 225, 261
  Evan Edward 231, 255
  Gainor 49, 96, 155, 157
  Griffith 54, 57, 59, 83, 97, 101, 102, 103, 105, 115, 132, 137, 138, 156, 257
  ap Howel 150
  Hugh 47, 95, 128
  James 173
  ap John 22, 24, 25, 27, 28, 29, 33, 104, 110, 120, 124, 149, 150, 181, 175-181, 249
  Jonett 111
  Lewis 173
  Margaret 21, 96, 131
  Rees 49

Robert 21, 224, 268, 276
Robert Cadwalader 92
Robert David 111
Robert Ellis 257
Thomas 99, 114
Thomas ap Hugh 21
Thomas Thomas 173
ap Thomas 22, 25, 33, 41, 45, 46, 47, 54, 58, 59, 64, 99, 109, 114, 115, 116, 129, 137, 138, 155, 157, 158, 161, 240, 255, 261, 270
William 72, 95, 106, 133, 267, 268
ap William 131
JOHNES Jonett 154
  Sarah 216
JOHNS Arthur S. 74
  Thomas 259
JOHNSON Rev. Richard 236, 239
JONES of London, Edward 219
JONES Anne 121, 161, 225
  Aquilla 77
  Awbrey 156
  Beula 77
  Cadwalader 54, 59, 100, 122, 275
  Daniel 99, 256
  David 86, 97, 107, 115, 121, 154, 163, 165, 174, 198, 203, 222, 225, 236, 249, 269, 270
  Dr. Edward 25, 33, 41, 42, 45, 46, 47, 53, 55, 58, 60, 63, 64, 78, 79, 83, 92, 104, 107, 116, 117, 120, 121, 124, 130, 138, 147, 155, 158, 161, 172, 191, 193, 199, 203, 231, 245, 249, 250, 257, 261, 263, 264, 270
  Edward 73, 98, 148, 174, 208, 214, 216, 222, 225, 226

Edward, Jr. 54, 55, 57, 58, 71, 77, 78, 80, 83, 88, 89, 91
Elizabeth 77, 91, 92, 102, 122, 154
Elizabeth M. 190
Elizabeth W. 269, 272, 273
Ellen 121, 225, 270
Ellis 214, 216, 221, 223
Evan 73, 77, 89, 91, 120, 132, 134, 135, 264
Ezekiel 77
Fred. Rhinelander 74
Gabriel 89
Gainor 129, 154
Gerrard 122, 135, 153
Griffith 121, 136, 174, 260, 275
Hannah 76, 158
Henry 249
Hugh 48, 54, 56, 57, 59, 90, 91, 106, 108, 216, 225, 246, 257
Hugh, Jr. 216
Isaac 269, 271, 272
J. Awbrey 77
Jacob 77, 130, 158
James 198, 256, 269, 271
James Lewis, Jr. 130
Jane 76, 216
Janne 135
John 73, 76, 77, 78, 121, 135, 146, 165, 224
Jonathan 70, 73, 75, 76, 77, 81, 102, 121, 155, 156, 158, 173, 192, 199, 264
Jonathan, Jr. 77, 121
Jonett 154
Joseph 225
Katherine 102, 122, 158, 198, 246, 261
Lewis 121, 158, 257
Lowry 76, 77, 122, 134, 247
Margaret 135
Martha 70, 74
Mary 73, 76, 103, 158, 199
Matthew 163, 256, 259, 275

INDEX

Owen 76, 130, 135, 156, 158
Col. Owen 76, 156
Paul 122
Penelope 77
Peter 237, 257
Priscilla 102
Prudence 77
Rebecca 76, 130, 158
Rees 48, 56, 106, 107, 131, 132, 138, 161, 216, 257
Richard 15, 54, 57, 132, 134, 135, 137, 222, 225, 231, 247
Robert 54, 59, 60, 81, 84, 91, 102, 103, 117, 121, 129, 132, 136, 153, 156, 164, 165, 173, 180, 222, 225, 229, 247, 255, 257, 262, 267, 268, 270
Roger 146
Salvenas 77
Sarah 76, 92, 135
Solomon 149, 151
Susanna 76
Thomas 21, 54, 59, 73, 77, 80, 86, 91, 100, 107, 118, 120, 129, 136, 141, 142, 148, 149, 158, 192, 214, 216, 217, 224, 249, 257, 262
Walter 118
William 47, 48, 57, 99, 104, 106, 136, 181, 268
JORDAN Dr. John W. 169

KEITE Martha 179
KELLY John 107
  William 204, 232, 253
KENDERDINE Margaret 226
  Thomas 226
KINCHNER Francis 174
KINSEY David 214, 217, 249
KINSEY John 249

LATCH Rudolph 130
LAWRENCE Ann 142
  Daniel 164, 166, 244, 256

David 87, 165, 198, 199, 200, 204, 218, 227, 245, 258
Eleanor 87, 245
Henry 86, 87, 164, 165, 166, 245, 246
Margaret 245
Mary 158
Rachel 245
Rebecca 87
Thomas 87, 225, 245
William Thomas 86
LEACEY Col. 238
LEACOCK John 130
LEHNMAN Thomas 223
LEVICK Anna Lucile 274
  Charles Mather 274
  Ebenezer 272, 273
  Elizabeth W. 274
  Florence 274
  Henry Lewis 274, 285
  Dr. James J. 19, 24, 27, 109, 117, 161, 272, 275
  Jane Foulke 274
  Lewis Jones 22, 109, 114, 118, 268, 269, 274
  Louise Jamart 274, 285
  Mary Sabina 274
  Samuel Jones 269, 272, 273
  Samuel J., Jr. 274
  Suzanne 274
  William E. 274
  William Manlove 273
LEWIS Abraham 232
  Alice 196
  Amos 165, 204
  Ann 165, 253
  Benjamin 230
  Betty 203
  Cadwalader 118
  Caleb 164
  Daniel 226
  David 152, 164, 199, 217, 230, 232, 256, 258, 263
  ap David 25, 33
  Davis Levis 247
  Edmond 165
  Eleanor 230
  Elizabeth 165, 197, 201

Ellen Ann 165
Ellis 122, 240, 271
Enoch 165
Evan 165, 178
George H. 247
Griffith 152, 180, 221
Hannah 166
Henry 165, 173, 195, 197, 199, 200, 204, 215, 221, 230, 253, 255, 256, 258, 269, 270
Henry, Jr. 196, 197
Howell 132
Isaac 122
J. Howard, Jr. 133
James 24, 98, 165, 166, 196, 271
James, Jr. 197
Jesse 165
John 195, 196, 200, 204, 229, 256, 258
John, Jr. 195, 196, 258
Jonathan 164
Joseph 166
Josiah 229
Katherine 166, 271
Levi 165
Lewis 165, 178, 197
Lydia T. 165
Margaret 173, 197, 203
Martha 164
Mary 164, 178, 230
Morgan 106
Nathan 165
Osborn G. L. 247
Owen 115, 132, 152,

[289]

INDEX

154, 180, 198, 219, 220, 221, 224, 235, 243, 271
Owen, Jr. 219, 224, 236
Peregrine 165
Philip 229
Ralph 95, 163, 164, 196, 204, 218, 232, 245, 256, 258, 261
Robert 132
Ruth 164
Samuel 164, 176, 197, 198, 200, 232, 256, 265
Samuel, Jr. 176
Samuel B. 247
Sarah 166, 229
Sion Griffith 234
Stephen 229
Thomas 203
Tryon 165
William 95, 164, 165, 166, 199, 218, 237, 247, 256, 258
William, Jr. 165
LIGHTNER 146
LIPPINCOTT Mary 170
LLEWELLYN Alexander 98
Andrew 271
Ann 153
David 151, 173, 202, 204, 232, 245
Griffith 153, 173, 248
Hannah 201
John 204
Mary 153, 173
Maurice 196
Morris 153, 199, 201, 202, 204, 227, 229, 232, 249, 255, 258, 263
LLOYD Charles 24, 33, 25, 29, 52, 55, 75, 80, 124, 131, 141, 142, 145, 149, 150, 183, 185, 249
Judge David 146, 147, 148, 219, 225, 228, 229
David 129, 147, 165, 216, 247, 251, 260
Deborah 183
Edward 241
Elizabeth 143, 248
Evan 248, 256
Francis 202, 222, 227, 245
Gainor 247
Gwen 247

Hannah 247
Howard W. 184, 247
Col. Hugh 247
Jane 248
John 72, 79, 105, 106, 136, 137, 143, 214, 217, 218, 222, 223, 226, 228, 248, 261
Joseph 222
Lowry 135, 247, 264
Mary 222
Rev. Morgan 23, 189
Patience 146
Rees 84, 135, 247
Richard 135, 247, 248
Robert 72, 79, 105, 106, 122, 134, 135, 137, 138, 156, 246, 247, 257, 264
Sampson 149
Sarah 247, 248
Gov. Thomas 52, 55, 75, 80, 99, 124, 141, 143, 145, 147, 149, 155, 174, 183, 188, 210, 219, 225, 237, 242
Thomas 47, 48, 56, 86, 134, 136, 137, 138, 151, 222, 246, 247
Thomas, Jr. 247, 248
William 153, 248
William Supplee 247
LODOVICUS ap Robert 114
LOGAN Judge James 147, 191, 208, 268
LONGWORTHY Sarah 107
LORT Elizabeth 142
Robert 261
Sir Roger 142
Sampson 142
LOWER Thomas 275
LOWRY John Evan 231
LUKENS Jawood 73, 190

MARGARET John William 131
MAURICE ap Edward 109
MAURICE Humphrey Morgan 115
McCALL Archibald 74
Col. Geo. A. 74

MacVEAGH Edmund 260
Wayne 216
MALIN Mary 211
MARCHANT Thomas 197
MARIS Elizabeth 178
George 82, 159
Hannah 159
Jesse 159
John 165
Richard 178
MARKHAM Dep. Gov. Wm. 67, 69
MARRIOT Samuel 104
MARSH Richard 174
MARSHALL Samuel 133, 247
MARUIN Edward 174
MATHER Charles 269
Rev. Cotton 17, 186
Isaac 274
Joseph 274
Mary 269
Richard 274
Samuel 136
Susanna M. 269, 274
MATTHEWS Col. 77
MAUD Margery 189
Joshua 183, 189
MAURICE David 200
Edward 118
Ellis 213, 215, 243
MAYS John 166
MEDLICOT 124
MEIGS Mrs. Arthur V. 73, 130, 190
MELE Bryan
MELLOR John 29
MENDENHALL James 211
MEREDITH Daniel 231
David 81, 214, 216, 217, 222, 223, 224, 228, 249, 255, 256, 258
John 224, 275
Katherine 224
Mary 224
Meredith 224
Richard 224
Samuel 74
Samuel R. 74
Sarah 81, 224
METEER Ann 212
Thomas 211
Thomas, Jr. 212
MICHINAR John 275

[290]

INDEX

MILES Griffith 251
  Phoebe 223
  Richard 214, 217, 223
  Ruth 223
  Samuel 217, 222, 223, 231, 258
  Tamar 223
MILLER Jane 163
  John 28
  S. Bevan 74
MILLINGTON John 249
MILLS Samuel 249
MIRICK David 264
MOLINEAUX Henry 176
MONTGOMERY William 81
MOORE Deborah 145
  Edward 226, 252
  John 149, 257
  Mordecai 97, 122, 146, 183, 249
  Richard 182, 183, 215, 216, 222, 224, 229
  Thomas 121
  William 174
MORCE Mary 197
MORDANT William 249
MORE John 218
MORGAN Blanch 218
  Cadwalader 47, 48, 54, 56, 57, 79, 80, 95, 101, 105, 106, 108, 125, 127, 128, 132, 133, 135, 137, 138, 216, 257, 275
  David 197, 227, 257
  David, Jr. 227
  Edward 218, 248
  Elizabeth 227, 263
  Evan 227
  Hannah 216
  Humphrey 218
  James 106, 216, 221
  Jane 79
  John 106, 107, 215, 216, 221, 226, 227, 248, 256, 258, 275
  John Price 77
  Joseph 248
  Katherine 218, 227
  Lewis 107
  Owen 218, 257
  Sarah 216
  Thomas 263
  William 22, 83, 89, 96, 105, 263

MORICE David 215
MORRIS, Anthony, Jr. 171
  Daniel 159, 222, 231
  David 198, 203, 215, 225
  Edward 120
  Ellen 271, 284
  Ellis 23, 152, 154, 219, 220, 224, 236, 239, 243
  Evan 269, 272
  Gainor 272
  Israel 174
  Jane 22
  John 252, 271
  Joshua 269
  Lewis 111
  Mary 203, 269, 274
  Morris 269, 272
  Thomas 141, 149
MORTIMER James 173, 203
  Margaret 173
MURREY Col. 238
MUSGROVE/MUSGRAVE Alice 197
  Lewis 197
  Margaret 197, 198
  Peregrine 200, 232, 241, 243, 271
  William 170

NANCARRO John 76
NEALSON 148
NEEDHAM Dr. 182
NEILSON Lewis Winthrop 274
  Winthrop C. 274
NICHOLAS Edward 133, 252
NORRIS 146
  Hannah 237
  Isaac 101, 146, 237
  Mary 145
  Thomas 130

OGDEN John 159
  William 159
OLIVER Evan 214, 217, 224, 249
  Winifred 252
ORMS/ORME Richard 178, 179, 191, 215
OSBORNE Elizabeth 260
  Charles 146

  Peter 247
ORIN William 174
OWEN Anne 49, 262
  Edward 47, 48, 55, 72, 83, 95, 103, 142, 160, 213
  Elinor 104
  Ellin 21, 96, 155
  Elizabeth 49, 134, 158, 179, 220, 261
  Esther 158
  Evan 22, 75, 77, 83, 105, 148, 149, 154, 155, 157, 220
  ap Evan 22, 155, 267, 268
  Evan Robert 101
  Gainor 22, 76, 158, 199
  Dr. Griffith 25, 83, 104, 160, 161, 177, 188, 191, 219
  Dr. Griffith, Jr. 104
  Griffith 55, 75, 101, 197, 229, 245, 261
  Hannah 159, 160
  Harry 235
  Hugh Evan 81
  Humphrey 49, 115, 132, 152, 180, 220, 221
  Humphrey Hugh 179
  Jane 101, 136, 155, 160, 240
  Janne 96
  John 49, 84, 104, 132, 151, 157, 159, 180, 220, 257
  Joshua 150, 151, 157, 180, 231, 257
  Lewis 98, 104, 115, 152, 154, 160, 213, 215, 220, 224, 236, 243
  Mably 81
  Owen 159
  Peter 21
  Rebecca 151, 154, 157
  Richard 149, 151, 152, 180, 221
  Robert 21, 25, 70, 75, 76, 80, 83, 96, 97, 99, 101, 102, 104, 105, 109, 111, 116, 118, 120, 121, 132, 138, 146, 149, 151, 152, 154, 157, 176, 180,

INDEX

220, 221, 227, 235, 246, 257, 263
Robert, Jr. 159
Roland 49, 115, 119, 132, 152, 154, 198, 213, 215, 219, 224, 236, 243, 271
Sarah 104, 161
Sidney 158
Tacy 159
Thomas 95, 234, 258, 262, 264
William 125, 126
OWENS John 156

PAINTER Elinor 204
George 103, 199, 230, 244
Susanna 103
PALMER Martha 77
John 130
Thomas 130
William 77
PARDO Letice 197
PARKER John 176
PARR Elizabeth 189
PARRY Edward 222
Rev. Harry 113
Henry 143, 222
Hugh 222
John 165
Llewellyn 210
Owen 175, 177
Robert 222
Thomas 216, 217, 222, 226
Thomas, Jr. 222
PARSONS Thomas 174
PASCHALL --- 81
Hannah 283
Thomas 135, 200
Thomas, Jr. 201
William 247
PASTORIUS Fra. Dan. 145
PAUL James 122
John 131
PEARSON Katherine 173, 203
Mary 173, 203
Robert 173
Thomas 173, 203
PEARSALL William 74
PEMBERTON Abigail 201
Phineas 201

PENN Guilielma 173
William 17, 22, 98, 173, 267
PENNINGTON William Jr. 124, 173
PENNOCK Christopher 124, 201
John 124
Nathaniel 201
PENNYPACKER Samuiel W. 170
PENROSE Sarah 274
PEROT Mary William 133
PERROT John 197
PETER Rees 218, 220
PETERS William 174
PHILIP ap Evan 221
PHILLIPS Jane 222
Philip 222, 251
Phoebe 251
PHILLIPIN Mary 199
PICKERING Charles 188
PINNIARD Marie 160
POTTER Gen. James 237
POTTS Arthur 74
David 262
Thomas 255
POWEL/POWELL David 36, 51, 52, 71, 98, 148, 173, 228, 231, 232, 249, 250, 254, 255
Elizbeth 150
Ellis 235
Evan 252
John 150, 252
Joseph 254
Robert 227
Rowland 198, 215, 217, 244, 245
Thomas 252, 254
William 174, 219, 249
POYER John 153, 200, 204, 229, 232, 241, 249, 253, 255
PREES Ann 161
David 146, 200, 256
Edward 79
James 98
John 161
Mary 161
Phebe 161
Rees 161, 172, 255
Richard 133, 161, 229
Sarah 161
William 114

PREESON Capt. William 161
PRESTON Rachel 145
Richard 87
Samuel 146
PRICE David 146, 200, 215, 225, 228, 257
Edward 78, 79, 81, 107, 133, 264
Ellis 81, 234
Esther 82
Evan 136
Gwenllen 200, 229
Hannah 132, 133, 200
Henry 229
Isaac 229, 257
Isaac, Jr. 229
James 213, 215, 225, 228, 252
Jane 81, 82, 132
John 81, 200
Katherine 115, 220
Margaret 229
Mary 107, 229
Philip 229, 237, 257
Rees 78, 81, 82, 130, 153, 204
Richard 83, 96, 105, 111, 118, 133
Rowland 204
PRICHARD Edward 25, 171, 249, 253
Elizabeth 163, 164, 166, 204, 232
Katherine 163, 164, 166, 232
Thomas 48, 56, 83, 96, 97, 132, 136, 166
PRIEST Edward 82
PRIS Katherine 203
PROTHERO Evan 259
PUGH Ann 224, 225
David 146, 203, 224, 251, 255, 257, 267
Edward 267
Eleanor 248
Elizabeth 225
Ellin 225
Ellis 213, 215, 218, 224, 243, 267
Evan 224, 268
Henry 225, 248, 264
Hugh 225, 237
James 251, 255, 261
Jane 225
Jesse 225

INDEX

Job 225
Katherine 222, 225, 248
Moses 225
Richard 275
Robert 96, 125, 126, 225
Roger 225
Thomas 225, 275
William 225
PUSEY Caleb 206
Owen 177

QUANDRILL Hannah 212
Capt. John 212

RATCLIFF Richard 98
RAWLE Wm. Henry 74
RAWLINS David 97
READ Harmon Pumpelly 74
John 74
Judge John M. 74
REDMAN John 101
REECE/REES/REESE Daniel 215, 229
David 196, 215, 229, 241
Edward 22, 47, 48, 53, 57, 58, 60, 71, 80, 81, 82, 102, 105, 138, 146, 154, 216, 223, 239, 257, 264
Eleanor 215
Elizbeth 152, 173, 215
Ellin 49
Ellis 49
Evan 47, 48, 55, 56, 59, 70, 83, 96, 97, 105, 122, 127, 152, 154, 198, 216, 256, 271
Gwen 49, 215
Henry 215
Hugh 115, 152, 154, 220, 221
Humphrey 225
Isaac 215, 229
John 56, 173, 215, 223, 226, 229
John William 47, 79, 96, 106, 122, 131, 133, 136, 161, 247, 261, 264
Lettice 229
Lewis 215
Margaret 215
Mary 229
Miriam 215, 229

Philip 215, 229
Rebecca 229
ap Rees 226
Rees 81, 252, 264
Richard 54, 220
Samuel 199, 215, 229
Sarah 229
Sidney 122, 129
Thomas 164, 176, 199, 215, 217, 229, 256, 257, 258, 261
REINALD Humphrey 152, 180, 220
REYNOLD Ann 105
REYNOLDS Humphrey 49
RHOADS James 159
RHODE Adam 208
RHODERICK David 149, 150, 257
Evan 255
Thomas 142
RHYDD John 149, 150
RHYTHERCH/RHYDDERCH
John 141, 142, 149, 150
RICHARD ap Evan 166
Gryffyth Rhys 107, 133
John 82, 163, 164, 232, 258, 259, 261
Morris 262
Rhys Grywwyth 79
Rees Jones 56, 58
Robert 220
Robert Thomas 126
Rowland 108, 257, 275
Thomas 47, 48
ap Thomas 25, 33, 147, 148, 207, 249
RICHARDS Bridget 161
Hannah 132, 161
John 161, 261
Lewis 164
Susan 161
Thomas 198, 271
RICHARDSON Charles 73, 133, 190
Joseph 170
Samuel 159, 170
RIDER Tryall 175, 176, 179, 191
RIDGWAY Charles 133
RIGHT Henry 249
RINGGOLD Adm. Cadw. 74
ROADES Adam 198, 217
ROBB Henry B. 74, 190

ROBERT ap Cadwalader 269, 271
ap David 48, 63, 64, 79, 82
Ellis 275
Evan 267, 268
ap Evan 267
Griffith 154, 220
ap Hugh 96, 125, 267, 268
Jane 115, 154, 155, 225
Janne 220
John 101, 198, 225, 226, 271
John Evan 115
Katherine 86, 117
Lewis 220
Margaret 154, 220
Morris 101
Owen Humphrey 103
Owen Lewis 239
Roger 225
Theodore 220, 245
Thomas Morris 126
ROBERTS Aaron 107
Abel 107, 216, 251, 256
Alban 129, 131
Algernon 130
Col. Algernon 130
Algernon S. 130
Dr. A. Sidney 130
Ann 131, 177, 180, 225, 266
Awbrey 103
Benjamin 130
Edward 100, 103, 130, 154, 180
Elizabeth 129, 151
Ellis 107, 225, 251, 262
Evan 107
Gainor 47, 56, 70, 84, 86, 95, 96, 106, 107, 125, 126
George B. 73, 130, 133, 190
George T. 130
Hannah 180
Hugh 21, 25, 47, 49, 53, 54, 57, 59, 60, 70, 80, 84, 85, 86, 89, 95, 96, 103, 110, 116, 117, 119, 120, 122, 125, 134, 136, 137, 138, 147, 148, 150, 154,

[293]

INDEX

155, 156, 160, 166, 170, 176, 207, 208, 219, 234, 241, 246, 257, 261, 262, 266
Isaac 130, 126
Jane 84, 155, 219, 269
Job 269, 272
John 25, 72, 78, 89, 90, 95, 101, 102, 103, 105, 107, 108, 124, 125, 130, 132, 134, 136, 138, 151, 153, 156, 158, 174, 175, 178, 179, 200, 212, 213, 214, 215, 216, 219, 221, 224, 225, 245, 257, 261, 262, 269, 271, 272, 275
John Jr. 76, 129, 130, 180, 247, 269, 272
John, 3d 247
Jonathan 130
Joseph 180
Katherine 96, 107, 127
Margaret 84, 129, 239
Martha 73
Matthew 180
Morris 275
Moses 106
Owen 53, 54, 58, 102, 103, 122, 129, 170, 173, 177, 180, 225, 229, 237, 247, 262
Percival 130
Phebe 122
Phineas 129, 131
Rachel 107
Rebecca 180
Rees 129, 131
Richard 126, 127, 225
Robert 53, 54, 58, 80, 84, 102, 106, 122, 129, 130, 156, 158, 173, 180, 246, 257
Roger 83, 96, 97, 105
Sarah 212
Sidney 131
Tacy 130
Thomas 265
Titus 131
William 180, 247, 256, 257, 261
ROGER John 225, 271
  ap John 24, 28
ROSS Charles W. 74

ROTHEROE/ROTHERS Rees 195, 199, 204
ROULES B. 249
ROWE Grace 200
  William 196, 200, 244
ROWEN Evan 241
ROWLAND Ann 154
  Edward Humphrey 235
  Henry J. 74
  Hugh 132
  Thomas 254
ROWLES Bertha 244
RUDYARD Thomas 255
RUSSELL Elizabeth 274
  John 274
RUTTER Samuel 76
RYTHARCH Rees 199

SANDIFORD Ralph 265
SAMUEL Humphrey Hugh 81
  Daniel 49
  Hugh 216, 250, 251, 261
  Joseph 49
  Lydia 49
  Margaret 216
  Rebecca 49
SANBURN Daniel 98
SANDERS Henry 253
  William 104
SCARLETT John 153
SCHLEY Cadwalader 74
  William 74
SCHREW George N. 74
SCOTHARN Ann 82
SCOTSON George 174
SCOTT William 98
SCOURFIELD Maurice 196, 232
SELLERS Hannah 247
  Samuel 247
  Sarah 247
SHARLOW William 119, 121, 124, 174, 207, 208, 255
SHARPLESS Blanche 219
  Isaac 17
  William 261
SHEPHERD 241
SHIPPEN Edward 191
SHOBER Samuel L. 74
SHOEMAKER 146
SHORT Adam 188
SIBILL Hugh Gwynn 150
SIMONS John 203, 249

SIMSON John 174
SINEX Eli 212
  John Henry 212
  Thomas 212
SINKLER William 173
SIXMITH Bruen 189
  Ester 189
  William 189
SIXSINTH Lucien 176
SIXSMITH Bryan 185
SKONE James 197
  Margaret 197
SKURFIELD Maurice 196
SKY William 65
SMEDLEY Hannah 192
SMITH Abraham L. 73, 190, 245
  Benjamin H. 20, 73, 190, 245
  Francis 145, 147
  Dr. George 73, 161
  Henry 197
  Mary 197
  William 145, 174
SOUTHWORTH Alice 189
  John 189
  Mary 176, 179, 189, 191
STADLEMAN William 130, 264
STAFFORD Elizabeth 220
  Richard 220
  Richard, Jr. 220
STALKER Thomas 211
STEEL 202
  James 171, 177
STEINMETZ John 74
  Joseph A. 190
STEPHEN ab Evan 217, 218
  ap Evan 228
STEPHENS John 228
  Richard F. 74
STEWARDSON Mary H. 190
  Mrs. Thomas 190
STORY Enoch 146, 223, 228
  Marcy 146
  Mary 146
  Patience 146
STOUT Elizabeth 229
SULLIVAN Gen. 238
SULLIVANT Joseph 274
SYMCOCK John 174
SYMMONS Thomas 232

TAYLOR Capt. 97
  Roland L. 74

[294]

INDEX

Thomas 175, 178, 191, 242
Thomas, Jr. 178
THOMAS Abel 55, 86, 107, 132, 135, 137, 174, 257
Ann 218, 223
Awbrey 173
Cadwalader 21, 49, 109, 138, 155, 157
Daniel 176, 218, 257
David 223
Edward 98, 141, 142, 150, 173, 230, 247, 262
ap Edward 114
Elizabeth 49, 114, 173, 203, 211
Ellin 155, 225
Esther 72
Evan 87, 164, 173, 195, 196, 199, 232, 261
ap Evan 267
George 211, 212
Grace 211
Hannah 211
Henry 195
Herbert 173
Hester 173
Howell 166
Hugh 256
ap Hugh 81
Hugh Evan 109, 110
Humphrey 249
Jacob 108
James 166, 173, 180, 200, 202, 227, 241, 245, 253, 254, 257
James, Jr. 202, 257
John 49, 54, 72, 109, 153, 173, 203, 249, 250, 256
John Evan 231, 249, 255
John Thomas 153, 173
Katherine 95, 100, 117, 119, 150, 173, 203, 257
Litter 22, 114
Lowry 133
Margaret 141, 142, 149, 173, 203
Mary 164, 211
Morris 173
Nathan 100, 173, 180, 196, 203, 204, 227, 254
Nathan, Jr. 203
Owen 173, 196, 203, 232, 252, 253, 257, 262

Rees 77, 95, 138, 154, 167, 171, 172, 215, 225, 229, 237, 257
Rees, Jr. 172
Rees Evan 133
Richard 55, 71, 100, 229
Col. Richard 210, 211
Richard, Jr. 84, 207, 211
Richard, 3d 211
Richard 4th 211
ab Richard 132, 133, 136
Richard Evan 166
ap Robert 133
Robert Lloyd 299
Solomon 193
Thomas 173, 223, 225
Watkins 166
William 152, 166, 172, 173, 214, 218, 220, 221, 225, 256, 275
THOMSON Charles 237, 238
TILGHMAN Richard A. 73
TOLAND Robert 73, 77
TOUNSON Anthony 197
TOWNSEND Edward Y. 133
Henry Troth 133
John W. 133
TRAVIS John 74
TREVOR John 28
TRIMBLE John 211
Joseph 211
William 211
TROTH William P. 133
TUNES/TUNIS Anthony 78, 264
TURNER Robert 260, 266, 267
TUDOR Mary 161

VAUGHAN Edward 49, 157
Jane 103, 161
John 180
Robert 99, 103, 118, 119, 120, 122, 154, 160, 161, 198, 262, 271
Thomas 119
VAUGHN Gawen 109
VAUX 146

VERNON Rebecca 134
VINCENT Robert 264

WAINWRIGHT 146
WAKER (Vaikaw, Walker)
Mary 203
John 55, 252
Lewis 200, 203, 217
WALLIS Philip 257
WALN 146
WALTER John 177
Richard 54, 55, 59, 83, 84, 257
WARLEY Daniel, Jr. 239
WARNER Col. Isaac 130
John 174
Tacy 130
William 69, 174
WATKIN Edward 275
John 47, 48, 54, 136, 137
WATKINS John 48, 57, 99
Richard 226
WATSON John 226
WATTS Bridget 261
Elizabeth 261
Hannah 262
Jean 261
Thomas 252
WAYNE Thomas 120
WEAVER John 146
WELLES John 275
WEST Joseph 159
WESTON Deborah 197
WETHERILL Elizabeth 272
Mary 272
WHARTON 146
Joseph 160
Rachel 204
Robert 245, 256
Thomas, Jr. 237
WHEELDON Isaac 176
WHEELER Andrew 128, 219
S. Bowman 190
WHITE Richard 241
WHITPAIN John 104
Richard 171
WIGES Henry 98
WILCOX Barnabas 119, 174
WILLIAM David 229
ap Edward 48, 63, 64, 79, 80, 84, 85, 92, 99, 121, 216, 245, 248
Elizabeth 96
Evan 232, 258

[295]

INDEX

Hugh 276
John 22, 49, 56, 57, 80, 115, 133, 215, 220
ap John 104, 267
ap Owen 96
Robert 54, 55, 59, 147, 148, 257
Robert Ellis 275
Thomas Hugh 275
WILLIAMS Anthony 240
  Charles 190
  Daniel 87
  Edward 87, 246, 257, 264
  Edward, Jr. 87
  Eleanor 87
  Elizabeth 70, 86, 114, 115, 225
  Ellen 87
  Ellis 71
  Evan 163, 260
  Hugh 191, 215, 216, 225
  Humphrey 262
  Jane 87
  John 105, 106, 231, 237, 244, 246, 251, 257
  J. Randall 190
  Joseph 87
  Katherine 86
  Lewis 248
  Lumley 252
  Margaret 260
  Mary 87
  Robert 71, 86, 208
  Sarah 87
  Susanna 225
  Thomas 114
WILLIAMSON John 275
  Robert 275
WILLING 146
WILLIS Jacob 260
WILSON George 97
  Henrietta 274, 275
WISTER Alexander W. 73
  Daniel 76, 77
  Israel J. 73
  John 156
  Col. Lewis 156
  Dr. Owen Jones 73
  Rodman 73, 190
  Wm. Wynne 73
WOOD Ann 159
  Eleanor 169
  George 169
  John 169

  Joseph 119
  William 119, 124, 174, 207, 208
WOODVILLE William, Jr. 74
WOODLIFFE Nathan 226
WORM William 264
WORRELL John 221, 230
  Mary 230
  Peter 230
WYNNE Elizabeth 116, 188, 189, 192
  Hannah 153, 192, 193
  James 192
  John 21, 77, 113, 174, 181, 192
  Sir John 182
  Jonathan 174, 177, 178, 184, 188, 190, 192
  Martha 192
  Mary 73, 192, 193
  Morris 152
  Owen 112
  Rebecca 189, 193
  Sarah 192
  Sidney 192, 193
  Thomas 153, 182, 249, 255
  Dr. Thomas 25, 33, 72, 73, 104, 120, 138, 153, 161, 164, 175, 189, 210, 257
  Tibitha 193
  William 182

YOCUM James 73
YOUNG Peter 100
  Sarah 146

ZANE Robert 267

www.ingramcontent.com/pod-product-compliance
Lightning Source LLC
Chambersburg PA
CBHW060555230426
43670CB00011B/1835